We, the British

We, the British

IVOR RICHARD

Doubleday & Company, Inc., Garden City,
New York   1983

Library of Congress Cataloging in Publication Data

Richard, Ivor, 1932–
  We, the British.

  Includes index.
  1. Great Britain—Politics and government—
1964–   . 2. Great Britain—Economic
conditions—1945–   . 3. National
characteristics, British.   I. Title.
DA589.7.R5   1983   941.085
ISBN: 0-385-14531-4
Library of Congress Catalog Card Number 80-2623

To My Children—David, Alun and Kate

Grateful acknowledgment is made to the following for permission to reprint their copyrighted material:

"Lament" by Dylan Thomas from *Poems of Dylan Thomas*. Copyright 1952 by Dylan Thomas. Reprinted by permission of New Directions Publishing Corporation and David Higham Associates Limited.

The excerpt from *England's Hour* by Vera Brittain is included with the permission of her literary executors.

CONTENTS

The
People

THE UNITED KINGDOM AND THE BRITISH

Britain is such an enigma to most people that few of them even get the name right. The French press quite normally speaks of *les anglais* when it means the British Government; Americans are more familiar than most with the term *U.K.*—which goes nicely with *U.S.*—yet tend to think the country is called Great Britain. The BBC, in weather reports broadcast from London, frequently enrages Scottish and Welsh opinion by speaking about the North, Scotland, and other *regions*—when it should talk about the different *nations* that make up the United Kingdom of Great Britain (England, Wales, and Scotland) and Northern Ireland. And being British is, of course, quite different from actually coming from the U.K.

One of the more ludicrous aspects of the ending of the Empire is that vast quantities of ink have been spilled, and legislative, judicial, and journalistic energy used up, in trying to define exactly who the British are. After the Second World War a Labour government came to power under Clement Attlee pledged to end British rule in India. Independent India and Pakistan were born, with their own heads of state and government, membership of the United Nations, and all the other trappings of nationhood, including—perhaps more important than anything else—the ability to define their own citizenship. The Attlee government decided at the same time to keep the link with the former dominions and colonies by forming a loose association of free nations called the Commonwealth—linked together by their common heritage of British rule, the English language, and British legal traditions under the King or Queen of the United Kingdom either as head of state or, for those independent nations which preferred a republican constitution, as Head of the Commonwealth. While India and Pakistan, in 1947, went their own way, the Attlee government decided to retain the link with the former Empire by making every citizen of any Commonwealth country, as well as the British in Britain and the citizens of the remaining colonies, "British citizens."

In 1948, then, the British Nationality Act gave the full rights of British citizenship—including the right to enter and leave the United Kingdom freely and the right to vote and stand for election —to all the citizens of the British Commonwealth. Today millions of Indians, Canadians, Kenyans, Jamaicans, and Nigerians— though not the Pakistanis after Pakistan's withdrawal from the Commonwealth in 1972—remain, like all Commonwealth citizens, British subjects under British law. But a succession of immigration and nationality laws, beginning with the first immigration controls over Commonwealth citizens—the Commonwealth Immigrants Act of 1962—and culminating in the British Nationality Act of 1981, have now finally narrowed the definition of who may enter and leave the U.K. freely down to something like a normal definition of citizenship: those born in the country to U.K. residents, and, subject to certain conditions, their children.

The debate about Britain's immigration and nationality laws has often been bitter and highly controversial—with, as we shall see later, frequent racial overtones—but British citizenship is still technically held, under the 1948 Act, by all citizens of all Commonwealth countries. There is nothing to stop an Indian or a Ugandan from standing for the House of Commons—provided he (or she) fulfils the usual criteria—or, if he can get into the country and register as an elector, from voting in British elections. No matter how people may feel in the independent Commonwealth countries concerned, under British law about a third of the population of the world remains "British."

Actually feeling British is, of course, different from the legal position. There are some people in the United Kingdom—the highly nationalist, or republican, element of Northern Ireland's Roman Catholic population, for example—who do not particularly want to be British; and there are others, many more in number, and scattered throughout the world, who desperately want to remain British and who wanted to have no part of the decolonization process. These groups include the Gibraltarians, 25,000 British citizens whose patriotic fervour was demonstrated when the Prince and Princess of Wales visited the Rock at the beginning of their Mediterranean honeymoon in August 1981, and the 1,500 or so Falkland Islanders, whose windswept islands have many more sheep than people. In both cases the local population wants to remain British rather than be incorporated into the neighbouring nations, Spain and Argentina respectively. This fact and its acceptance by the British Government led in 1982 to what would have hitherto seemed inconceivable—war with Argentina. The result of that will be to make the Falkland Islanders even less inclined in the future to envisage any weakening of their connection with Britain. While the Gibraltarians are a unique racial mixture—including Spanish, British, Moroccan, and Genoese blood—the Falkland Islanders are, in the main, of pure British, that is, United Kingdom, stock.

Another consequence of the loss of Empire, in addition to the parliamentary sport of passing laws separating the "real" British from the purely honorific, has been the increasing emphasis, within the U.K., on national and regional differences. The English monarchs brought Wales into the kingdom in 1536, added Scot-

land in 1707, and Ireland in 1800. In 1922 the Irish Free State
left the kingdom, taking with it twenty-six of the thirty-two counties on the island, and leaving Northern Ireland as a predominantly Protestant province owing allegiance to the United Kingdom. There are now Nationalist parties in Scotland and Wales,
some of whose members would like to see their countries independent, and there is an increasingly strong body of opinion in Northern Ireland that sees the answer to the province's problems in an
independent Ulster.

Following some spectacular electoral successes by the Scottish
Nationalists in the 1970s, the Labour government of James Callaghan planned to devolve a measure of political power to Scotland
and Wales, involving the setting-up of a Welsh Assembly in Cardiff
and a Scottish Assembly in Edinburgh. But the proposals failed to
get the required 40 per cent majority vote of the entire electorate
in referenda held in 1979, and the splendid buildings prepared to
house the Assemblies have never been used. The Conservative
government of Margaret Thatcher, which succeeded Callaghan's in
May 1979, thought it best to let sleeping dogs lie. Indeed, in that
same election, the Scottish voters seemed to shift back to some extent to their traditional allegiance, the Labour Party.

But whether or not the political controversy over devolution is
dead, the increasing self-confidence of the Welsh and the Scots
continues to assert itself. Because—in yet another typical anomaly
—the individual nations of the U.K. enter their own teams separately for the World Cup soccer competition, Scottish players,
but not the English, were able to get to the final rounds in Argentina in 1978, and—although their team did disastrously—the Scots
managed to turn the whole thing into a huge patriotic outburst. In
Wales the number of Welsh speakers has continued to decline—
from about half the population of Wales at the turn of the century
to around 20 per cent in 1971—but there has been an increasing
effort to teach Welsh and to make Welsh acceptable for official
purposes, together with more and more broadcasts in Welsh on
both radio and television. In Scotland, where the Gaelic language
is confined largely to the islands of the North-West, the BBC has
now opened a local radio station that broadcasts almost wholly in
Gaelic. Meanwhile, in both Scotland and Wales, a militant minority has resorted to terrorist tactics. These have been particularly

noticeable in Wales, where there have been arson attacks, in Welsh-speaking districts, on the holiday homes of English residents.

Yes, despite these pressures, the kingdom remains fundamentally united. Indeed, although there are probably half a million Welsh speakers, around 75,000 who understand Gaelic, and thousands more recent immigrants whose mother tongue is Punjabi, Greek, Urdu, or Polish, English remains the national language. There are, of course, many varieties of English, and experts can place people by their accent to within a few miles of their birthplace. There are no proper dialects—as there are, for example, in Italy—but Lowland Scots is still a very distinctive form of English, with a vocabulary of its own (immortalized in the poetry of Robert Burns), and in England accents as different as "scouse" (Liverpool), "broad Yorkshire," and, in London, "cockney" continue to flourish. The BBC, which until recently allowed only "received" or "Oxbridge" English to be spoken on its air waves, has now—and above all with the recent expansion of local radio stations—allowed regional and local accents to be heard. The exception is the BBC World Service, which still broadcasts to the world in the sort of clipped tones that used to characterize *all* of the BBC's output.

The possession of the language, and the sharing of a million and one idioms and recognizable regional or class allusions in speech, are the factors that probably make a person British. The language is now the major world language: not for Britons the satisfaction of the Swedes, the Dutch, or the Bulgarians at possessing a language and a literature that few foreigners can penetrate. Their language is the international language of commerce, if not always of diplomacy, and it is the language of multinational corporations and international bureaucracies. But that English is, in a sense, a different English from the one spoken in Britain, a more solid and predictable language than the infinitely variable spoken word of Scotland, Ireland, England, and Wales. Millions the world over learn the language of business and public affairs; the language of cricket and gardening, of the pub and the working men's club, is impenetrable even to many born into it.

Another especially British characteristic is allegiance to the monarchy. The monarchy remains, as Bagehot put it, the "cere-

monial" part of government, which the British keep separate
from the actual functioning of government, which he called the
"efficient" part. The 500 millions throughout the world who
watched the royal wedding on their television sets in the summer
of 1981 enjoyed the pageantry and splendour, but few probably
reflected that the separation of the symbolic from the real, of the
head of state from the head of government, was a uniquely British
way of handling the business of government. In Britain the Royal
Family attracts all the respect and adulation that in other countries are attached to the office of the President or other leader,
while the Prime Minister, and he or she alone, actually rules the
country through his or her Cabinet of ministers answerable to the
House of Commons. The Queen reigns but does not rule.
Strangely enough, when things are going badly for the *government*
—when the popularity of the Prime Minister is at a low ebb—it
seems as though the monarchy actually increases in importance
and popularity. No one thinks of blaming the Queen for the recession or for unemployment. Rather, the population seems to feel
sympathy for the Queen that her ministers and her government are
doing such a bad job, feeling the need to express more strongly
than ever feelings of pride in the nation and in the ceremonial,
unchanging part of the government. A tiny minority feels that the
Royal Family squanders its money on frivolities and is too
wealthy; for many, the advantage of a hereditary as opposed to an
elected, or meritocratic, head of state, is that the position is literally unreachable and beyond anyone's dreams. The fairy-tale side
of the monarchy—the state coaches, footmen in wigs, and the
rest—is thus a secret world where the British seek an escape from
the drab realities of European statehood.

Whether there is a national character—or whether the United
Kingdom contains several national characters—is not an easy question to determine. Most of the old clichés about the British once
had some basis in fact, but times change. London, only thirty
years ago, was a sombre and serious city compared with the gaiety
of post-Liberation Paris. Yet in the sixties—when the term "swinging London" was coined—commentators said that all the national
clichés about England (staid, conservative, puritanical, hard-
working, not interested in wine, women, or song) and France
(stylish, frivolous, fashion-conscious, food-loving, and sexy)

should be reversed. Aspects of the old puritanical attitudes coexist alongside a thriving fashion industry and a new interest in good food, and the traditional reserve of the Englishman (who will rarely talk to his neighbour in a railway carriage) has to be seen in the context of the wild (and often deplorable) behaviour of British football fans at home and abroad. The British in general may be unpolitical and irreligious, but there is a lively political life in Britain and "fifty-seven varieties" of political party, and the churches, after decades of steady decline in attendance, are now beginning to attract larger congregations.

Neither is there, in purely physical terms, any readily identifiable British "race." The Celts are supposed to be stocky and dark, the Vikings tall and blond; something like 20,000 black slaves vanished into the population in the eighteenth century; there were large Jewish immigrations from Eastern Europe at the end of the last century and the beginning of this; after the Second World War thousands of displaced people from Eastern Europe, including Poles, Lithuanians, Estonians, and Ukrainians, settled in Britain's industrial cities: while the fifties, sixties, and seventies saw immigration from the Caribbean and the Indian subcontinent, so that now something like 4 per cent of the total population is black or brown. The Jewish community is particularly well represented in business and the arts and in the legal profession.

Yet although Anglo-Saxon names remain the norm and many British people think the typical Englishman is tall and blond and called Smith or Robinson—as he probably is—and although Britain is far from being the "melting pot" of the United States, there really is no such thing as the "British race." Since Greeks and Phoenicians traded with the ancient Britons, the islands' inhabitants have had constant contact with other peoples and races. When at the beginning of the Christian Era the Romans colonized Britain, some of the original Britons—the Celts, the speakers of Cornish, Welsh, and Gaelic—fled to the western corners of the islands where their ancestors still live and where (except for Cornwall) the ancient languages are still spoken. And many more Celts went westward when the Anglo-Saxons arrived. It was the Romans who gave Britain its basic road network and founded many fine cities (Bath, St. Albans, and Chester, for example). As the Roman Empire fell apart, it was the Anglo-Saxons from Germany who added a North European blend to the national racial mix. The later Vikings added a Nordic element. The Norman invasion in 1066 under William the Conqueror introduced the Norman French language and a new ruling class, which in turn brought a new legal system (Norman French terms still sprinkle English law) and political and social organization to the country.

Today's typical Briton might be from the East of the country (from one of the countless towns and villages whose names end in -by, showing that it was originally a settlement of Scandinavian origin) but born there (since the East is an area of expanding population) of parents whose families had themselves moved to England from, say, Scotland or Wales. His mother might be by origin a Scot on one side of her ancestry, whose family had come to Glasgow from the Gaelic-speaking Highlands in the middle of the last century, but who now regards herself as invincibly English; his father, a second-generation Welsh immigrant from the valleys. He grows up in a new urban development area near an older city, together with a handful of local children and many more, like himself, descended from immigrants from other parts of the U.K., and possibly a handful of black or brown children whose parents arrived from the West Indies or India or Pakistan in the fifties or early sixties. His appearance is anyone's guess, but he is probably less fair than the very blue-eyed Scandinavian type and is unlikely to be as dark or swarthy as a southern European or North African.

His schooling and housing, political behaviour, and hobbies and interests, as well as his aspirations for himself and his children, are typical of much of the population. There are thousands of people like him up and down the country. But the statistical average could not exist without a wide variety of non-typical types and a broad range of attitudes and approaches that no caricature can hope to convey. The statistically average may not be typical, in the sense that the national personality may be based on views of Welsh, Scottish, English, or Irish character that have no basis in identifiable reality. But the fact that national characteristics are thought to exist, or that they are attributed to large segments of the population of the United Kingdom, are highly relevant to any understanding of the British. In actual fact, such an average is more typical of the modern Briton than any kilt-wearing Scotsman called

Archie MacTavish is typical of the modern Scot, or any leek-eating hymn singer called Aneurin Goronwy Jones is a typical Welshman.

The same goes for the question of class. In recent years, British culture, from John Osborne's angry young men to the Beatles' Mersey sound, has begun to portray something other than upper-class Oxbridge types as typically English. The eighteenth-century aristocratic "milord" on his tour of continental noble houses and architectural monuments remains a common English caricature on the Continent. A new image has, however, now begun to appear, and it is of a loutish, foul-mouthed, unemployed rioter or football fan. This image seems equally puzzling to people abroad used to the caricature of the mild and slightly eccentric aristocratic Englishman. The reality is, of course, totally different: our average youngster is neither aristocratic nor a hooligan, and Britain, despite all the inherited baggage of ingrained class *attitudes,* is a fundamentally middle-class society. But, again, in recognizing the reality of our statistically more or less average youngster, we have to understand the norms and values of the statistically non-typical in order to form a clear picture of national class attitudes and stereotypes.

What is statistically typical, then, may not be representative, and this is, of course, particularly true of British culture. Almost by definition, those who create will be untypical, but their writings, their art, their music will in many ways be a product of the society of which they are a part. The aim here is to give an overall picture of a people and a country, combining GNP and monarchy, both strikes and unemployment and choirs and orchestras.

But the question remains: What is it that is typically British? There is an almost unwieldy load of inherited attitudes and structures, both in the culturally interesting but fundamentally harmless area of "priceless heritage," and in the more problematic area of resistance to change, unwillingness to adapt. For all its economic and social problems, and despite the rapid pace of change, Britain retains, as a society, a peacefulness that many visitors still find remarkable. There is a gentleness, a you-mind-your-own-business-and-we'll-mind-ours attitude in the population at large which borders on the indifferent but which marks the British off from many other peoples and societies. There is an absence of violence in British political life; a failure of ideology to grip any but a tiny minority of enthusiasts with political fanaticism, and an abiding characteristic of pragmatism in British politics. There is, too, the coexistence in the society of widely differing cultural, political, and religious attitudes embodied in institutions as quintessentially British as the BBC, the Church of England, and the Labour Party; but the lack of ambition of many Britons, whose positive side is the contentedness of the gardener and the amateur music-maker or dog-owner or pigeon-keeper, has a negative side which is the failure of British industry to grasp new opportunities to compete in world markets.

THE WELSH

Taffy was a Welshman, Taffy was a thief,
Taffy came to my house and stole a leg of beef.

In many parts of Britain the Welshman is seen as devious and hypocritical. Like all national stereotypes, this is untrue in its comprehensiveness. But the reputation persists that the Welsh are untrustworthy, two-faced, unreliable, and persons against whom one should be on one's guard.

Some of this stems from the fact that Welsh is a separate and living language, spoken by half a million people, approximately one-fifth of the population, and taught in all schools in Wales.

Unlike Irish, the official language of Ireland, Welsh is neither artificial as a national language nor virtually extinct. Unlike Gaelic in Scotland, it has not been confined to one remote geographical region of the country. Within thirty miles of the border with England there are towns where Welsh is not merely spoken but the main and natural language, where one will hear it far more in the streets, shops, and factories than English, and indeed where until recently little English was used. There are Welsh newspapers and Welsh radio and TV, and the language of the nonconformist chapels is still Welsh rather than English. In some areas, school is conducted in Welsh, English being a fluent but second language.

The incomprehensibility of Welsh to the English and the "clubbishness" of those who speak it is a recipe for communications failure, the legacy of which still persists. Add to this the fact that Welsh tended to be the language of the working class and English that of the land-owners, managers, and professional classes, and it is hardly surprising that national stereotypes emerged.

It is said that a Welshman cannot answer a straight question directly and will only rarely disagree bluntly in a situation where to do so would result in offence. H. V. Morton, in his book *In Search of Wales,* tells of once going up Snowdon (Wales's highest mountain) when the weather was fine at the bottom and cloudy at the summit. Before he left he asked a local whether he would see anything from the top and received the reply, "Yes, you probably will." Of course he saw nothing, the mountain being covered in cloud. He reflected that in a similar situation a Scotsman would have said, "Of course not, man, you will see nothing at all," but concluded that the Welshman had not intended to mislead, only to warn.

One needs to be conscious of nuances in Wales. The word "yes" is quite capable of meaning "no" if uttered in a certain hesitant way, drawn out and with a silent pause afterwards. To take it at face value is foolhardy; one has to listen for the tone in which it is said, not merely the actual word used. This comprehension takes a long time to acquire, and few English people have either the time or the opportunity to acquire it.

Along with this Celtic ability to conceal there goes a fluency in the use of words, especially from the pulpit. The Welsh have a joy in listening to formal language used to excess that is unrivalled in Britain. A Methodist congregation expects (and gets) its money's worth on Sundays in rural Wales: spontaneous prayer, with a lack of ritual, and "proper" sermons preached by a minister whose flow of language is expected to be intense and moving whether the service is in Welsh or English.

The nineteenth century produced great preachers in Wales, some of whom are remembered to this day. John Elias was one such. It is said that the power of his oratory was so great that people would come from miles around to hear him preach. But then, "preach" is hardly the right word. It was not a sermon, it was a performance with a sense of theatre and enough dread to give it spice. The story is told of his preaching in a small village in mid-Wales on the way the finger of God touched every man. At the height of his peroration he flung out his arm, having carefully arranged the candles beforehand so that the huge shadow of his finger fell upon the wall. Seeing this monstrous arm, the congregation fled.

There is indeed a Welsh word for such oratorical intensity: *hwyl*. When someone has the hwyl, whether in chapel or in Parliament, it means that he is charged with such verbal power that the listener reels from its effect. The hwyl does not come often, but every preacher worth his salt experiences it at some time or other.

This verbal felicity has produced not only preachers but also poets and politicians. One of the great word-masters of the century, Dylan Thomas, was Welsh, born in Swansea and living in Laugharne, a small fishing village in Carmarthenshire, the origin of the town of Llaregyb in *Under Milk Wood*. He was a man of violent tastes and tumbling words, and the adjectives poured from him. Take, for example, these verses from his poem "Lament":

> *When I was a windy boy and a bit*
> *And the black spit of the chapel fold,*
> *(Sighed the old ram rod, dying of women),*
> *I tiptoed shy in the gooseberry wood,*
> *The rude owl cried like a telltale tit,*
> *I skipped in a blush as the big girls rolled*
> *Ninepin down on the donkeys' common,*
> *And on seesaw sunday nights I wooed*

Whoever I would with my wicked eyes,
The whole of the moon I could love and leave
All the green leaved little weddings' wives
In the coal black bush and let them grieve.

When I was a gusty man and a half
And the black beast of the beetles' pews,
(Sighed the old ram rod, dying of bitches),
Not a boy and a bit in the wick-
Dipping moon and drunk as a new dropped calf,
I whistled all night in the twisted flues,
Midwives grew in the midnight ditches,
And the sizzling beds of the town cried, Quick!—
Whenever I dove in a breast high shoal,
Wherever I ramped in the clover quilts,
Whatsoever I did in the coal-
Black night, I left my quivering prints.

It was the romanticism of the man that produced this flood of language, a romanticism about which, like many Welshmen, he felt intensely guilty. There is something about the grey and the rain of South Wales that produces twin feelings of social rebellion and personal guilt.

The worst type of Welshman is the one who has not only forgotten his roots but deliberately suppressed them. London is full of oversmooth Celts trying to compete on equal terms with the products of Eton and Harrow. To meet a Mr. Davies who has felt obliged to hyphenate his name to Gwynn-Davies, and has acquired the manners, bearing, and pretensions of an Anglicized *grand bourgeois,* is to see a person who has not only forgotten his origins but denied them. It is sad that his sole remaining connection with Wales is his name, and even that he has felt the need to prettify.

One reason for the Welsh sense of latent aggression towards the English is their history, and particularly that of the late nineteenth and early twentieth centuries. Wales is much closer to England than is Scotland, and was therefore conquered earlier; its rulers have until recently always been foreign. It is a surprising paradox that, despite this, the Welsh have succeeded in preserving their language far more effectively than either the Scots or the Irish.

Repression always produces reaction, and the attempts by the English to stamp out the Welsh language (at one time, for example, it was forbidden for Welsh to be spoken, let alone taught, in the schools) produced a strong countermovement. The chapels preserved the language in the nineteenth century, and an increasing national consciousness in the twentieth has tried to extend it.

If the rulers of Wales were foreign, so, too, were the industrialists. Of the great names in Welsh industrial development, few were actually Welsh themselves. Guest, Keen, Baldwin, Mond, the industrialists of nineteenth-century South Wales, were all Englishmen who came to Wales to make their millions. There is a saying in the mining valleys that the English came and took the money and "left us with the muck." They created a society in which the valleys were despoiled, the language suppressed, the culture undermined, and the Welsh dispersed to England. *How Green Was My Valley,* if overdrawn, is not entirely romantic imagination. The lot of the Welsh miner was no worse than that of his Yorkshire or Durham counterpart, but at least there the exploiter was seen to be native.

Wales was for many years sharply divided along class lines, and a consciousness of social distinction and personal separation was strong. In some areas it still is. No one who knows the industrial history of South Wales should be in the least surprised at the past militancy of its workers, and John L. Lewis would have been a highly recognizable figure had his father stayed in the land of his birth.

But if the Welsh were angry, they were also shrewd. Education, they realized, was the way out for the children, in the nineteenth century through the chapels and Sunday schools, and later through the grammar schools and universities. Formal education almost came to be worshipped as an end in itself.

When I was a boy in South Wales, the lists of passes or failures in any examination from the most elementary in piano-playing to university entrance to Oxford and Cambridge were published in great detail in all the local newspapers. Proud were the parents of those who had passed, and retiring were those of the ones who had failed. "Hasn't he done well" was the accolade the mothers most liked to hear, and it was not merely for the social cachet that success bought a bright child. It was that there was at least the prospect of that child's escaping the drudgery of the valleys. This is also why Wales has produced so many teachers, a white-collar, apparently intellectual occupation.

For generations Wales sent its brightest away to England, North and South America, Australia, New Zealand, and South Africa. For a nation whose population even today is not 3 million, it is a remarkable story. Four men of Welsh birth or descent signed the Declaration of Independence, and Thomas Jefferson allegedly was Welsh himself. The Welsh diaspora is an extraordinary story, though perhaps one mirrored by the Scots and the Irish.

A Welshman is difficult to know. Revelation does not come easily to him unless under the influence of either alcohol or words. The Welsh are strong drinkers, finding there some strange justification for revealing themselves. When drunk they are rarely violent, passing from jocose to lachrymose without much pause at the bellicose stage. When either happy or sad they sing their hymns, invariably in four-part harmony and usually too loud. The pubs of the valleys on a Saturday night (before the days of TV) were choirs in miniature, except that they always lacked female voices, for the drinking parlours of South Wales were places few women ventured into. At "stop tap," the hour when the licensing laws demand that landlords cease serving alcohol, the choirs were transferred to the street. It is strange, too, that a Welshman, if he sings alone, will get morose, whereas if he can harmonize, then he enjoys it more. To hear anything like it today, one needs to go to a rugby international match at Cardiff Arms Park, particularly if the other team is England. Sixty thousand Welshmen singing hymns in harmony at a sporting event is a frightening sound. Most opponents reckon it is worth six points to Wales before the game even starts.

Music in Wales is not, of course, confined to the pubs, but it is peculiarly oral. Save for the harp, there is not a great tradition of instrumental music in Wales. Many indeed learn to sing their part not from normal notation but from a strange, somewhat esoteric, form called tonic sol-fa, which does away with complications, such as key signatures or modulations. This works perfectly well for hymns but is a little too simplistic for oratorio, the other great Welsh tradition. Most people in Wales have at least a nodding acquaintance with the great oratorios, particularly the *Messiah* and

Mendelssohn's *Elijah.* Small indeed is the town in South Wales where one performance of each is not given each year.

The first time I heard Handel's *Messiah* was in a chapel in my home town of Ammanford. In the vestry as one entered was a pile of scores. If one wanted to sing it, one went upstairs with the choir; if one wanted to listen, one sat downstairs—except for the "Hallelujah" Chorus, which everyone knew and sang. The assumption was that if one took a score, one knew the work sufficiently well to be able to participate. The orchestra was scratch, though the organist knew his part backwards. Together it made an enthusiastic, if unrehearsed, performance, and one I like to think Handel himself would have approved of.

The tradition still persists. Each year the National Eisteddfod of Wales is held, a strange week-long Welsh cultural love-in, with competitions for poetry, singing, and, most prestigious of all, the "chief choral." The choir that wins that prize has something of the status of a winning football team and is treated as such in its home town. When English choirs started winning regularly a few years ago, it caused consternation and disbelief in the valleys.

The Eisteddfod is a curious blend of Celtic nationalism and nineteenth-century mock-paganism. There is a druidic circle and a company of bards and druids, many of whom are nonconformist ministers playing at being pagans. They dress up in what are believed to be druidic robes, and ceremonies take place involving a horn of plenty and a sheathed sword representing peace (though nothing for fertility). It is all relatively harmless symbolism invented in the last century. The serious side of the Eisteddfod, however, is a deliberate attempt to enhance the status of culture in Wales. For one week in August, radio, TV, and the press report it fully, and while it seems a strange event to many English-speaking Welshmen, since all the proceedings are in Welsh, it helps to preserve the reality of the language and the image of Wales as the home of a living culture. Most of the poetry is, unfortunately, untranslatable, and little of it has in fact been translated into English. If the test of great writing is the extent to which it can be appreciated and understood in other languages, little of Welsh literature would seem to qualify as great. The best-known piece of "Welsh" writing translated into English is still *The Mabinogion,* a collection of mediaeval tales, somewhat akin to the

Icelandic sagas, even though the most popular version is that produced by a Scotswoman, Lady Charlotte Guest, in the first half of the last century.

One should not seek Welsh fluency solely in Welsh, nor for that matter in the written word at all. One should seek it in the speakers.

In British politics this century there have been two giants of spontaneous oratory, both Welsh: David Lloyd George and Aneurin Bevan. Churchill's speeches were always written in advance, carefully constructed, rehearsed, and performed. Lloyd George and Bevan were both natural debaters of immense skill and spontaneity. They could each thrill the House of Commons with a flow of English unrivalled in their time. In 1909, when Lloyd George was Chancellor of the Exchequer, the House of Lords unconstitutionally rejected his budget. Discussing the peerage, he said: "They have no qualifications—at least, they *need* not have any. No testimonials are required. There are no credentials. They do not even need a medical certificate. They need not be sound either in body, or in mind. They only require a certificate of birth—just to prove that they are the first of the litter. You would not choose a spaniel on these principles. . . ." He had probably the greatest command of the spoken word of any British leader of the twentieth century. Yet his writings are dull, almost turgid; too many details tend to submerge the argument.

Both men had a strong sense of the dramatic. One of Lloyd George's conscious tricks, which he had learned from Welsh preachers in action, was always to start a speech softly, working up the volume when all had craned forward to make sure they could hear. Neither had a particularly good voice. Lloyd George's was high, and Bevan had a lisp and a partial stutter. Yet when the flow was on, they were impossible to resist. Not for them the conscious well-turned phrase of a Churchill. They relied on the passion and vehemence of the language to carry the day. Aneurin Bevan was never Prime Minister, and Lloyd George never held office after 1922, yet memory of their parliamentary abilities still persisted even as late as 1964, when I first entered the House of Commons. There were still some MPs in Parliament then who had heard the great debate of May 1940 when Chamberlain fell and Churchill came to power. To those who were there, Lloyd

George's speech in that debate was the greatest spontaneous parliamentary performance they had ever heard—particularly if they happened to be Welsh.

More than most, the Welsh seem to have a strong belief in the power of language. It is sometimes more important that an argument should be passionately put than that it should be right. They seem to believe that passion convinces, and in this they are of course wrong. But what a splendid illusion.

The nineteenth century was supposed to be the era of the Scots in British government. If so, the late twentieth century is that of the Welsh. There are thirty-two parliamentary seats in Wales, but many more MPs who are Welsh, which means that areas of England and Scotland are represented by Welshmen. In the last Labour government, the Prime Minister, James Callaghan, represented South-East Cardiff; the Leader of the House of Commons, Michael Foot, sat for Ebbw Vale; the Lord Chancellor, Lord Elwyn-Jones, came from Llanelli; the Home Secretary, Merlyn Rees, was from the Glamorgan valleys; the Secretary of State for Wales, John Morris, was of course Welsh; and the Foreign Secretary, Dr. David Owen, was part-Welsh by origin. In the Foreign Office itself, two of the Ministers of State, Lord Goronwy-Roberts and Ted Rowlands, were Welsh, and I was the Ambassador to the United Nations. There was a distinct Welsh lilt in the upper reaches of British diplomacy.

Wales is, in short, a good place to have come from. Given the centralized nature of British institutions, it is, however, hardly surprising that too few Welsh people stay behind. The stage is perhaps too small and the level of education too high for Wales to be able to accommodate all its brightest. They have enriched English life, though at the expense of the relative impoverishment of that of Wales itself. It is a trend which, despite the efforts of the Welsh nationalist movements in recent years, seems likely to continue.

THE SCOTS

Despite its basic lack of political sovereignty, Scotland is in many ways a separate nation. It is not a state in any federal sense, certainly not an independent nation, and could for example in no way claim a seat in the United Nations. It is, however, far more than the sum of the twelve regions that make it up.

Scotland has recognized borders that have remained unchanged for centuries and a system of law quite distinct from that of the rest of the U.K. The established church is Presbyterian, not Episcopalian, the system of local government is distinctive, mayors are provosts, towns are burghs, and Scottish education has a tradition and organization different from those of England and Wales. In Scotland many functions of government, administered by separate ministries in England and Wales, come under the control of one member of the Cabinet, the Secretary of State for Scotland. Sport is organized on a national basis; the Scottish national soccer team, for example, takes part as Scots, not Britons, in the Soccer World Cup. In 1978 Scotland was the only team from the U.K. which competed in the final stages, England having been eliminated in the qualifying rounds. Scotland is thus a separate geographical entity, and there is no Scotsman living who fails to know that that is what he is.

Scotland's distinctiveness is in many ways a product of its history. It was a separate kingdom for centuries until James VI of Scotland, the son of Mary Queen of Scots, became James I of England on the death of Queen Elizabeth. The union of the two nations was uneasy until the Act of Union of 1707, and even thereafter Scottish traditions and allegiance led to two rebellions against the English Crown, that of the Old Pretender (son of James II) in 1715 and that of his son Bonnie Prince Charlie in 1745. In recent years the Scottish National Party has become a major political force in Scotland on a platform that includes separation and independence.

What, then, makes the Scots still a nation? It is, in the end, the perception that they are that makes them so, despite the extent to which they are integrated into the U.K. as a whole. Scottish MPs sit at Westminster, and it is the British Parliament that imposes the taxes and distributes the benefits. Scotland's government is different but not independent.

Unlike the case in Wales, there is in Scotland no national language other than English, for Gaelic speaking is now confined to some remote areas of the Highlands and islands. There is little really distinctive in the culture, save perhaps for caber-tossing and the bagpipes, and yet the fact remains that Scotland feels different, is different, and is likely to remain so as long as the people themselves feel this to be the case.

Visitors to Edinburgh cannot long imagine themselves to be still in England. The architecture is distinctive, seeming to demand rain and fog. The city earned the nickname Auld Reekie, and all the anti-pollution acts of successive governments have failed to change it. The air may be cleaner, but the atmosphere remains.

Britain is in many ways much less homogeneous than the

United States, for all its size and regional history. Boston and Houston have much more affinity than do Edinburgh and London, or Glasgow and Manchester, for that matter. The unusual thing about Scotland is that it has managed over 250 years to preserve a sense of national identity while lacking the overt political framework to sustain it. In the past, distance may have contributed to this phenomenon, but it is remarkable that political nationalism in Scotland has grown at precisely the time when travel and communications have been made easier. The Lowlander and the Highlander feel an affinity for each other far greater than does the Lowlander for his immediate English neighbour. The former identify themselves as Scots, the latter as English.

The principal exports of Scotland are its whisky and its people. The word *whisky* itself derives from the Gaelic *uisge beatha,* "the water of life," a derivation it shares with other raw spirits. Its great advantage is that it can be drunk long or short. If one puts ice and soda into it, it hardly matters which brand one drinks, since the soda dilutes and the ice desensitizes. Most of the scotch usually bought is at any event blended. The Johnnie Walkers, Haigs, and Dewar's are all mixtures of a number of different whiskies. Some emerge from the blender's art tasteful, some bland: it is all a matter of taste—though I often wonder why such a pallid scotch as Cutty Sark is so popular in America. But the real joy of scotch whisky is in the unblended malts, a pure spirit that depends for its taste not on the skill of the blender but on the quality of the water and the peat used in its distillation. There are literally hundreds of malt whiskies, the best known of which are probably Glenlivet, Glen Grant, Glen Fiddich, Glenmorangie, Glenfarclas, and Laphroaig; they range from the sweet Glenmorangie to the extremely peaty Laphroaig. They should be drunk either neat or with only a small drop of water as pure as one can get it. In no circumstances should they be iced or subdued with soda. They deserve to be savoured. As an after-dinner drink, instead of cognac, they are immensely superior. Moreover, they have the great advantage of being so numerous as to give the prospective aficionado an almost limitless opportunity for personal experiment. Once you are addicted, the task will happily prove to be lifelong. Malts warm in the same way a good Havana should, and, since U.S. citizens are denied the latter, it would seem an ideal opportunity for trying the former. Many are, however, kept and drunk in Scotland itself. They are produced in local distilleries and therefore only in very limited quantities. I once found one called Glen Coe, 100 proof and very smooth, but I have never seen it in England, let alone in America.

The Scots themselves seem to treat their whisky with contempt, even disdain. Once in John o'Groats, near the most northerly point of the Scottish mainland, I was surprised to see the locals drinking it mixed with the equivalent of 7-Up. It is a habit which, while it produces spiked lemonade, has little else to recommend it. The resultant brew is sickly sweet and the flavour of the scotch is successfully concealed. But if the object is to conceal the scotch, why bother to drink it in the first place? Gin, vodka, or even moonshine would do just as well.

The Scots are, however, serious drinkers. To them (as to the Irish) alcohol is not social lubrication but a means of release. When in drink, the Irish fight, the Welsh sing, and the Scots become garrulously loquacious. A Scottish football crowd, particularly when in England, tends to be brutish. After one Scotland-England game at Wembley, the centre of London was littered with celebrating Scots for three days after the match was over, a few heads were broken, and some arrests were made. They take their pleasures earnestly, as befits a dour northern people, not quite with the blackness of the Scandinavians but certainly without the somewhat tolerant, even carefree, attitude of the English.

Whatever he is, the Scot is not a good loser. When Scotland was beaten in the 1978 Soccer World Cup, it became a national disaster. The inquest went on for weeks, the manager nearly lost his job, and the team itself was an object of derision. When shortly afterwards it beat England at Wembley, it was as if national honour had been restored, and the historical defeats of Flodden and Culloden avenged. If sport is sometimes an indicator of national identification, then the Scots take it very seriously indeed.

The history of Scottish emigration is, if anything, more remarkable, if less romanticized, even than the Irish. The Highland clearances of the nineteenth century, when crofts were demolished to make way for sheep herding, meant poverty in the Highlands. In the early nineteenth century the Highlands supported a considerable population, mainly of small tenant farmers who made a

poor living from the poor land. Later, large numbers of Highlanders emigrated, and only recently has the population begun
to climb again with a deliberate attempt by government inter-
ventionist policies to introduce some industry. But it is a slow
process, and the young tend to drift from the land to the cities or
even further abroad.

As immigrants and traders, the Scottish were and are superb:
hard-working, disciplined, thrifty, canny businessmen, and honest
administrators. The history of Canada, Australia, New Zealand,
South Africa, and the United States is in part the history of the
overseas Scot. Canada, in particular, attracted many in the nineteenth century, and both its map and its politics illustrate this:
the Mackenzie River; Canadian Prime Ministers Sir John Alex-
ander Macdonald and McKenzie King, and British Prime Minister
Bonar Law and Cabinet minister and press baron Lord Beaverbrook (both of whom re-emigrated to England), as well as a host
of others, are examples of the astonishing spread of Scots across
the globe. In the United States there are Aberdeen (Maryland,
South Dakota, and Washington), the McKenzie River in Oregon,
McPherson counties in Kansas, Nebraska, and South Dakota.
Three men of Scottish descent signed the Declaration of Independence, and two other signers were part Scottish. President
Monroe's father was of Scottish descent, and Presidents Truman
and Hayes had Scottish blood in their veins.

The Scottish emigrants mostly went not out of altruism but
from necessity. When Cecil Rhodes first opened up to the West
that part of Africa which is now Zimbabwe (formerly Rhodesia)
there is a story told of his summoning a meeting of merchants in
what is now Bulawayo, to tell them of his plans for the future of
central Africa. He lectured them on their duty to generations yet
unborn and concluded with a ringing plea that they should not
forget posterity. It is said that after a long pause one Scottish
trader broke the silence with: "But, Mr. Rhodes, I'll have you
know I didna come here for posterity."

They may not have come for posterity, but they helped to shape
it. The stereotype of the Scot is that he is narrow in his outlook,
careful with money, if not actually tight, dour, stubborn in his
views, a man of few but well-chosen words, honest and straight in
his dealings, with a Calvinistic bent to his religion and a strong

sense of hell-fire and damnation, a stickler for the proprieties, a good and careful administrator, a person conscious of his history and tradition and very much separated from the English. Scots make, it is said, good if unimaginative civil servants and politicians, well-trained and reliable doctors and lawyers, effective if conservative bankers, strict and disciplinarian teachers, and careful scientists. It is said they are good on the details but lack a strong sense of vision. Like most national stereotypes, it is, of course, only partially true. Rutherford, who first split the atom, was of Scottish ancestry. So, for that matter, was Andrew Carnegie, who not only made his millions as a successful entrepreneur against intense competition but also then gave much of them away. In many small Scottish towns (as in many U.S. cities, including New York) there exists, even today, a Carnegie library. They are monuments to his generosity and benevolence (and perhaps his sense of guilt). Scotland has not, however, produced political giants in the Lloyd George or Churchill mould. They have been more of the Bonar Law type, careful rather than bold, and cautious rather than inventive. Harold Macmillan was perhaps an exception, but his family had lived in England for three generations (and his mother was American). It is said that the Scots make excellent deputies. They can be the backbone of an organization but rarely its guiding or creative force.

A Scot is not easy to know well. There is a closeness about him which is difficult to penetrate. It can be mistaken by an outsider for insularity, remoteness, or arrogance, and natural gregariousness is not his most obvious quality. But there is of course another side. Scotland has produced in Burns one of the truly great romantic poets of the English language. Once one has learned the dialect, there is a simple beauty to his poetry that is unique. If the English only read him more, his reputation would surely be as high south of the border as it is north of it. A man of humble birth, who led a wild life, he produced some of the most beautiful love poetry ever written. Take the following, for example:

> *Nae gentle dames, though e'er sae fair,*
> *Shall ever be my muse's care:*
> *Their titles a' are empty show;*
> *Gi'e me my Highland Lassie, O.*

Within the glen sae bushy, O,
Aboon the plains sae rushy, O,
I set me down wi' right good will,
To sing my Highland Lassie, O.

Oh, were yon hills and valleys mine,
Yon palace and yon gardens fine;
The world then the love should know
I bear my Highland Lassie, O.

But fickle fortune frowns on me,
And I maun cross the raging sea;
But while my crimson currents flow,
I'll love my Highland Lassie, O.

Although through foreign climes I range,
I know her heart will never change,
For her bosom burns with honour's glow,
My faithful Highland Lassie, O.

For her I'll dare the billows' roar,
For her I'll trace the distant shore,
That Indian wealth may lustre throw
Around my Highland Lassie, O.

She has my heart, she has my hand,
By sacred truth and honour's band:
'Till the mortal stroke shall lay me low
I'm thine, my Highland Lassie, O!

Fareweel the glen sae bushy, O!
Fareweel the plain sae rushy, O!
To other lands I now must go,
To sing my Highland Lassie, O!

Burns himself wrote of this poem: "My Highland Lassie was a warm-hearted, charming young creature, as ever blest a man with generous love. After a pretty long tract of the most ardent reciprocal attachment, we met by appointment, on the second Sunday of May, in a sequestered spot by the banks of the Ayr, where we spent the day in taking a farewell, before she should embark for the West Highlands, to arrange matters among her friends for our

projected change of life. At the close of autumn she crossed the
sea to meet me at Greenock, where she had scarce landed when
she was seized with a malignant fever, which hurried my dear girl
to the grave, before I could even hear of her illness."

The worship of Burns by Scots (including those who have never
read him) is little short of adulation. I cannot imagine the English
celebrating a Shakespeare Day the way the Scots celebrate Burns
Night. Perhaps they should. I am never quite sure, however,
whether the ceremonial eating of haggis on that occasion is a trib-
ute to the fact that it is an excellent way of eating otherwise inedi-
ble offal or to the fact that Burns succeeded in writing a poem in
its honour.

> Fair fa' your honest sonsie face,
> Great chieftain o' the puddin'-race!

Good haggis well cooked and served is an experience everyone
should go through. It is a thrifty peasant dish: offal and oatmeal,
mixed and seasoned and boiled in a sheep's stomach. It sounds un-
appetizing, but then so does pâté de foie gras when reduced to its
origins.

Burns was essentially a "common" poet. One writer on Scotland says firmly that he clearly belongs to the "social realistic
18th Century mould" (whatever that may mean). Perhaps it is
true rather to say that he just does not fit into any one of the usually recognized categories. He used words superbly to speak to
simple people in a way that has rarely been equalled. The Russians see him as the vanguard of the proletarian revolution, and he
is read a great deal in the Soviet Union, though perhaps in the way
Dickens is studied there, more as social commentary than as art.
Burns wrote almost entirely in the Lowland Scots vernacular,
which for an Anglo-Saxon makes the reading difficult until one
has mastered the idiom. Once one can understand the local usage,
however, much of his poetry emerges as simple yet great. It is well
worth taking the time and trouble needed to read him.

There seems to be a correlation between what we like to think
of as national character and the land from which it springs. To understand the Scots, one has to go to Scotland, and not merely to
Edinburgh or Glasgow. Edinburgh is a city that produces history,

learning, and the arts. Glasgow is a modern thrusting industrial city that exudes enterprise and work. But to see Scotland, one must go north to the Highlands. They are one of the few wild places left in Europe, and to stand at sunset on Cape Wrath at the extreme north-west point of the Scottish mainland, where there is nothing but ocean between there and the North Pole, is unforgettable. It is desolate, wildly beautiful, and humbling. I imagine the same is true of the Himalayas or Alaska, though the mountains of Scotland are lower and the land is more peopled.

The Highlanders are hard on the surface (they have to be), soft and slow speakers with a considered use of words, economical and thrifty in their language, as if that, too, is something to be treasured and not spent prodigally. *Dour* is an adjective often misused about the Scots. It really means that they think before they utter and then make sure that you understand exactly what it was they wanted to convey. Not for them a tumble of verbiage, nor, for that matter, a great deal of wit.

Much of Scottish humour tends to be rough and urban. The most famous Scottish comedian of the twentieth century was probably Sir Harry Lauder, and his most famous act was probably that of the Glasgow working man who sang when drunk:

> *I belong to Glasgie,*
> *Dear old Glasgie toon,*
> *But there's something the matter with Glasgie,*
> *For it's going roond and roond.*
> *I'm only a common old working chap,*
> *As anyone here can see,*
> *But when I get a couple of drinks on a Saturday,*
> *Glasgie belongs to me.*

It is a song one hears regularly in any liquid Scottish gathering and obviously has touched a chord in the Scottish soul.

The Scottish National Party members did not want only Glasgow to belong to them, but all of Scotland. Surprisingly, perhaps, separatism became a live issue in British politics in the 1970s. At one time dissatisfaction with Westminster was so live that the SNP had eleven members in the House of Commons. The government at the time was a minority Labour one, and the action of the SNP

in joining the Conservatives and Liberals in voting against that
government on a confidence motion precipitated the 1979 general
election and Mrs. Thatcher's premiership. It also produced a
memorable phrase from Jim Callaghan, the then Prime Minister
and Leader of the Labour Party, who turned to the Nationalists
during the debate and said, "It must be the only occasion in history when the turkeys have voted in favour of an early Christ-
mas," and he was right. When the election was held, the Nationalist representation in the House of Commons fell to two and their
vote in Scotland declined from 30.4 per cent in 1974 to 17.3 per
cent in 1979.

The fact was that they had peaked. The people of Scotland and
Wales had been asked to vote in 1979 in separate referenda on
whether they wished a measure of devolution of power from Westminster with Assemblies in both Cardiff and Edinburgh. The
Welsh peacefully rejected this notion. The Scots voted 52 per cent
to 48 per cent in favour, but since the proposal required 40 per
cent of the entire electorate to carry, it also failed in Scotland.
Lord Randolph Churchill once said, "Trust the people," and in
this decision the people were almost certainly right. For an Assembly in Edinburgh to be meaningful it would have to have
power, particularly that of raising taxes. By the government's proposals for devolution, this power was still to be reserved to Westminster. If it had had the right to raise taxes, Scotland would be
well down the road towards separation from the rest of the U.K.,
which many Scots were much too canny to want. On the other
hand, without this power the Assembly would have become just
one more unit of local government, a proposal for which there
was little enthusiasm. So the support was tepid and devolution
failed. The SNP then withdrew its support from the government,
which fell, and with it fell many of the Scottish National Party
MPs.

Nationalism could rise again, though the benefits of North Sea
oil seem now to have made this less rather than more likely. It
appears to have been based not only on a strong sense of national
identity, which of course still exists, but also on the feeling that
Scotland, like Wales, was too low on the list of national priorities,
that it was a long way from London and tended to be treated as
such. Nationalism was never a popular demand for separation and

nation-statehood for Scotland. Provided that British Governments in the future recognize the depth and validity of this feeling, nationalism is unlikely to regain the strength it so recently appeared to have, and Scotland will remain part of the United Kingdom.

THE IRISH

The English do not understand the Irish. But then neither do the Americans, for all their romantic attachment to an island almost as remote from them as this year's Fourth of July is from 1776. But if we do not fully understand the Irish, at least we in Britain have had to live with the problems of Ulster.

Ireland is not, never has been, and in my view is hardly likely to be, one peacefully united, independent entity. Its divisions lie too deep in history, tradition, religion, and blood.

In the thirteenth century there was an Irish Parliament, though it was confined to Irish settlers, as the native Irish were not represented. In 1494 the Irish Parliament passed Poynings' Law, which provided for all Irish bills to be submitted to Henry VII and his council in London, where they might be approved or rejected. At that time English authority was concentrated mainly in the Pale area around Dublin. Ulster was then ruled by powerful, independent, and wild chiefs.

Under Elizabeth I, attempts were made to extend English sovereignty to Ulster and substantial English and Scottish immigration took place. While the native Irish were Roman Catholic, the immigrants were not. The Scots were Presbyterian and the English mostly Anglicans. Throughout the seventeenth century, Protestant authority was strengthened, mainly as a result of Cromwell and of the defeat of the Catholic James II by his successor Prince William of Orange in July 1690 (an event still celebrated pretentiously, on July 12, as a public holiday in Northern Ireland). Thereafter the history of Ireland is that of the increasingly turbulent relationship between the Catholic majority in the thirty-two counties of Ireland as a whole, the Protestant majority in the six counties of Ulster, and successive British Governments at Westminster.

In 1920, after the Easter Rising of 1916 and a guerrilla campaign, waged mainly in the South of Ireland by the then IRA (Irish Republican Army), the British Parliament passed the Government of Ireland Act. This provided for two Parliaments, one for Southern Ireland and one for Ulster, which comprised the six counties of Antrim, Armagh, Down, Fermanagh, Londonderry, and Tyrone and the county boroughs of Londonderry and Belfast. Wide powers were to be devolved to each Parliament, and the Act envisaged the creation of a Council of Ireland, consisting of representatives from both the South and the North, designed to promote cooperation and encourage ultimate reunion within the U.K. The whole of Ireland was to remain part of the U.K.

These arrangements were reluctantly accepted by the North but failed to satisfy Sinn Fein, the main nationalist party in the South, which boycotted the new Parliament, while the IRA continued with the war. The Council of Ireland never met.

In 1922 a treaty was concluded with the "rebel" nationalist movement and the Irish Free State came into being as a self-governing state within the U.K. Thereafter the nationalist cause in the South disintegrated. Part of it wanted and accepted the treaty, while part wished to continue the struggle for a united Ireland. The Irish Republic has continued independent, and Northern Ireland has continued to be part of the U.K. to this day. Whatever one thinks today of the 1922 settlement (and attitudes differ widely, depending from which side of the Atlantic one is considering it), it was at least a genuine political attempt to deal with the underlying realities of the situation in Ireland, realities that persist today.

The central fact of Irish politics is still the existence in Ulster of approximately one million Protestants who in successive elections over some 150 years have consistently demonstrated their bitter opposition to union with the South. Even if the rest of Britain were to decide to withdraw its political, economic, and military support from Northern Ireland, that fact would remain unchanged. It is, moreover, a fact well recognized in Dublin, where on Northern Ireland there is a far greater clarity of view than seems to exist in some quarters of North America. The people there are, after all, somewhat nearer to the problem. It is this also which accounts for the (in all the circumstances) quite astonishing identity of approach between Dublin and successive British Governments. I cannot imagine that any government in Dublin would wish to find itself saddled with the problems of trying to coerce or pacify such a large number of unwilling and militant potential citizens. The mind recoils from the prospect.

Nor is it any answer to wish them elsewhere or to invoke the curse of Cromwell. The Protestants in Ulster are not there as imperialist settlers of recent origin. Indeed, their derivative title is some decades better than either that of the English in North America or for that matter the Dutch in South Africa. There is no metropolitan power to which they can return, and it would be a queer sort of political morality which determined that after four hundred years of continuous presence they should now be shipped back to Scotland or England.

The issue in Ulster is not one of forcible integration of the six counties into the Irish Republic. It is how to adjust the relationships between the one million Protestants and the half million Catholics who live there, in ways that guarantee to all the population equality of economic, social, and political treatment. The leg-

acy of the past is the bitterness of the present, and in looking at
Northern Ireland, like Chesterton,

I tell you naught for your comfort,
Yea, naught for your desire,
Save that the sky grows darker yet
And the sea rises higher.

Ulster will get worse before it gets better, and it will get better
only when the issue of forcible unification is rejected. In other
words, the sooner it is accepted on both sides of the Atlantic that
you cannot force a million people into a unity they do not wish,
the sooner we can proceed to more radical policies designed to
achieve the integration and equality of all its inhabitants. I believe
this is now accepted in London and Dublin. It were as well if it
came to be equally accepted in the United States.

The attitude of many British people towards Ulster is very simple. They wish it would go away. It is widely regarded as wholly
anachronistic that people should be so divided on grounds of
religion, divisions, moreover, that seem to be stridently expressed,
even enjoyed, by the extremist leaders. But while many people
in Britain wish it would go away, they nevertheless seem to be
able to perceive why it will not. Unless and until the majority
of the population of Northern Ireland accept the principle of unity
(and in my view that is an extremely long-term prospect), there is
absolutely no reason why Britain should allow an unwelcome unification to be forced upon them by the present IRA, who do not
seem to represent the views of the 500,000 Catholics in the North,
let alone the Irish Government in the South. We really cannot
permit a small group of urban terrorists to coerce a million people
into a course of action to which they are deeply and sincerely opposed. This is not to say that the Protestants of Ulster should have
a permanent veto on British Government policies. It is, however,
to recognize that they do have to be persuaded and led, not forced.

From this principle flows an obligation which it is difficult to
discharge: that of attempting to maintain law and order in Northern Ireland. British soldiers will have to remain in Ulster until the
violence comes to an end. If the Irish Government can then
persuade the majority in Ulster of the benefits of unity, and if that

majority then opt for association with the South, no one would be more delighted than I. The rest of Britain gains nothing economically from Ulster—quite the contrary is true. In short, what we are trying to do is to discharge an obligation laid on this generation by our predecessors.

There are approximately one million Irish people living in Britain itself. By a quirk of our electoral and immigration systems, they are allowed free access to Britain and a vote in British elections. The constituency I represented in Parliament for ten years had a large Irish population. It was both welcome and accepted. Many of the Irish in Liverpool or London remain Irish citizens. They are not there as prospective U.K. citizens but more as immigrant workers who, despite their allegiance to what is in theory a foreign country, are accepted on a basis of equality with the rest of us. As far as I know, they are under no legal, social, or political disabilities, though this is not true of English people living in the Republic. They do not have a vote, nor can they be members of the Irish Parliament, the Dáil. There are many Southern Irish citizens in the British Army and, despite Irish neutrality in World War II (an act that many British still find difficult to forgive), many Irish then served with distinction.

While the British have tended to accept the anomaly of the Irish connection, the Irish have tended to deepen it, perhaps understandably wishing to emphasize their independence and freedom of action. Until the latest "troubles" in Ulster the British hardly considered the Irish in Britain as a major issue. They still do not, except when some particular act of terrorism brings it again to their attention. The assassination of Lord Mountbatten or of Conservative MP and aide to Mrs. Thatcher Mr. Airey Neave, or some particularly senseless act of violence in Ulster itself, creates a consciousness for a time, but it has never yet manifested itself in action against the Irish actually living in Britain. Despite the deaths in Northern Ireland and the steady commitment of British soldiers, no political party has espoused an anti-Irish policy. There have been no reprisals on the mainland, nor has there even been a serious move towards the disenfranchisement of those Irish citizens living in Britain. It is a display of patience and understanding that I find astonishing. Much of it is due perhaps to the way in which the British (and particularly the English) have tended to view the Irish over the years.

National characteristics in the end quite often turn out to be other people's misperceptions. The Scots are supposed to be mean, the Welsh devious, the English tolerant, the Irish eccentric. None of these is, of course, entirely true. There are as many devious Aberdonians as there are careful savers in Cardiff, and English tolerance has certainly not always extended to racial integration. But all the others seem to agree on the uniqueness (and eccentricity) of the Irish. It is probably due to the fact that Ireland is an island and hence "over the water." There seems to be something mystically separating about a channel, whether it be St. George's (between Wales and Ireland) or the English Channel between us and France. The people on one side, even if they are naturally outgoing and gregarious, seem to feel a difference and distinctiveness from those on the other. Particularly is this true if one of the two peoples has over the years tended to migrate towards the other.

There are two distinct strands to the mainland's perception of the Irish, each of which is fallacious. One regards an Irishman as fey, other-worldly, mystical, charming, word-master, and poetic, someone who might just actually believe in leprechauns, and indeed who comes from a country where leprechauns might just actually exist. To these observers, the Irish have produced mystics, faith-healers, playwrights, critics, actors, writers, soothsayers, necromancers, musicians, dancers, and romantics. The Irish they think of are Shaw, Wilde, Yeats, Synge, Joyce, Behan, and Beckett, most of whom were obliged to emigrate from Ireland to make their names and reputations abroad, usually in London or Paris. If the experience of these emigrants is to be accepted at face value, life in Ireland was one in which talent abounded but opportunity did not.

The other strand is darker and equally unrealistic. It sees the Irish as feckless, drunken, violent, spendthrift, hard-working manual labourers but rarely to be entrusted with executive responsibility, priest-ridden, superstitious, overfecund, and irresponsible. Life in Ireland to these observers is hard and poor, dominated by peasant agriculture and the Catholic Church. The Irish pubs of Hammersmith (London) or Liverpool on a Saturday night are almost foreign territory into which mere Englishmen enter at their peril, lest they find themselves assailed with personal responsibility for the woes of Ireland extending back to Cromwell and beyond.

Ireland is what it is: a small country attached tenuously to Europe through its connections with Britain and the EEC, relatively non-industrialized and with an agricultural system more akin to the French than the English. It is developing slowly, but its raw materials are few and its industrial skills are as yet unrealized.

It is a country of deep piety, with an attachment to the Catholic Church unmatched in Europe, outside Italy or Poland. Its people are the mixture one would expect of a country slowly moving from an agricultural economy to an industrialized one. Managerial skills are slowly developing, though almost all the development capital has to come from abroad. Its politics are confused and still dominated by the North and the special relationship with Britain. Waving the bloody shirt of the "troubles" (though in this case the shirt is green, not red) is still legitimate politics in the South, and the Orange fear of "Popery" is very much alive in the North.

Towards the problem of Irish unity there is considerable apathy in Britain as a whole. Many do not understand why a battle in 1690 should still be celebrated so vehemently in Ulster. Nor do many comprehend in a time of increasing ecumenism the bitterness with which some Protestant clergy in the North rail against the Pope and the Catholic Church. Many English still regard the Irish as eccentric figures of fun, fighting old battles that the rest of the world has long since forgotten. On the whole the regard is affectionate, except towards the IRA. One hopes it will remain so.

The Irish have been and remain great emigrants. From the time of the great potato famines of the 1840s, when the English sat and watched a people starve, to the present day, Irish men and women have left their homeland and created new lives overseas. In the United States, over 16 million people are of Irish descent. They have enriched the host countries with their energy, their liveliness, their traditions, and their capacities. Paradoxically, their grandchildren still find it necessary to blame the English for the infinitely higher standards of living they now enjoy as third- or fourth-generation immigrants. One would have hoped that by now the ancient and justified grievances might perhaps have dimmed.

The British-Irish connection is unique, legally, economically, and constitutionally. Poor Roger Casement found it impossible in 1916 to recruit more than a handful of Irish prisoners of war to fight on the German side against the English, and the same was true in World War II. Despite Ireland's neutrality, many Irish served in Britain's armed forces when there was neither obligation nor necessity. Until recently the economies of the two countries were closely coordinated to such an extent that the currencies were almost identical. Britain is overwhelmingly the largest market for Irish goods, nearly half of Ireland's exports going to the U.K. in 1979.

There is thus an overt political detachment between the two countries that is not matched by the degree of contact at personal or business level. The only major problem (and it is one held in common) is the future of the North, and even over this issue the support for the IRA in the South is more imagined than real—a contribution to a collecting box in a pub, an expressed support for the "boys in Belfast," or a veneration for the genuine independence fighters of 1916. Few in the South would welcome the problems that the million Protestants would bring, and fewer, I think, would be prepared to face those problems if it meant the weakening of the Irish economy that further separation from Britain would entail.

We tolerate and even enjoy each other most of the time, though I expect the Irish understand the British rather better than the other way round. After all, they have over the years had to make the greater effort.

THE NEWCOMERS

Somewhat under 4 per cent of the British population is now black or brown, but since black and brown people, almost without exception, are to be found only in the major cities, the average figure gives a false impression: in large areas of the country there are virtually no "minority ethnic groups," while in parts of London, Birmingham, Manchester, and Leeds the proportion can be as high as between a third and a half. The change in the appearance of these inner-city areas has therefore been dramatic. Thirty years ago, apart from a few black people living in old ports such as Liverpool and Cardiff, the British population was virtually 100 per cent white. But the arrival of black and brown people in Britain's—and above all in England's—cities has been only one of a number of dramatic changes that have affected those cities since the end of World War II.

The first "colonials" to decide to settle in Britain after the war were West Indians from such islands as Jamaica and Trinidad who had served in the British Army or the RAF, had been stationed in Britain during the war, and had acquired a wife or girl-friend and felt that a new future beckoned them back to England. By 1948 the word had got around, and entire shiploads of West Indians were arriving in Britian: indeed, the *Empire Windrush,* a former troop carrier, was diverted to the "immigrant" route and its first trip is now seen symbolically as the beginning of the wave of black and brown immigration to Britain.

Like all immigrants, the first West Indians saw Britain as a land of opportunity as much for their children as for themselves. They therefore showed the usual immigrant determination to get on, to put up with tough conditions and to work long hours in the hope that their children would know something better. They probably also inculcated their children with high expectations about the fu-ture—expectations that have all too often been unrealized. The West Indians found accommodation and jobs where they could, and since their arrival coincided with massive public housing ("council house") programmes and slum clearance schemes—part of the post-war Labour government's pledge to make the country a land fit for returning heroes—many ordinary English people were at the same time moving out of the inner-city areas into new towns and new suburbs. The immigrants therefore tended to move into older housing in city-centre areas. They settled where there were jobs, and these were often in the public service sector where pay may have been reasonable but where hours (for example, for bus drivers) were what is now called "unsocial."

The black and brown population thus mirrored Britain's econ-omy and housing situation. Where there were virtually no vacant jobs—such as in the towns and cities of Scotland or in the West of England—there were no blacks. Where dramatic changes were tak-ing place in the living and working conditions of ordinary English people—in London and the South-East, for example—blacks were part of the process. London families were getting smaller, too, and, particularly in the sixties and seventies, it began to be normal for wives to go out to work. Larger Victorian houses were thus being abandoned for two- or three-bedroomed council houses; from the fifties onwards a general change in the life-style of the British working class was bringing car ownership and continental holidays within the reach of millions for the first time. Nine-to-five jobs were part of this new life-style, and the immigrants were the people prepared to put up with old-style housing and work longer hours, thus facilitating the upward mobility of the native English.

By the mid-fifties, immigration from the West Indies was running at tens of thousands of workers a year. London Transport actually opened recruitment offices in Barbados and in Trinidad at that time to recruit staff for London's buses and underground. By then new gaps were appearing in the work-force, as traditional jobs in the mills and textile factories of the North of England were shunned by local workers. Employers in Bradford, for example, began to recruit Indians and Pakistanis, and a chain reaction started as individual immigrants began to find jobs for their brothers and cousins. In some cases entire factories in the North of England were staffed by Indians or Pakistanis from a single village, all because one trail-blazer had begun the process and then been used to find other workers to fill more vacant jobs. By the early sixties, Asians were beginning to appear in large numbers, not so much in London as in the East and West Midlands, Yorkshire, and the Manchester area.

It was in the early sixties that the "open door" policy for Commonwealth immigrants was finally ended by a Conservative government with the passing of the Commonwealth Immigrants Act of 1962. But despite increasing tension in areas of black and brown settlement and the beginnings of a white backlash, the Labour Party, under the leadership of Hugh Gaitskell, steadfastly opposed the new law. They saw it as racially motivated and as an attack on the idealistic view of the Commonwealth as a worldwide multiracial association. But underlying realities were different. The British economy, after a decade and a half of steady growth and low inflation, was beginning to show clear signs of the "stagflation" that was in later years to be its chronic affliction. Jobs were not so easy to come by: indeed, the children born to the post-war "baby boom" were beginning to come onto the labour market.

There was thus a crude economic rationale for the ending of the open-door policy. But in many ways the new law was liberal. The ban was on new workers or "heads of families"—the family members of immigrants who had *already* entered were still able to join them. And the law affected only those with "colonial" or local citizenship—not those with U.K.-based British citizenship. In the future the arrival of the wives and families—often ladies and children in brightly coloured saris—and the arrival of waves of British citizens (like the Asian Ugandans who had retained British citizenship and were expelled *en masse* by Idi Amin in 1971) puzzled British people who had been told that immigration had virtually stopped. It also provided a ready political market for those prepared to whip up fears in the white population about unending black or brown "invasions," and allowed politicians like Enoch Powell, then a Conservative member of Parliament for a West Midlands constituency, to claim that officials were not implementing the closed-door policy and were fiddling the statistics.

The result was a steady stream of legislation designed to make immigration more difficult—the Commonwealth Immigrants Act of 1968, which introduced a voucher system for U.K. citizens without a previous connection with the U.K.; the Immigration Act of 1971, which brought the old Aliens Acts and the new Commonwealth immigrant laws into line; and, in 1981, a British Nationality Act that made it much more difficult for British citizens not actually descended from Britons and living in Britain to transmit their citizenship to their children. At the same time, successive governments introduced legislation to outlaw racial discrimination, beginning with the first Race Relations Act in 1966. As American cities burned in the series of race riots that racked the States in the sixties, Britain remained astonishingly complacent about race relations and inner-city questions. Yet surveys showed that black and brown people—even British-born children of immigrants—found it much more difficult to get employment than white children with the same or even worse qualifications.

By the early 1980s black and brown people were part of the British scene. As old-fashioned corner shops disappeared from city streets, unable to face competition from the supermarket chains, the "Paki-shop"—misnamed because most of them were owned, not by Pakistanis, but by Indians from East Africa—appeared to fulfil a vital service. Asian families, prepared to join together and work long hours, set up shops, often with sub-post offices, which sold everything from milk to sealing-wax, from vegetables to skipping-ropes. Since the opening hours of most British shops are apparently based on the assumption that housewives do the shopping (the nine-to-six opening times being virtually impossible for anyone working more or less normal office or factory hours) the Asians were able to exploit this example of British inflexibility to earn a livelihood. The ambition of many Asian immigrant families seemed to lie in the direction of shopkeeping, the typical activity of those who, in East Africa, had formed the intermediate shopkeeping and clerking classes between the British colonialists and the African masses. In a largely hostile—or at least indifferent—environment, the Asian immigrants were sustained by their powerful religious traditions. Sikh and Hindu temples began to appear, and mosques—sometimes financially aided by a different class of immigrant, rich Arab investors and businessmen from London's West End—became commonplace in the larger cities.

The Asians, then, seemed destined to be the later equivalent of the Jews of the turn of the century: enterprising newcomers, hardworking and determined to get on, but with a religious and cultural background that both sustained them and separated them from the rest of the population. Children of Indian and Pakistani origin, teachers said, were doing well in school, particularly in mathematics and music. The host population seemed to regard the Asians in much the same way that, nearly a century before, they had regarded the Jewish migrants from Eastern Europe. Asians were seen as successful businessmen and admired for their hard work and family-centredness, but also resented for the same reasons, even feared as people with cultures and patterns of behaviour that the ordinary Briton found rather frighteningly impenetrable.

The blacks, on the other hand—the descendants of the West Indian immigrants of the fifties and early sixties—seemed, on the whole, destined to play a less economically successful role in British life. Black footballers and athletes became commonplace by the seventies—but often black athletes wondered whether they should represent Britain or their parents' country of origin, such as Jamaica, in international athletic events. There were successful black entertainers and artists—Trevor McDonald of the new TV

Channel 4, formerly of Independent Television News and of the now defunct BBC Caribbean Service, became Britain's first black national newscaster, and later ITN diplomatic correspondent—and of course cricket provided a traditional outlet for West Indian skills and aptitudes. But the average black family remained trapped in the inner-city areas, where social services, schools, and other amenities were under most strain and employment opportunities most limited. It therefore seemed as though the American pattern was being repeated, on a smaller scale, in England's major cities. Successful working-class whites were increasingly moving to the suburbs, where amenities were good, with, for example, new schools being built in spacious surroundings, while the immigrants and those unable to aspire to the suburbs remained concentrated in increasingly impoverished inner-city districts. Local authorities in those areas often tried to remedy some of the deprivation by raising the rates (local taxes levied on house-owners), and these stiff rises often had the same effect as similar taxes in the States: they drove out more and more of the middle-income residents, who resented being asked to take on the financial burden of a community that had been created as a result of national policies.

The London Borough of Lambeth, a part of inner London running south and south-west of the River Thames from a point approximately opposite the House of Commons or Charing Cross, is typical. Lambeth includes both a typical inner-city area, Brixton, where many blacks and immigrants live, and, further south, a typical middle-class area, Streatham. Its range of housing goes from the so-called gentrified areas—areas of old housing which had gone into decay but which are now being renovated and becoming more fashionable—where well-off people who work in the West End or the City now live, to dilapidated multi-occupied tenements where black and Irish families live alongside the poorest segments of society—the very old, large one-parent families, young "squatters"—and so on. By 1981 the rates in Lambeth had risen so high that for many residents they were higher than their rents. A "rates rebellion" against the local left-wing Labour administration of Councillor Ted Knight seemed inevitable.

It was in Brixton in April that the inner-city riots of 1981 began. For several days youths, many of them black, fought police, broke shop windows, and set buildings on fire. Fortunately no one died—*The Economist* magazine described the whole affair as typically British: the rioters were, it said, disorganized and hardly knew what their target was, and the police were equally bemused and muddled. Millions of pounds' worth of damage was, however, caused to property even if no lives were lost. Many youths blamed the police for being repressive and racist; the police said that, in a situation of social deprivation, it was they who were being given the job, as one officer put it, of keeping the lid on the dustbin. Mrs. Thatcher's government set up an inquiry and promised aid to the inner cities. But, at the same time, her government had launched a campaign against what it considered to be free-spending local authorities—of which Lambeth was typical—and had sided with local Conservatives who had campaigned against high rates.

Later, in July, there were further riots, following more or less the same pattern. Generally speaking, youths, often but by no means always black, began battles with the police that ended with violence and damage to property, including the looting of shops. Rioting was particularly ferocious in Liverpool, where the only death occurred—that of a handicapped boy, not involved in the riots, who was struck by a police vehicle. Liverpool, one of the country's major ports in the eighteenth and nineteenth centuries— and, ironically, the original centre of the slave and sugar trade with the West Indies—had become an economically depressed area, and its inner-city area, Toxteth, a place with a reputation for racial tension and police harshness.

All of these events were profoundly shocking for Britain's self-image. People blamed Mrs. Thatcher's economic policies, the governments whose immigration policies had allowed blacks into the country, and the police: people were quick to apportion blame according to their own views and prejudices, with (generally speaking) the left calling for more subsidies and state intervention, and the right for more discipline and tougher policing. But youth unemployment was the underlying theme. Thousands of British young people were leaving school in the early eighties with no hope of obtaining employment. In the inner-city areas—and, significantly, in Northern Ireland—youth unemployment was often well over 50 per cent, and for areas such as Northern Ireland and Brixton the prospect was of jobs being available for only about a quarter of all school-leavers. Few would deny, whatever their views of Mrs. Thatcher or the police, or however strong their racial prejudices, that the rage and frustration of the most energetic section of the population had *something* to do with the 1981 riots.

But if 1981 was a bad year for the cities, 1982 proved calmer. Nevertheless, profound difficulties remain and the problems of integrating our black and brown fellow-citizens are yet to be solved. While the shock of the 1981 rioting has stimulated an intense public debate over what to do about the inner cities, the actions which the government has so far taken have been slow and extremely limited in scope. It would be a foolishly optimistic man who could say that there is now no possibility of a repetition of what happened in 1981. I am neither so optimistic nor, I hope, so foolish. So long as there remains in Britain a sizeable proportion of our population living in deprived areas who themselves feel that they are discriminated against on account of the colour of their skins, so long is there a real danger of renewed violence in our streets.

Business, Work, and Wealth

BRITAIN'S ECONOMIC DECLINE

A well-known and penetrating commentator on British economic and social affairs, the late Sir Andrew Shonfield, wrote in 1958:

> Here is a vicious circle with a vengeance: Britain's slow rate of economic growth, which is not matched by any slowness on the part of anybody to demand a rising standard of living, causes the rise in prices; this rise carried on over a period of years results in higher and higher demands for money wages; and that in turn drives up the price level further. On the other side the remedies which are applied, with the intention of creating a psychology of

restraint through the restriction of output, tend to impose a further check on the growth of British industry.

Shonfield's diagnosis remains true today. The slow rate of growth of the British economy—consistently slower than growth in the economies of other European countries—has meant that, as trade unions have pressed for wage increases to maintain standards of living, so the policies adopted to deal with inflation have effectively reduced the real value of wage increases and slowed down industrial output. Simple explanations such as lazy British workers, incompetent managers, greedy unions, or the class structure all overlook the key and basic fact: Britain's economy has a very long record of comparatively low growth. For Shonfield, a look at capital accumulation and investment—particularly at net fixed investment as a proportion of the net national product—provided the simple reason. Britain has tended to spend capital rather than to invest it productively.

But this is not something new. Over one hundred years ago, at the Paris Great Exhibition of 1867, the British were shocked to find that other European countries and the United States walked off with the same prizes which, at the previous British exhibition in 1851, Britain had taken easily. Fear of German competition in particular seems to have been commonplace in British industry for at least one hundred years, and far-sighted politicians were then already pointing out that it was inevitable that the first country to have an industrial revolution should enjoy a head start in world markets, and equally inevitable that newcomers would catch up and eventually overtake. But that explanation does not tell us why Germany, twice defeated in war with its industry largely wiped out, has been able to bounce back so fast and so effectively: its economy—that of West Germany, the Federal Republic—is now twice the size of Britain's.

Britain's economic problems, then, go further back even than the trade union movement, which some people now blame for the whole sorry syndrome. Some of the problem is statistical: depending on whatever preconceived ideas people have, they can usually find the statistics to back their case. Britain's share of world trade, for example, has been declining since about 1800. Some people might claim, therefore, that Britain's decline as an economic power dates from the eighteenth century; but world trade as such had hardly started in 1800 and Britain's share of a vastly expanding world trade remained constant at about a quarter for the whole of the nineteenth century. In terms of shares of world trade, at the beginning of World War II, in 1939, Britain, with 12.1 per cent, and the United States, with 13.5 per cent, were the world leaders. At the end of the war, while Britain had maintained its share, with 11.5 per cent, the American share had gone up to 21.8 per cent. By 1975 Britain had slipped to 5.0 per cent and the United States to 12.2 per cent, while West Germany and Japan had reached 10.3 per cent and 6.4 per cent respectively, having started virtually from zero in 1945. But in absolute terms a slightly different picture emerges. British exports expanded fourfold between 1939 and 1976. You could thus argue that British exports continued to expand, but that others entered the field and did rather better.

One factor that cannot be overlooked is the former British Empire. Shonfield points out that British industrial performance in normal peacetime years this century has been consistently worse than that of Britain's main competitors with the exception of the period of the Great Depression in the 1930s. It was then that Britain's European competitors were particularly badly hit as outlets closed because of the recession, while Britain, at the centre of an Empire producing raw materials, was able to expand imperial trade and keep things going much better. Shonfield actually concluded that, had it not been for this breathing space which imperial trade afforded, and the military successes in the two world wars, Britain's decline would have been much more steep—and much more apparent. Political success both in imperial trade and then, later, in decolonizing the Empire, and the astonishing victories in the two major wars of the twentieth century, somehow postponed the day of reckoning. Other commentators would go further, suggesting that Britain's early industrial and trading successes were built on the captive markets of Empire and that British industry and exporters had never learned to compete in a modern sense with rivals from other industrial countries. The imperialist mentality, according to this school of thought, had never given way to the more modern, adaptable entrepreneurial approach.

But if Britain's economic decline has been a long-term affair—
and it may even be that other nations which followed Britain into
the industrial revolution will also follow it into stagflation—
several facts are, today, indisputable. The first is that, comparatively speaking, Britain has done particularly badly in *recent*
years. The second point is that Britain remains far more dependent on external trade than does, for example, the United States.

To look at Britain's recent economic performance, we need to
look at average annual growth rates and at average gross domestic
product per capita figures for Britain and its main competitors. As
for growth rates, these have been consistently lower for the United
Kingdom than for its competitors for at least twenty years. For the
period 1967–78 the average rate of growth for all the main Western economic countries (the OECD) was 3.8 per cent; for Britain
it was 2.3 per cent, compared with Germany's 3.8 per cent, Japan's
7.2 per cent, and the United States' 3.0 per cent. If we take 100 as
the index of U.S. real GDP per capita in 1975, Britain's rate was
62, compared to Germany's 79 and Japan's 65; if we go back to
1967, we find Britain at 61 and Japan at 50. So if Britain, until
the sixties, had done reasonably well by its own standards though
not in comparison to its rivals, since then the position has been
one of bad performance even by the rather low British standards.
This was the basic conclusion of the Brookings Institution study,
Britain's Economic Performance, published in 1980.

The other key fact about Britain's economic performance is the
country's extreme vulnerability to external factors, or, put differently, its very high reliance on international trade. In terms
of exports per head of population, Britain, until the late sixties,
had the highest rate in the world; it is still second only to Germany. In recent years there has been an adverse trade balance:
between 1970 and 1979 exports rose by 49 per cent, imports by
78 per cent. Britain's best market was, until the mid-seventies, the
United States; now the Federal Republic of Germany is Britain's
single best customer, and while British exports to the world in
general rose by 8 per cent in 1979, for example, exports to the
European Community rose by 30 per cent, and by the early eighties exports to the EEC were accounting for nearly a half of Britain's total exports. But the trade deficit even with the European

Community was still massive: over £2.5 billion at the end of the seventies.

The Brookings study concluded that, while conditions for all major trading nations had been difficult since the seventies—with raw material price rises in the early seventies, followed by the massive rise in world oil prices in 1973—Britain had somehow weathered the storm less well than her competitors. Why was this? A number of possible explanations were looked at in the Brookings study, including the possibility that an "output" gap was harming production, that external factors were responsible for domestic inflation, and that policy-making by governments had been seriously deficient. Basically, the Brookings researchers concluded that adjustments to Britain's international financial position—for example, by securing a better international balance of payments—had been secured by a number of mechanisms, above all by manipulation of the exchange rate and the running of the economy below full capacity (and incidentally creating unemployment), which in turn had adversely affected the country's export performance. One of the Brookings studies found that rising import prices had indeed been one of the components of domestic inflation, but thought that the labour market played a key role. Partly as a result of the unpredictability of real wage levels caused by variations in the exchange rate, wage increases were a major factor in short-term inflation and in long-term productivity. Brookings points out that in the seventies 93 per cent of the *money* rise in GDP went straight into inflation: in other words, a great deal of the effort expended by trade unionists in demanding higher wages, and of employers in resisting them, was a complete waste of time. Brookings' basic conclusion: "Britain's economic malaise stems largely from its productivity problem, whose origins lie deep in the social system." Some of the answer lay in increased industrial investment, especially in small firms, and a real depreciation of sterling (at that time being maintained at an artificially high level by a combination of high domestic interest rates and the value of Britain's North Sea oil).

A combination of factors—a long-term reliance on inherited imperial markets; the complications of the world role of sterling and the difficulties of accepting its reduced world role; the push for high wage levels, with increases financed by inflation rather than through increased production; and a severe lack of productive investment—therefore lie behind Britain's recent abysmal economic performance. The vicious circle described by Shonfield has not yet been broken. Indeed, recent years have seen the polarization of political attitudes in the two major political parties as the Conservatives (who have seen themselves as the party of employers) and the Labour Party (historically the political wing of the trade union movement) have tended to espouse philosophies and to advocate solutions in the economic sphere that tend to lay the blame on the other "side." Economic policy, in fact, has been so central to the political debate in Britain in recent years that it has sometimes seemed that politics was only about economics. The Thatcher government's basic policy—control of the money supply, with less and less involvement by government in economic activity—could be contrasted with the "alternative economic strategy" of the Labour left, involving more nationalization, increased government investment in industry, and import controls. The duality of the political debate somehow reinforced the view that explanations and solutions were easy. Half the country, it appeared—the Tory voters—thought trade unionists were lazy and greedy, with communist and left-wing leaders who needed to be shot; while the other, Labour-voting, half, thought honest British working men were being increasingly exploited by vicious and desperate capitalist bosses. The political system therefore mirrored the class divisions, tended to see solutions as one-sided, and almost completely failed to focus on the international dimensions of Britain's predicament. Few politicians were prepared to recognize that it takes two sides to make a relationship, and that if the relationship goes wrong or sour it takes two to mend it. While Mrs. Thatcher ploughed on with her economic policy—which the Brookings report said would certainly cause short-term economic disruption—left-wingers continued to assert that the answer lay in more "socialism," conveniently blaming Mrs. Thatcher for events that in many cases were not the result of her policies at all but caused by changes in the international economic system. As the politicians shouted their slogans, the unemployment figures climbed to unprecedentedly high levels, nearly 3.5 million by the summer of 1982. Increasingly, employment expanded in those areas of the economy where employers felt that the big unions (which they perceived as the major problem) were not in control, so small firms, employing non-union labour (and, increasingly, female labour), began to do well as many giants went bankrupt and large areas of industrial Britain, particularly in the Midlands, saw traditional firms go to the wall.

EMPLOYMENT, JOBS, AND THE TRADE UNION MOVEMENT

While many industrial nations—especially the newly industrialized countries such as Brazil and Korea—still have a large agricultural population, and many European countries such as France and Italy have seen their agricultural population decline dramatically this century, Britain's labour force began to move out of agriculture into the cities and urban employment with the enclosure movement in the mid-eighteenth century. By the middle of the last century, only just over a quarter of Britain's population was engaged in agriculture, a situation not reached in continental Europe until the recent post-war period. Indeed, these demographic factors are often ignored by economists seeking explanations for Britain's poor economic performance. Until recently France, Germany, and Italy had a steady stream of able-bodied workers available for their industry as people left the land. When this source of labour dried up, France and Germany recruited hundreds of thousands of immigrant workers from such countries as Algeria, Portugal, Yugoslavia, and Turkey. While, as we have seen, Britain took in some hundreds of thousands of Commonwealth immigrants during the same period, these were admitted as families for settlement; on the Continent, particularly in Germany, the "guest-workers" came as workers, without their families and on the clear understanding that they would in due course return home.

This is a major difference between Britain and all the other Western industrial countries. The British population has been essentially urban for a long time—though this is not to say that, even with less than 3 per cent of the population now engaged in it, Britain does not possess an efficient and highly productive agricultural sector. Few British families can remember when part of the family tilled the land, unlike, for example, the French, for whom urbanization has, for many families, taken place within living memory. British workers have been settled in their ways, therefore, for a long time—have been better housed, with a smaller average family size, for longer than their European neighbours. And British industry in recent years has not had the mobile labour force, cheap in social infrastructure costs, which other European countries have had as a result first of urbanization and later of the influx of guest-workers. Even the United States has had a recent history more similar to that of continental Europe than that of Britain, as millions of "illegals" have swelled the labour force and have been, by definition, more mobile and adaptable than the settled American worker. The question is whether there is an endemic "British sickness" or whether, as other countries whose industrial revolutions came later catch up with British social patterns, they, too, will show the same symptoms of slow growth and low productivity. With political pressure forcing an end to immigration in Europe and a much tougher policy on illegal immigration in the United States, it could well be that in terms both of the adaptability of the labour force and of consumption (there being fewer families suddenly experiencing a large rise in their standard of living) the United States and the continental European economies are actually travelling the same route as the British.

The other spectacular change in the labour force—which the British and American economies have experienced in much the same way and at about the same time—has been the massive move, since the sixties, into the service sector, with over half the working population in both countries now engaged in the provision of services. "Services" covers everything from hotels and betting shops to health services and car repairing to research and development services. But, to take one example only, the number of people engaged in the provision of educational services in Britain doubled (from 881,000 to 1,620,000) between 1959 and 1973. There has been a steady movement out of manual work; even *skilled* manual work now accounts for less than a third of the labour force. Indeed, during the seventies, service sector jobs rose by 1.7 million, while employment in manufacturing fell by 1.1 million.

The picture that emerges is very different from the usual image of the British worker as an amiable, conservative, uneducated elderly male manual factory worker. The British worker is increasingly someone with education or training and unlikely to be engaged in either manual work or in industry. The British worker is still, however, likely to be male, but, as we have seen, employers are tending to recruit more female than male workers for a variety of economic and social reasons. At the end of the 1970s there were almost 400,000 more jobs in Britain than in 1969, but while the number of employed men fell by over 600,000, the number of employed women increased by over a million. The service sector, in fact, employs more women than men.

About half of all British workers are members of a trade union. Trade union membership grew substantially in the early years of this century, declined in the twenties (probably as a result of the recession and unemployment) but began rising in the mid-thirties and is now at its highest level ever. In the early part of the century there were over 1,200 separate trade unions; by the end of 1978 there were only 462. If, however, you consider that 207 unions had fewer than 500 members, the picture becomes clear: trade union membership has been increasing as the number of unions has been declining, and large amalgamated unions are now the norm. At the end of the 1970s the 26 largest unions each had over 100,000 members and between them accounted for over 80 per cent of all trade union membership.

The Brookings study tried to answer the question: Do trade unions cause inflation (by pushing for higher wages unmatched by increasing productivity) or does inflation cause trade unions (by making workers seek the protection of trade union negotiators in protecting the real value of their earnings)? In Britain the way people answer that question would be largely determined by their political position, and objectivity is very difficult, but the facts suggest that workers have sought the protection of trade unions at times of inflation rather than being pushed by unions into inflation-causing wage demands. Over the last ten years—when inflation in Britain has been worse than ever, at one point risking "hyper-inflation"—trade union membership has increased by nearly a third. Increasingly, trade union membership and wage militancy has been spreading into white-collar sectors—including bank clerks, insurance company employees, and the lower grades of the civil service.

But while the number of different unions is steadily decreasing, the overall number of unions remains high in comparison with those in other countries. Whereas in the United States all the workers in one factory or even industry will be organized in one single union, British unions, with only one major exception—in the coal mines, where the National Union of Mineworkers remains the one industry-related union in Britain—organize workers by grade or craft. Thus in an engineering factory, for example, the skilled workers will probably be organized by the engineering union, while the unskilled will be members of one of the giant "general" unions, and the office staff may be members of yet another union. When the board of British Rail starts wage negotiations with the railroad employees, it has to deal with three unions: the Associated Society of Locomotive Engineers and Firemen (representing the actual locomotive drivers, ranging from highly paid drivers of inter-city express trains to much less well paid drivers of local goods trains), the National Union of Railwaymen (representing the porters, signalmen, guards, and other rail staff), and the Transport Salaried Staffs' Association (representing the ticket clerks). In the motor car industry literally dozens of different unions may be involved in negotiations at any one time.

Trade unions are not, however, divided on religious lines, as in continental Europe. Most trade unions have a clear political affiliation with the Labour Party (which came into existence in the last quarter of the nineteenth century to secure the election of trade union representatives to Parliament) and all are affiliated to the single trade union confederation, the Trades Union Congress (TUC). The TUC is organized through a General Council, where senior officials of member trade unions sit, with a permanent staff headed by a general secretary. Although the trade union movement itself is deeply divided politically—with most union executive committees split between Labour supporters and the Labour left and the Communists—the Trades Union Congress as such restricts itself to pronouncements about economic and other policy matters of interest to trade unionists. Its officials sit on government committees and, together with the employers' representatives grouped in the Confederation of British Industry (CBI), are routinely consulted by government on economic and other matters.

The "Labour Movement" in Britain consists of the trade unions and the national and local organizations of the Labour Party. To an extent unknown in the United States, trade union officials seek and obtain political office in Britain through the medium of the Labour Party. The former general secretary of the giant Transport and General Workers' Union, Frank Cousins, a veteran of bitter disputes involving dockers and busmen, entered Harold Wilson's Cabinet in 1964 as Minister of Technology, while the Labour Prime Minister from 1976 to 1979, James Callaghan, was a trade union organizer of tax employees before entering the House of Commons. The Labour Party's National Executive Committee has trade union as well as political representatives, and the annual conference of the party is attended not only by Labour MPs and representatives of constituency Labour parties, but also by delegations representing affiliated trade unions. After a special conference held in January 1981 to alter the system of selection of the Labour leader, trade unions will now have a 40 per cent say through an electoral college in choosing the next leader of the

Labour Party. Senior members of the trade union movement, on retirement from their union jobs and on leaving the TUC General Council, are often made life peers and sit in the House of Lords. Previous general secretaries of the TUC, like Lord Citrine or the late Lord Feather, thus ended their political lives alongside the representatives of the hereditary aristocracy, and a previous left-wing Engineering Union leader, a man loathed in his time by many Conservatives, now sits in the House of Lords as Lord Scanlon.

The British Communist Party, which in general elections can barely manage to get 20,000 votes in the country as a whole, is highly active in trade union affairs and has party members on the national executive committees of many of the most important British unions. This seems to have been the result of a deliberate policy by the Communists, who decided to concentrate on obtaining industrial power rather than political office through the ballot box. Key union leaders like the leader of the Scottish miners, Mick McGahey, or (until his dismissal in 1980) a key union negotiator in British Leyland's factories in the West Midlands, Derek Robinson, are communists. Increasingly the Communists seek alliances in trade union affairs with Labour left-wingers, forming the so-called broad left alliance. In addition, Trotskyites have managed to gain influence in some quarters, particularly in white-collar unions. They tend to set up so-called rank and file committees demanding more active or revolutionary policies from trade union leaders whom they often accuse of being out-of-touch bureaucrats.

It is this highly political trade union activity that marks Britain off from many other countries. Although some trade union leaders will claim that they are merely professional negotiators, the very structure of the trade union movement and the Labour Party forces all active trade unionists to take up a political position. The Conservative Party, simply because it needs a majority of votes to obtain power, obviously has the support of a large number of trade union members, and has made strenuous efforts to get individual members of unions to "negotiate out" of the political, pro-Labour Party, side of trade union membership. By law, trade unions have to keep their industrial and political funds separate, and a member may opt not to contribute to the union's political activities. This is called "opting out of the political levy," and Conservatives claim a great deal of success in persuading their supporters to opt out. One union that has grown considerably in recent years as white-collar wage militancy has increased has been the Association of Scientific, Technical and Managerial Staffs, whose leaders include Labour left-wingers and communists. But large numbers of the ordinary members, while applauding union success in bargaining for higher wages, clearly do not support the political complexion of the union's leaders, and many thousands have opted out.

Because unions often have leaders with outspoken political views, and because trade unions can easily be portrayed as scapegoats at times of economic and social tension, the trade union movement and its policies and practices have been at the centre of the political debate in Britain in recent years. There have been isolated individuals to whom the description "trade union wreckers" can be fairly applied and there have obviously been political extremists at work in the trade union movement. But the image of Britain as a country permanently on strike is simply false. Official statistics show that in the five years 1974–78 eight major industrial countries, including the United States, Italy, and Australia, lost more working days through strikes and industrial disputes than Britain, while Germany, Japan, France, and the Netherlands lost fewer. (The international statistics are based on a selection of industries only; they include mining, manufacturing, construction, and transport.) Within Britain, strikes and industrial disputes occurred almost solely within large firms and very rarely in small establishments. Vast numbers of businesses—well over 90 per cent of the total—and at least 80 per cent of British workers are never involved in strike action.

Britain has known more strikes in the past than in recent years. Seen over time, the first twenty years of this century seem to have been the worst as far as Britain's strike record is concerned. There followed a period of very few big strikes, doubtless as a result of the world recession, and then, in the 1970s, major strikes in several major industries, including the mines and the postal services. But these strikes were strikes called to press claims against *government* pay policy, since in both cases the employers were, directly or indirectly, the government and the issue was government pay policy. Many of the most controversial strikes in Britain in recent years have been called to protest government pay freezes and incomes policies rather than as political moves against individual employers. Far from being revolutionary in inspiration, such strikes have usually been called by unions anxious to maintain differentials and concerned that, when wage "ceilings" are introduced, it is not their members who are unfairly affected by an arbitrary cut-off point. Since there is an annual "pay round," whereby unions, one after the other, put in their claims for next year's pay rise—beginning towards the end of the summer—whenever a government decides that an arbitrary figure of 5 or 6 or 8 per cent will govern pay rises, some unions are bound to be caught.

Increasingly, unions, like businesses, are becoming large amalgamated organizations. Union organization is not merely normal but compulsory for at least 5 million British workers: the "closed shop" exists not only in single-union industries such as mining but also in printing (where the unions virtually control recruitment and where access to highly paid jobs in London's newspaper industry, for example, is largely restricted to the relatives of union members); metal manufacturing; food, drink, and tobacco firms; clothing and footwear; gas; water; electricity; transport; and communications. The Conservative government's Industrial Relations Act in 1971 tried to outlaw the closed shop, and in August 1981 the European Court of Human Rights ruled that three railway workers, who had been dismissed for failing to join a union, had been denied their freedom to decide for themselves whether or not to join a trade union. Pressure is strong in Conservative Party circles for more action to curb compulsory union membership, but many employers clearly favour the closed shop, since the 1971 Act could not have been nullified without full co-operation between employers and unions. In fact, the picture that emerges is of large firms increasingly deducting union dues directly from wages, providing an office for the union convener and the shop stewards (the union representatives in the different departments or "shops" in a factory or business), and insisting that people employed by them should join the union.

Things are thus very far from the picture conjured up by the two extremes of the British political spectrum. The leftist paints trade unionists as strugglers against the vicious exploitation of capitalists, whereas the rightist sees enterprise being stifled by communists and agitators. Both, in other words, see a much more individualistic world than is in fact the case. In most industries, national negotiations between national union and employer representatives determine wage rises, and a collective relationship exists between unions and employers in which both agree on centralization and an equilibrium of power. Employers have therefore agreed on an extension of the closed shop because they recognize that increased union membership means a stronger union and a better bargaining partner. "Good industrial relations" depend on fair collective bargaining and on the bargains being carried out; the closed shop seems to assist this process and therefore to contribute to good industrial relations. It is, of course, part of the labour relations scene in a number of countries (including the United States, where valid union security agreements may be negotiated except where state law prohibits them), though illegal in others, including Germany.

One reason why many employers favour the closed shop and a strong trade union is that, once a collective agreement has been reached, the union officials can help ensure that the agreement is properly observed. As we have seen, most industrial disputes do occur in large undertakings, and they are often caused by what is called unofficial action. This is completely different from the industry-wide stoppage called in protest at national policy; such localized disputes often do not have union backing, which is why they are termed "unofficial." *Most* British strikes appear to be "unofficial" and in contravention of agreed procedures. There is thus a common interest between employer and union in maintaining collective bargains. There is not much research available on the subject of "unofficial" disputes, but they seem to be unpredictable and often highly personal in nature; they may, for example, have to do with relations between a specific foreman or manager and a worker or group of workers.

The history of government attempts to end the compulsory closed shop shows that legislation in this field is not necessarily effective. But a combination of media concern about strikes—developed at times almost to the point of national neurosis—and a belief by some economists and senior civil servants that poor productivity was caused by strikes and industrial disputes have forced all governments and opposition parties since the 1960s to promise to do something about industrial relations. The Wilson government in the late sixties produced a discussion document entitled *In Place of Strife* that proposed giving legal force to collective agreements and provided for compulsory "cooling-off periods" and official arbitration procedures in industrial disputes. Many employers, and many Whitehall officials, favoured the moves towards making the observance of collective bargains legally binding, but the trade union movement, led by the TUC, strongly opposed bringing the law into industrial relations. In the early seventies the Heath government brought in its Industrial Relations Act, involving the establishing of a special Industrial Relations Court, but it never received trade union support and much of the legislation was repealed by the Labour government of Harold Wilson when it came to power in 1974. In her turn, Mrs. Thatcher, on entering No. 10 Downing Street in 1979, assured her supporters that individual freedom would be protected against union abuses of power, but her then Employment Secretary, James Prior, preferred a cautious and pragmatic approach and resisted attempts to bring in draconian legislation. Repeatedly, political concern about union power, strikes, and industrial relations—often presented to the electorate in extremely over-simplified terms—has foundered against the rock of accepted, non-legal practices followed not only by the trade union movement but also (and this is often forgotten) by most big employers.

While strikes and trade union militancy have often been put forward as the explanation for Britain's industrial ills, another and allied phenomenon, overmanning, has now become the fashionable cliché for those seeking simple, instant reasons or excuses for the British disease. Conservative ministers in the eighties, such as the then Trade Secretary, John Biffen, were actually prepared to argue that unemployment, though unpleasant for some individuals, would ultimately help the British economy because it would result in the shedding of surplus labour. So for those who did not find the low levels of investment convincing as an explanation for poor British economic performances, or who did not think the explanation lay in the nature of the labour force in Britain compared with that in continental Europe or the United States, or who thought trade unions were not so destructive or strike-prone as to be responsible for all the failures, the slogan "overmanning" became the answer. "Overmanning" does at least have the advantage of not being a one-sided explanation; short-sighted capitalists may have failed to invest, and greedy trade union leaders may have preferred disruption to co-operation, but overmanning is a phenomenon for which *both* sides of industry must be blamed. Indeed, if overmanning is the real culprit, it must be caused by an over-cosy relationship between unions and employers rather than by the alleged propensity to confrontation.

The facts are, indeed, clear. Productivity (the ratio of output to the number of persons employed) has risen more slowly in Britain than in any of the other major industrial countries—yet until the 1950s Britain's record was consistently better than that of the others. By 1971 American productivity was precisely *double* that of Britain's, and French and German productivity about 50 per cent higher. The government think-tank, the Central Policy Review Staff, in a report in 1975 on the British automobile industry, found that vehicle assembly in Britain took 100 per cent more man-hours than it did in continental Europe. Not all British industry had such a poor record (in glass, carpets, and brick-making the record was much better), but the overall trend is clear. British productivity is low and may be getting even lower. Explanations are not easy—the Brookings study thought the phenomenon was supported by values deeply imbedded in British society. "The mutual tolerance," wrote economist Richard E. Caves, "which makes the daily life in Britain so attractive to many foreigners indeed prompts an acquiescence in things as they are and a willingness to cope with imperfection rather than make a scene."

There are, of course, other explanations. In some industries with poor productivity records there are rules and restrictive practices between, say, craft and general unions that adversely affect production. And the generalized use of overtime—though formally an extra, in fact commonly accepted by workers and employers alike—may harm productivity by appearing to make more time available to complete certain tasks. The quality of British management, and its alleged tendency to improvise rather than to plan ahead, and, to paraphrase Caves, to muddle through rather than seek clear solutions to production problems, may also be to blame.

But if British industry and British workers fail to keep up with internationally accepted norms of productivity, then, for a country so dependent on foreign trade, and one pledged through GATT and the European Community to maintain a high degree of free trade, there is only one answer: the least efficient go to the wall. Later we will look at British industry and how it is organized, and we will see that there is already evidence that British industries that do things well are achieving success in international markets, while the inefficient and those with poor productivity records are indeed going to the wall. For the worker, this means fewer jobs.

Unemployment in Britain, as in other industrial countries, has risen sharply since the oil price rise of 1973. But it has been worse than in comparable countries, and particularly bad in those parts of the country where declining industries were located: in Northern Ireland, Scotland, and the North of England (shipbuilding), in Scotland and Wales, where many coal mines have been closed, and in Scotland, Wales, and certain parts of England where large steel plants have closed. Unemployment did not reach 1 million until the mid-seventies but exceeded 3 million in 1982. Jobs have been declining in number while the work-force has been growing. The outlook for young people is particularly bleak, especially in depressed areas like Northern Ireland and in inner-city areas. Our average youngster is relatively well placed, in a prosperous eastern area where redundancies have occurred but both his parents have escaped; there are some job vacancies for young people and about 60 per cent of school-leavers end up with jobs. In Notting Hill, in London, where his parents met and lived, his chances would be far less. In Wales his cousins also face a bleak future.

BUSINESS AND INDUSTRY, MONEY AND WEALTH

While the British have been busy arguing about how to deal with trade unions and industrial relations, the remarkable fact is that foreigners have decided to invest in the country and often seem to have more confidence in its future than the British themselves. By 1975 American multinationals accounted for almost 17 per cent of the net *output* of the U.K. engineering industry—even though the actual foreign *ownership* of British industry is usually estimated at something like 2 per cent of the total. In fact, foreign investors were particularly active in Britain's engineering and chemical industries, and above all in industries making use of new technologies. This is in marked contrast to British investment abroad, which has tended to go into traditional, non-technology-oriented industries.

The changes in British industry since the Second World War have been enormous. Of the 200 largest companies in Britain in 1948, 179 had disappeared by 1972, mainly through mergers and amalgamations. As is the case with the trade unions, firms have been getting larger, and within Europe Britain has some of the largest plants and factories of all—although, as we have seen, small firms are, for a variety of reasons, the ones that seem to be doing best in the 1980s. But among Britain's most successful firms are large groups making food and drink (British chocolates, cookies, and sweets, or candies, are highly successful in the export markets of Europe and the United States, and although the British import large quantities of wine, alcohol, especially whisky, is also a highly successful British export, earning over £1 billion in 1980), tobacco (British cigarettes and quality pipe tobaccos remain popular throughout the world), textiles (despite contraction in the face of cheap imports, some brand names of British clothes, such as the St. Michael brand marketed in Britain by Marks and Spencer, are phenomenally successful in export markets), paper, and building materials. The metal and steel industries, and of course shipbuilding, have been declining, and there is some evidence that some sectors of industry are simply disappearing in the face of competition from other countries of the European Community. The British aircraft industry, for example, last produced a large commercial jet airliner—the VC-10—in the late 1950s, and has not managed to produce a commercially successful successor to the BAC-111 to compete against the newer versions of the Boeing 737 and the DC-9 for the shorter-haul air passenger market. Here, as elsewhere, a European pattern is emerging as large numbers of European enterprises combine to produce joint ventures like the European Airbus (for which the British made the wings) or the Jaguar fighter. Alternatively, British industry competes successfully with American industry to provide components for American aircraft (such as Rolls-Royce engines on 747s and for the Tri-Star). British firms no longer run the railroads of Africa and Latin America, but railway equipment is another successful British export, with British companies involved in renewal programmes in Hong Kong, Zimbabwe, and Peru.

Internationally, British goods are still famous for style and quality. British sports cars have consistently been popular in the United States, and despite attempts by the Taiwanese and the Ecuadorians to produce rival whiskies, scotch remains inimitable. Clothes, especially suits made from Scottish tweeds, and high-quality British shoes remain *de rigueur* for the fashionable the world over. The advantage of the English language gives British book publishing an automatic world outlet that the Finns or the Czechs, for example, do not have. But your electric toaster or shaver is less likely to be British than a few years ago, and it is very unlikely that your television set or transistor radio is made in the U.K. British Governments have tried to use government funds to promote British research and activity in the microchip field, to ensure that Britain does not lag behind in this field, too; in nuclear research for peaceful purposes, British scientists still remain in the forefront.

The myth of the British businessman holds that, when he is not playing cat-and-mouse with the trade unions or dealing with strikes and disruptions, he is having to hand over what little money he makes to the taxman. Yet another simple pretext for British industrial shortcoming thus looms into sight: the sole reason for it all, says one school of thought, particularly popular in the saloon bars of pubs in the London suburbs, is that high tax-rates stifle initiative. Strangely enough, however, it is people lower down the scale, rather than the company directors and businessmen, who pay proportionately more income tax in Britain than elsewhere. About 13 per cent of the average worker's earnings goes in income tax in Britain; in many countries—including France and Germany—no tax would be paid on average British earnings, and in the United States only about 2 per cent. (The average British income would of course be considerably *lower* than in the United States, so the tax paid on the average *American* income would be a better comparison. Average earnings in the U.K. in 1980, for a person in non-agricultural employment, were £2.63 an hour— about $5.75 at the exchange rate then—compared with $7.27 in the United States for a person in non-agricultural, manufacturing employment.) The British pay more tax than the Americans but less than the Belgians, Dutch, Swedes, and Germans. But, as if to compensate for fairly high personal taxes, the British tax system is lenient on corporations and gives great scope for avoidance (the legal way of arranging one's affairs to avoid tax—when tax is withheld illegally it becomes tax evasion). A great deal of effort and ingenuity, which some people think might otherwise be used in the creation of genuine wealth, therefore goes into schemes to avoid tax. The Brookings report commented: "For an outsider, it is difficult to understand how a country that imposed a maximum nominal tax rate of 98 percent on investment income also adopted capital consumption allowances that virtually wiped out the corporate tax on industrial and commercial companies, provided relief for almost half the remaining corporate tax on any dividends that are paid, taxed realized capital gains at a maximum rate of thirty percent while providing reduced rates for the first £9500 of gains, and exempted capital gains transferred at death." Wealth still largely escapes the British taxman, and attempts to broaden the tax base have still not produced a wealth tax.

The British tax system is therefore not so much a brake on initiative and hard work (and such evidence as there is suggests that the desire to earn more is stronger than any disincentive effect caused by high taxation) as a confused structure built up over the years as a result of attempts at reform that have generally avoided tackling problems raised either by entrenched interest groups or by the taxmen themselves. While foreigners may think that British taxes are high, the Briton regards anyone who actually pays the theoretically high levels of tax as so stupid that he deserves to lose his money. As with so much else in British life, the appearance and the reality are different; and as so often, the subtle differences between appearance and reality give rise to a rhetorical ambiguity that allows people of opposed views to claim that things are whatever they want to claim they are. Thus a Conservative advocate of private enterprise might claim that the tax system was driving people of initiative abroad by killing initiative, and in theory at least he would be right. The socialist could with equal reason claim that the system unfairly penalized the middle-to-lower-income families and, with the help of the accountants, allowed the rich to get off lightly. Immensely elaborate schemes set up by the Vestey family might be cited: by funnelling income abroad, the family—which owns meat companies and butchers' shops—managed to pay no taxes at all for year after year. The truth would, however, be different: the British tax system does little to encourage productive investment, penalizes wage and salary earners as opposed to investors and businessmen, and has so many special allowances that it is both inequitable and extremely complicated to administer.

Most people in jobs in Britain work either for the government or a nationalized industry, or else for a large privately owned conglomerate.

In Britain, the largest employers are public corporations such as the Post Office, the National Coal Board, and British Leyland, but nearly one hundred British companies have net assets over £250 million, and in terms of annual sales four of the top twenty industrial groups in Europe are British. We have already seen that, in Britain, it is large firms and plants that are strike-prone, with many smaller businesses never experiencing industrial action. Managers and investors know this, which means there has been a move away from investment in large plants in recent years. If, as seems likely, large plants are necessary in some fields for efficiency, this could be one interesting way in which the British make things difficult for themselves. But the large firms are concentrated in certain fields only; in industries such as oil refining, motor cars, aircraft, chemicals, and electronics a small number of large groups dominate the field, while countless small firms are active in other fields. Excluding farms, there are reckoned to be about 1.8 million private enterprises in Britain. While transport, energy, and communications are almost totally in the public sector, virtually all manufacturing (except steel, shipbuilding, and aerospace), construction, and other industries are in the hands of private enterprise.

The "City" of London is not only the name of a famous square mile of history; it is also the term normally and currently used in business and government to refer to Britain's financial institutions. Many countries have several capitals, one for government, another for finance or industry. In Italy and Germany, industry is concentrated in Milan and Frankfurt while government is carried out from the capitals, Rome and Bonn. In Britain, typically, the situation is ambiguous: Parliament and government as well as finance and banking are concentrated in London, but in two such different parts of London that you could almost say that finance and government had different capitals. The City of London is only one square mile—basically the EC2 postal district—but it has its own municipal council, police force, and Lord Mayor. (The Lord Mayor of London does not run London at all, but is a largely ceremonial figure presiding over the "square mile," while the political boss of the great metropolis, the chairman of the Greater London Council, is a far less well known figure.) The City is separate and special in many ways; some would say that the separation of industry and finance, based on ancient class distinctions, with "gentlemen" going into the City and "tradesmen" into industry, is still damagingly persistent.

The central financial institution in Britain is the Bank of England, set up by royal charter in 1694 and nationalized by the Labour government in 1946. It is the government's banker, and is basically in charge of the execution, through the clearing banks, of government exchange rate and interest rate policy. There are savings banks, a National Girobank, merchant banks, and other specialized institutions. The City is also the site of Britain's largest stock exchange. While it reigned supreme as the world financial center until at least 1914, the City has not ceased to play a major world role, and is still the place where many governments raise loans for big projects and where deals in basic commodities such as gold or coffee are done. Many commentators have praised the astonishing resilience and adaptability of the City. Anthony Sampson, writing in 1962, said: "the Dickensian-looking men in their mahogany parlours have turned from financing foreign governments to devising hire-purchase schemes; the Lloyd's underwriters have continued sitting in front of dog-eared ledgers, but now insuring atomic power stations and jet planes." In 1980 the Brookings study of the British economy echoed Sampson's view, praising the City for its adaptation to vast changes in the national and world economy and, incidentally, rejecting the view that Britain's financial institutions could be blamed for the country's industrial shortcomings.

The élite "accepting houses"—the small group of traditionally leading City investment banks—now have important clients in the

Middle East, and while family and connections are important for anyone hoping to join a City firm, a knowledge of a foreign language such as Arabic or even a degree in economics is now regarded as more of a help than in the past. Insurance companies, pension funds, and building societies, rather than the City grandees of popular mythology, now make many of the key financial decisions in the City. At the end of 1979 the total value of pension funds, in both the public and the private sectors, was approximately £40 billion, while the building societies had assets of just over that amount, and 20 per cent of world insurance business was still being transacted in the City of London. There have been constant criticisms that funds have tended to go for investment into countries whose industries compete with Britain's and, within Britain, to finance property investments rather than productive, wealth-creating activities. A feeling that British capital is not backing Britain lies behind demands from the Labour Party for new mechanisms for channelling funds into industry, and, on the party's left, for state control of, for example, the investment decisions of the pension funds. Meanwhile the City makes money for British investors in the Persian Gulf, in Malaysia, or in Brazil, and has become the centre of the Euro-currency market, holding billions of pounds in foreign currency—including, in 1979, about a hundred billion pounds in U.S. dollars.

The decline of the pound sterling is another story mirroring Britain's changing fortunes. The pound, which was worth $4.00 after the Second World War, has since depreciated more than any of the major Western currencies. In terms of purchasing power the pound slipped particularly badly in the early seventies, falling to 54 per cent of its 1970 level by 1975. This, in turn, was 32 per cent of its value twenty years before; the dollar and the German mark depreciated only about 50 per cent in the same twenty-year period. In terms of purchasing power in Britain, the fall has been dramatic: the pound of the beginning of the century is now worth, in terms of purchasing power, less than 5p—5 per cent of its original value. Politically, the pound has been an important symbol and even something of a national virility symbol: the decision to put the pound back to its pre-war level by adopting the gold standard in the twenties, or the decision of the Wilson government not to devalue on taking office in 1964, may have been dictated more by considerations of national prestige than by rational calculations of economic policy. In 1980 and 1981 British exporters complained that the high exchange value of the pound (which rose to over $2.40 in early 1981, having been at $1.80 in 1976) was damaging their chances in international markets, but the Thatcher government, seeing that a high pound made imports of essential commodities cheaper and therefore helped keep down inflation, took no action. It was the high interest rates in the United States during and after 1980 that finally caused the pound's value to go down—or rather, since most European currencies declined at about the same rate, caused a comparative increase in the world value of the dollar. The pound's role, until recently, as an international reserve currency has undoubtedly forced governments into action to defend the pound that has harmed the British economy. But British Governments have so far resisted any move by Britain into the European Monetary System—a so-called basket of European currencies which keep fluctuations in their relative value within certain agreed limits and which, some would argue, could be the forerunner of a new currency for the European Economic Community.

While business and commerce have the City, the government raises its funds from taxes. About half of the income of the government comes from income tax, and another large amount from indirect taxes—value added tax (VAT), and taxes on oil, wines and spirits, tobacco, and other sales. Local authorities get about 60 per cent of their income from the central government and about a quarter from the "rates," local property taxes. There are also national social security contributions, deducted, like income tax, from workers' pay by employers, which pay for social services, and a motor vehicle tax paid on every vehicle driven on the public roads. Originally the motor vehicle tax was intended to pay for road building and maintenance, but revenue now exceeds income actually spent on roads—just as social service *income* is not sufficient to pay for health services—and the government, in effect, lumps all income together, whatever its source.

Today the government is probably Britain's biggest landowner, though some traditional landowners, such as the Duke of Westminster (who owns much of central London) or the Duke of Bedford (who owns much of Bloomsbury, as well as a vast estate at

Woburn in Bedfordshire), still own the land they originally developed centuries ago. But through such institutions as the Forestry Commission the government has a flying start over any ordinary mortal. Yet property remains a major source of British wealth. Sampson saw the land as an essential part of the British way of life: he contrasted the urban bourgeoisie of Holland, France, or America, "content to live in apartments," with the British for whom the countryside remains the source of most of their values and habits, giving "strength to the amateur ideal, and reinforcing the distaste for trade." Whether or not this is still the case, the fact remains that the rich in Britain either already own land or, if they have recently become rich, aim to buy land. Even though the population density is one of the world's highest (in 1979 it was 356 to the square kilometre in England) the rural ideal—as gentleman farmer, not peasant—still grips the population. But more industrialists and City men, more companies and syndicates, and fewer dukes, now own Britain's rolling acres. Sixty-five per cent of Britain's farms are owner-occupied.

In fact, inequalities of wealth in Britain are declining. In 1923 the richest 1 per cent owned 61 per cent of the wealth, but by 1972 this had almost halved, to 32 per cent. Much of this change must be because of more general home-ownership, with over half of homes now owner-occupied. The share of the nation's wealth held by the least wealthy 80 per cent of the population rose between 1938 and 1972 from 8.4 per cent to 14.7 per cent. As far as actual personal income is concerned, there has been a steady increase in real terms—but a much lower real increase, in the past ten years, than in other Western industrial countries. International comparisons of income are difficult and in any case need to be related to purchasing power in the different countries. But the average British wage-earner, in 1977, had to work less time than colleagues in France and Germany, but more than an American, to earn money to pay for basic foodstuffs. Whatever international comparisons are made of Britain's overall economic performance, they show relative decline—decline from about the 1850s onwards —in Britain's relative success. Manchester and Birmingham are no longer the workshops of the world. But within Britain, standards of living have risen steadily, and despite unemployment, British workers have known a steady increase in earnings in real terms. For a variety of reasons, British workers have still been able to eat and drink what they enjoy. The British way of life has, despite all the economic problems, managed to survive.

THE SPECTRE OF NATIONALIZATION?

The largest public corporations in Britain include the National Coal Board, British Gas Corporation, the electricity industry, the British Steel Corporation, the Post Office, British Telecoms, British Rail, the National Freight Corporation, British Airways, and the National Bus Company. The docks and the Bank of England are also nationalized. In all, nationalized industries employ about 8 per cent of the work-force. But Britain's proportion of nationalized industry is about the average for Europe—lower than Italy's, higher than Germany's.

In addition to the obvious "commanding heights of the econ-

omy" that have been nationalized, chiefly in the period since
World War II, there are such peculiarities as the British Water-
ways Board (Canals and Rivers)—but only for transportation—
and the British National Oil Corporation, which owns the oil
under the seas around Britain but which licenses production rather
than producing in its own right.

Many of these industries have to compete in world markets,
usually with the nationalized industries of other countries: examples are steel, British Airways, shipbuilding, and aerospace. Some
even have to compete with other nationalized industries. The gas,
coal, and electricity boards are in direct competition with each
other as far as domestic use is concerned. British Airways has to
contend with a host of other international carriers all equally
state-owned, save for Pan Am and TWA, which are perhaps more
state-patronized than actually owned. In my experience, it
competes reasonably well, judging by the quality of its service and
the load factors it produces. In short, many nationalized industries
are not exempt from the pressures of the market-place, however
much they might like to be.

The precise relationship between a nationalized industry and
the government of the day is at best uneasy and at times uncertain.
No nationalized industry is actually run by the government of the
day. There is no minister for coal, or rail, or steel. There is, on the
other hand, a Department of Energy, and one for Transport. The
minister picks the chairman of the nationalized industry concerned
and would have to approve the other members of the board. In
extremis, the government can dismiss a chairman, but this is rare,
and can be relied upon to produce a major political row. In 1970,
for example, the incoming Conservative government sacked the
Labour-appointed chairman of the Post Office, Lord Hall. This
resulted in a censure debate in the House of Commons which, although won by the government, made it somewhat careful about
repeating the exercise. The managerial dilemma facing both the
government and the nationalized industries themselves has been
expressed succinctly in a "White Paper" published in March
1978. (In British parliamentary usage, a White Paper is a document expressing government views but not necessarily a definitive

statement of government policy. It is designed to promote discussion, not to express firm decisions.) The paper said:

> The central problem in evolving an acceptable relationship between the Government and the nationalized industries has always been how best to reconcile the boards' need for sufficient freedom to manage the industries with the Government's legitimate interests in them. The Government must be concerned in the strategies and operational decisions of public importance, of industries which are basic to the national economy; in seeing that these industries, which are not subject to the private sector discipline of the threat of bankruptcy, and are in some cases relatively free from market pressures, are efficient; and in ensuring that there is an acceptable return on the public capital invested in them.

Implicit in this statement of the dilemma is the recognition that a publicly owned industry is not subject to market disciplines in precisely the same way that a private company is alleged to be, and that therefore efficiency in the mercantile sense may have to be ensured by other methods. I say "alleged to be" deliberately. I simply do not believe that market forces in the economic purist's sense of the term are significantly more decisive on a major private commercial enterprise in America than they are on many of the major public enterprises in Britain today. Whether Lockheed had been privately or publicly owned, a similar rescue operation would have been necessary in 1971/72. If Ford or General Motors were faced with closure or bankruptcy, I suspect that public money would be found to help it back to solvency in much the same way as was done in Britain with Leyland. So far as rail transport is concerned, parts of the diminishing network in the United States are already in receipt of central government help. The approach is really not very different. On the whole (though not exclusively), the British have felt that a greater degree of public ownership was necessary in order to bring with it a sufficient amount of public control. In the United States, ownership and control in the largest corporations have become so separated that perhaps the need has not been as sharply perceived. Perhaps, too, corporate power in the United States has in recent years been exercised more responsibly.

A large corporation in the United States, particularly if it is one whose interests are diffuse, operates with a degree of independence from its stockholders which, to a foreigner, is remarkable. Such large corporations are the last feudal barons of the twentieth century, as well as being in many cases the last great private patrons of the arts. Their independence from their stockholders, save in the most legalistic sense, is now almost total. A conglomerate with diverse business interests ranging from property to brewing now operates in a way that its stockholders can hardly comprehend, let alone control. Big business is now very much in the hands of the managers, not the owners.

But managing a conglomerate is in reality not very different from managing a nationalized industry. The same disciplines are needed, and the same decision-making process exists. The main distinction is, I suppose, that a nationalized industry in theory has to be more responsive to social pressures and public need than does the theoretical board of directors of a conglomerate. Yet even that distinction is rapidly becoming blurred in practice. The pressures to avoid pollution, to placate the environmental lobby, to be seen as a "socially responsible" corporation, to avoid creating unemployment, even at the cost of some interference with the operation of the market, to be seen to be conscious of the needs of the larger community, to be perceived as appealing to the "higher things" in life via art purchases or sponsorship, the need to talk to labour and to proceed by consensus rather than confrontation with the labour force, the necessity of ensuring that Washington understands their problems and that they conform to federal thinking—all these are real pressures on the managers of an American conglomerate. Frank Abrams, when he was chairman of the board of directors of Standard Oil of New Jersey, summed up the role of the managers as follows: They had to conduct the affairs of the corporations "in such a way as to maintain an equitable and working balance among the claims of the various directly interested groups—stockholders, employees, customers and the public at large."

Whatever else this is, it is a long way from the day when the sole function of a corporation was perceived to be the maximization of its profits and little else besides. These developments seem to me to have produced in the American corporate psyche a degree of conscious national responsiveness which, though still imprecise and legally unformulated, is becoming more important. Parallel with this there has been a relative decline in the impact of personal consumption and hence overt competition on the real economic activity of the nation. Television advertising, while still important in some fields, such as motor cars, pet foods, beer, or toiletries, seems to be increasingly used to justify the social responsibility of corporations that do not depend on public choice, or even on public utility monopolies. Weyerhaeuser's advertisements do not emphasize its success in cutting down trees but its ecological foresight in planting more than it cut. Con Edison in New York, though a monopoly in the supply of electricity to Manhattan, endeavoured mightily to persuade those of us who lived there that it was "working harder to serve you better," a sentiment patently not universally shared by New Yorkers. Whether we think well or ill of Con Edison, we still have to take its product, and the expenditure on this type of advertising can be justified only on the basis that social responsibility has become a factor of greater significance in the corporate decision-making processes.

It is really not very different from the London Electricity Board or British Gas. The American steel industry flourishes with the general level of economic activity just as does the British. At the moment it (like the nationalized British steel industry) is trying to achieve a degree of protection from foreign imports of cheaper products but of a comparable quality, although anything less theoretically "capitalist" than protectionism is hard to imagine. It assumes that competition is desirable when applied domestically but that its ideological validity ceases when products are coming in from abroad.

I have a strong suspicion that if one were to bring together the chairman of the British Steel Corporation and the president of United States Steel, not only would their problems be very similar but so would their answers be. They are both faced with foreign competition, the need for new investment, the inability to forecast accurately and with certainty the size of the domestic market or the supply of raw materials, the need for fewer workers and consequential redundancies, and finally their mutual relations with their respective governments. The American might tend to express himself more in conventional market economy terms and the Englishman might put more emphasis on the industry-government relationship, but they would both nevertheless agree that they were operating a commercial enterprise in a mixed economy, that their business was to make a profit or at least avoid a loss, and that if left to themselves they could doubtless do better. In theory, the ultimate sanction of liquidation is present to U.S. Steel and absent to the British Steel Corporation. In practice, if the industry was large enough, influential enough, and important enough, I find it hard to believe that this ultimate sanction would in practice be more readily used in the United States than in Britain.

The problem in Britain (it exists in the United States, too, though perhaps less articulated) is therefore how to devise a relationship between the government and the nationalized industries which makes sense in commercial terms but which also satisfies the government's need generally to guide and assess. The National Economic Development Office, a semi-official organization, put it thus in its 1976 report:

> Their [i.e., the nationalized industries] importance as employers, suppliers and customers, and the economic and social implications of their actions make it right, as well as inevitable, that Government should take a close interest in their strategies. The issues of public policy involved are so large and politically sensitive that it is not realistic to suppose that they would ever be left for long to management alone to determine, subject only to periodic checks on their financial performance.

Governments in Britain have been, on the whole, reluctant to interfere with the normal operation of the nationalized industries. The last thing a minister wants is to make himself liable to questioning in the House of Commons on the details of administration. When the Post Office was actually run as a government department, the Postmaster General (the minister then directly responsible) would find questions on the order-paper of the House of Commons asking, for example, why a letter posted in Scunthorpe at 5:15 P.M. on Wednesday, January 20, 1968, did not reach its destination at 23 Wellington Road, Leeds, until March 17. The waste of parliamentary time was absurd. In 1969 the Post Office ceased to be a government department and became a nationalized industry. Thereafter the junior minister responsible for overall postal policy could, and did, take refuge in the response that he had no responsibility for its day-to-day administration, and that any such query should be addressed to the chairman of the Post Office Corporation. Had there been direct ministerial responsibility for running the other nationalized industries, I shudder to think of how many questions could and would have been asked about the late running of trains—why was the 4:52 P.M. from Portsmouth to Waterloo twenty-seven minutes late on February 17?—or operations out of Heathrow—why was British Airways flight No. 461 to Paris on November 18 overbooked, and why could not Mr. Bloggs get a seat?

Consequently, the present position in this delicate relationship is that a minister may give a board either general or specific directions on matters that appear to him to affect the national interest. There are a number of safeguards built into this power. A minister would first have to consult the industry in question. The direction would have to be given publicly in the form of a statutory instrument, debatable in Parliament. There would have to be an estimate of any extra costs to be incurred by the industry in following the direction; and as the ultimate sanction of all, since it would require Treasury approval, compensation could be payable by the government to cover that extra cost. The intention is that ministers should use their power sparingly and in such a way as to avoid any direct responsibility for the day-to-day running of the industry concerned.

The principle behind the British approach is simply that the nationalized industries are so fundamental to the running of the country and to its future prosperity that such vast power has to have an element of public accountability built into its operation. In a democracy, it is difficult to see who else can provide this public element other than the government of the day, which is, of course, under our system, answerable to Parliament itself. Subject to this, each industry operates on a commercial basis, and in a competitive way. Whatever else this strange blend of public accountability and private commercialism is, it is light-years away from the centrally planned economic systems of Eastern Europe, and not too different from the way in which the major industries operate in the United States. The main distinction is that we have institutionalized and thereby softened the process, since whatever else the House of Commons is, it is hardly a smoke-filled room, and ministerial intervention is in public rather than in private.

It may be that this mode of activity by the more important sections of an economy could prove a pattern for others. We are, I think, on the way to resolving this difficult question of how to make the critical parts of a mixed economy publicly responsive and in a visible way. Whereas the United States is no longer a capitalist society in the nineteenth-century freebooting sense, it is equally true that Britain is nothing like a centrally planned economy in the Marxist sense.

For the most part there is in Britain today a national consensus on the degree of centralization necessary to run the country. While decrying the nationalized industries in Parliament when in opposition, when in power a Conservative government is just as ready to nationalize when it becomes necessary to do so. In 1972 Edward Heath's government did precisely that when faced with the distinct possibility that Rolls-Royce might have to go into liquidation. The massive deal with Lockheed to supply aero engines for the new air bus had strained the resources of Rolls-Royce to breaking point. I well remember the atmosphere in Parliament at the time. A Conservative government faced with a very real threat of the bankruptcy of a major national asset, and one employing thousands of people, threw its professed ideology out of the window, produced the necessary cash, and nationalized the important parts of the company. There was, of course, a major political row over the decision, but it was a politician's row. Most people seemed to accept the necessity and indeed the wisdom of such a course. There were some learned articles in the heavier Sunday papers, but that the government of the day should seek to preserve a major national asset such as the leading aero-engine designer and producer in Europe, and possibly in the world, was not greatly disputed. The end result of the story was that part of Rolls-Royce was nationalized, while the company survived and is now turning a handsome profit, selling its engines to the United States and many other countries. On the other side, the Labour Party when in office has sometimes found itself obliged by national necessity to behave in ways that it would reject as undesirable and unsocialist when in opposition. The increase in health service charges, the cutting of public expenditure programmes: these unpleasant necessities are ones that a Labour government has had to accept. It has, more-over, deliberately refrained from any massive extension of the public sector of industry, just as the Conservatives have refrained from any massive denationalization, though it is as yet unclear precisely how far Mrs. Thatcher is prepared to go in the direction of further "privatization." The strength of the national consensus is that in both Conservative and Labour administrations each side has found itself having to accept and implement policies which were unpalatable to its own professed philosophies, but which had to be accepted because the interests of the nation demanded it. I am reminded somewhat of Churchill's eulogy on a parliamentary colleague whom he said had been a good Party man, "by which I mean, that he put his country before his party and his party before himself."

A LAND FLOWING WITH
MILK AND HONEY,
OIL AND GAS

Many an observer, looking at international economic statistics, and observing a country declining steadily from a position of world economic dominance over more than a century, has wondered why Great Britain Limited did not collapse and call in the liquidators long ago. Britain's economic decline had become obvious by 1914, yet Britain still managed to win a war; the decline continued, yet the British emerged victorious in World War II; after economic miracles in Germany and Italy, a triumphant upsurge in French economic strength, and a technological and trade blitzkrieg by the Japanese, Britain has still managed to survive into the eighties as a world power of considerable importance. It is a surprising story. Men and women from a tiny group of islands in north-west Europe—mainland Britain is only 600 miles (1000 km) from north to south and never more than 300 miles (500 km) from east to west—not only managed to run the world a century ago, but still manage to survive economically and to preserve their way of life. Part of the explanation must lie in the British Isles themselves, for, after an industrial revolution based on plentiful supplies of coal and water and a long period of imperial expansion, just as it appeared that the British would be impoverished and would withdraw to their island redoubt, discoveries of vast supplies of natural oil and gas, as well as more coal reserves, added a new lease on life to the country. In 1980 Britain became self-sufficient in energy.

The first North Sea oil was discovered in 1969. Until the 1960s it had been thought that energy needs would have to be met by imported oil. Prospecting began in full in 1964, and, after many years of drilling in some of the world's most difficult sea conditions, North Sea oil is now flowing so fast and so plentifully that the government target is for 5 million tons of oil exports by 1985. As recently as 1978 Britain had had to import 41 million tons. Oil and gas reserves off the coasts of Britain are reckoned to be worth over £300 billion, and success rates for prospectors are high. Massive investments have been made, often involving American corporations, and exploration is continuing, government policy being to make the reserves last at least until 1999. Exports of oil, mainly to Western European countries, are now boosting Britain's export figures and transforming Britain's foreign policy. Britain is almost unique in being an industrial country that is also a major oil producer, and while her allies, such as the United States, continue to press Middle Eastern oil producers, such as Saudi Arabia, to keep oil prices low, Britain stands to gain a good deal, as oil exports increase, from any rise in world oil prices. Although Britain has tended to support European Community moves towards the "Euro-Arab dialogue," the country is, in fact, much less dependent than France or Germany on Arab goodwill.

The natural gas story is much the same. Gas discoveries date from 1965, yet ten years later virtually all of Britain had abandoned the old "town" gas, made from coal, and was receiving natural gas from under the North Sea. The use of gas had begun over a hundred years before as the main source of lighting in London; now it is used above all in industry, particularly where careful control of high temperatures is required, and for central heating systems in private homes. Because of uncertainty about oil and electricity prices, people have been moving over to gas—despite the fact that, only fifteen years or so before, gas had seemed electricity's doomed rival, dirty and poisonous—and the nationalized gas industry is one of Britain's commercial success stories.

This sudden transformation of the British oil and gas industries has also transformed the parts of the country where the oil and gas are brought ashore. Most of the oil so far discovered is in the northern part of the North Sea, off the coasts of north-east England, the eastern Scottish mainland, and the Orkney and Shetland islands, and towns like Aberdeen in north-east Scotland and Lerwick in Shetland have suddenly become boom towns. The work is dangerous, involving periods on oil rigs often far out to sea, and helicopters ferry the men from the mainland out to the rigs. A disaster to an oil rig in the Norwegian sector of the North Sea and some well-publicized helicopter accidents have underlined the point, but wages are high. The gas comes mainly from further south, off the East Anglian coast of England, with the major shore pumping station being at Bacton in Norfolk. Transport facilities have also been transformed. There are regular flights between eastern England, Aberdeen, and Norway, and one British airline, British Caledonian, advertises its non-stop flights from Houston, Texas, to Gatwick (one of London's airports), with a link to Aberdeen for busy international oil executives. Because of the extremely hazardous nature of the sea conditions, many operations can only be carried out in summer, but the pay-off is that British offshore oil and gas technology is highly developed. Mexico, which has recently discovered its own vast reserves of offshore natural oil and gas, is expected to place orders for equipment with British firms.

Coal has been Britain's industrial backbone for centuries, but, like the gas industry, seemed doomed until recently. British Rail scrapped its last steam locomotives in the mid-sixties, and the electricity industry decided to go increasingly for oil-burning power stations and nuclear reactors as the major sources of electricity. Yet the massive rise in oil prices in 1973 suddenly made coal economical once more, the electricity industry went back to coal-burning power stations, governments began re-investing in coal technology, and by 1981 coal, formerly a major British export, was being exported again. The story says little for the far-sightedness of Britain's decision-makers, but the effects of the short-sightedness could at least be minimized because the coal was still there. Small and relatively uneconomical pits have been closed, but the National Coal Board's "Plan for Coal" has swung the decline into reverse by opening new colleries, often very deep underground. Production at Selby in Yorkshire, for example, will start in 1982 and produce about 10 million tons a year. Plans for further major developments in other parts of the country are being held up because of environmental objections, as in North Oxfordshire, which contains some of England's most beautiful and traditional rural landscape. Britain's miners—the "aristocracy of the working class"—after a strike in 1973 that virtually caused the fall of Edward Heath's Conservative government quickly appreciated the change in the world energy market, and pressed for and have obtained much higher wages than before. At the same time, investment in mining technology has been high, another field where Britain remains in the forefront in world terms. But exports of coal have not been particularly successful because Britain's major competitors, Poland and South Africa, lack free trade union bargaining procedures and have managed to keep export prices low. However, in 1981, as Poland collapsed into chaos and some countries, such as Denmark, were being criticized politically for importing coal from South Africa, the prospects for Britain's coal exports seemed better, and one big order came from Brazil. Although these prospects have not yet fully materialized, the future for coal is reasonably bright.

As it is, Britain has brought electricity to virtually all of its population and has the largest single centrally controlled grid in the world. Most of the supply comes from steam power stations (oil- or coal-burning) but much of Scotland's supply comes from hydroelectric plants and an increasing proportion of the national supply—now about 12 per cent—from nuclear reactors. In addition, there is an exchange cable with France, soon to be upgraded to enable large quantities of electricity to be exchanged (for example at mealtimes, which are different both because of the one-hour time difference and because the French take their midday meal at midday, the British take theirs a little later). Britain was the first country in the world to develop nuclear power on a commercial scale, with the opening of the Calder Hall power station in 1956, and now has eleven stations in operation. Mrs. Thatcher has no doubts about the future of nuclear power: her government is committed to ordering at least one new nuclear power station a year during the 1980s.

Oil, gas, and coal are not the only valuable commodities under the land and seas of Britain. About a quarter of Britain's tin needs are mined in Britain, much of it in the handful of remaining tin mines in Cornwall. Britain is a major world producer of some industrial minerals, such as china clay, fuller's earth, and gypsum. And Britain's special geographical position means it is well placed to harness the power of the tides. Even Britain's winds, predominantly from the south-west, provide a possible future source of energy and therefore of wealth.

But there are, of course, many minerals vital to industry that cannot be mined in Britain—another major factor governing foreign policy, since a number of key minerals, such as cobalt and vanadium (used for steel-making), have to be imported from South Africa. Another costly import is wood: not only timber, but newsprint. Considering the large sales of books and magazines in Britain, and the country's successful publishing industry, this is a major cost to Britain. Imports of wood and wood products cost about £3 billion a year in foreign exchange. This does not prevent the British paper industry from being a great export success— quality papers produced in Britain are still in demand all over the world. But with the country itself producing less than 10 per cent of its wood needs—despite attempts since the 1950s to plant forests, and a planned increase of the home-grown proportion to about 12 per cent over the next twenty years—this is a graphic illustration of Britain's dependence, despite its extraordinary resources, on international trade.

Although much of Britain was long ago probably wooded, only about 9 per cent of the total land surface is now woodland; 78 per cent of the land is used in one way or another for agriculture. Every year more land is taken for housing or road developments, yet agricultural productivity has kept pace with the shrinking land available for farming. The unhappy people are the naturalists, who complain that as farming becomes more and more efficient, many habitats for wild life disappear—marshy land is drained, so plants and animals that live in boggy conditions become more and more rare; weed-killers remove wildflowers that used to be a common sight in English wheat-fields; and as fields grow from meadow-size to rival Canadian prairies, hedgerows, the habitat of many British species of bird and animal, are swept away. But British agriculture is increasingly efficient and scientific, with research and advisory services provided by the Ministry of Agriculture. There was a time when country people hated townspeople who came at weekends and at holiday time to pollute the countryside; now many of the activists in the environmental lobby are people who live in towns and spend their time campaigning against farmers who use dangerous chemicals or who, as the environmentalists would see it, are apt to destroy the natural heritage recklessly.

The fact is that Britain imports about 40 per cent of her food needs. In almost all cases—for example, meat, butter, or wheat—Britain is becoming more, not less, self-sufficient. In 1968, 44 per cent of the wheat consumed in Britain was actually produced in the country, but by 1979 the percentage had risen to 74 per cent. For meat, the proportion rose from 72 per cent to 82 per cent; for cheese, from 44 per cent, to 69 per cent; and for butter, from 12 per cent to 42 per cent. In milk and eggs Britain is self-sufficient. But large imports of grain for feeding cattle are still necessary, and these come, in the main, from North America. Britain nevertheless exports wheat, in addition to meat. One gain the people of Paris and Amsterdam have had from Britain's membership in the European Common Market has been greatly increased exports of high-quality British beef and—when the French government lets it in—English lamb. It is now not uncommon, when motoring in a country lane in a rural part of the English West Country, to encounter a large French refrigerated truck from Paris, stocking up on prime British beef. Regular truck runs now go from northern Scotland with prime Scotch beef to the tables of Milan and Rome.

The changes in British agriculture and, more slowly but never-theless perceptibly, in the consumption habits of the British people engendered by the European Common Market are now becoming clear. The Empire, with its great dominions in Australia, Canada, and New Zealand, made food available cheaply for the British ta-ble—food like beef, mutton, and wheat that could also be pro-duced in Britain. As Britain entered the Common Market, these traditional sources of supply were supposed to be largely replaced —as part of the deal on entry, they taking (we hoped) our indus-trial exports—by supplies from continental Europe. French beef has tended to replace Argentine beef, Danish butter largely, though not totally, butter from New Zealand, and fruit from Italy at least some of the traditional South African imports: but all of these replacements, for a variety of reasons, are more expensive to the consumer. The result is that, with the assistance of Common Market programmes that boost farmers, British agriculture has been given an impetus to increase production as never before. There is even a small, but rapidly expanding, wine-making indus-try, mainly in the South of England. In the cases of the main food-stuffs, British supplies have increased, and, together with conti-nental imports, have made up for the shortfall from the traditional suppliers.

Although the myth persists (particularly in continental Europe) that Britain consists of housing estates, factories, and the occa-sional parkland, the fact is that the agriculture industry is not merely important but remarkably efficient and productive given the small size of the country. The climate may not—particularly on dull, rainy days in winter—be very enjoyable to live in, but it is ideal for grass, barley, wheat, and cattle, and a high degree of mechanization and efficiency is ensuring that it is made maximum use of. The British farmer is unlikely, too, to be the grass-chewing yokel of popular myth, but is almost certainly a trained expert— and probably a businessman as well.

Class and the British Way of Life

FORMATIVE INFLUENCES

We have already seen that, in terms of water, gas, and electricity, Britain is centrally administered, with almost 100 per cent coverage: while there are regional variations, with even linguistic minorities in some parts, Britain remains an astonishingly homogeneous country. National newspapers reach virtually all of the country, and although there are more and more local radio stations, radio and especially television are predominantly national in coverage. Politics—again, with some slight regional variations, particularly in Scotland—show roughly similar tendencies throughout the country. Consumer habits, tastes, and hobbies also seem to be evenly spread throughout the nation. Although there are regional dishes, whether haggis in Scotland or pasties in Cornwall, and although the timing of the main meal may vary between midday and evening, the normal eating preferences of the British do not vary much from place to place or from region to region.

Part of the reason for this homogeneity lies in geography. The British Isles are in any case small, and the British population is, numerically speaking, concentrated in England, and, within England, in the south-east part of the country. In 1979, population density in the United Kingdom was 228 per square kilometre, compared with 24 in the United States and 98 in France—but in England it was 356, and in South-East England, where over a third of the English population lives, the density was 619 per square kilometre. In the Netherlands, generally considered to be Europe's most densely populated country, the density in 1979 was 412; for Australia and Canada, just 2.

The other key fact about the physical conditions in which the British live is that housing standards are high, with most people living in houses and only one family in four living in an apartment. Amenities are generally good, with some form of central heating now the norm—only twenty-five years ago most British homes were heated by coal fires—and most homes having bathrooms and indoor toilets of their own. Half the British own their own homes, and most of the others rent from local authorities; there is practically no private housing market in rented accommodation except for high-cost short-term lets in the major cities. Half the British live in homes built since 1945. A large proportion of house-owners have a private garden, and many flat-dwellers, too, have a garden plot or access to communal gardens.

All of this goes to underline the truth of the old saying that the Englishman's home is his castle. No matter how mean and poky his residence, the Englishman, particularly if he has a patch of garden, and above all if he owns his house, feels that he is to some extent at least a member of the land-owning classes. Few British people have an ambition to set up a thriving business or to make a million in industry, yet a love of the countryside, a longing to be a country gent, is deeply embedded in the British—and especially the English—character. As he tends his vegetable patch or walks his dog, the Englishman, even if he lives miles from any open country and by the side of a motorway, communes with nature.

All of this may seem very strange in a people who are more

urban than practically any other people in the world. There are, as we have seen, no peasants or class of small farmers in Britain, as there are in most of continental Europe—and the British were the first to have an industrial revolution and the first to move en masse to the cities. Yet this relationship with the countryside lies behind much that outsiders find strange or mysterious in British society. An industrialized, urbanized, and highly literate people maintain, at least in its trappings, a class structure, with a monarchy and aristocracy, whose origins lie deep in pre-industrial society.

There are other important historical and geographical features unique to Britain. The idea of the "island fastness," and of the home as a castle or stronghold to which one retreats in privacy, obviously has something to do with the fact that the country has not—unlike anywhere else in Europe—been successfully invaded since the year 1066, and has known only one military dictatorship since then. The mere fact that Great Britain is an island, though a cliché and the object of many jokes (for example, continentals claim that a British newspaper once carried the headline "FOG IN CHANNEL: CONTINENT CUT OFF"), is central. As the late Denis Brogan, a Cambridge political scholar, wrote, "Because she was an island, England escaped that militarization that overtook Europe in the late sixteenth and early seventeenth centuries. She escaped the identification of the gentry with an officer class. . . ." While France was in arms and in the process of revolution, and Prussians and other Germans were arming for war, Britain had what Brogan called "a rather random handful of gentry controlling a small army of poor men." The British character and British history owe a good deal to these influences: tiny Britain could embark on the creation of an enormous world-wide empire precisely because it felt secure in its island fastness and did not have to arm to the teeth against revolution or invasion. The huge importance of the Navy, and the love of the sea, second only to the rural ideal, also derive from these simple facts, while British attitudes to foreigners—that they get excited and have revolutions whereas the British are calm, collected, and rational—and to politics all have their roots in this heritage.

What of the climate? Madame de Staël, the classical French writer of the beginning of the last century, pioneered the theory

that climate was a major influence on the institutions and literature of a country. She contrasted Ossian, a poet then in vogue, as
a product of Scotland's misty hills, with Homer, whom she saw as
a product of the hard sunlight of Greece. The weather in Britain
changes all the time and gives the British their favourite topic of
conversation:

"Bit wintry, isn't it?"

"Yes, but I expect it'll brighten up later."

Exchanges like this are the life-blood of social contact between
British people, simply because the ever-changing climate offers a
constant source of speculation and comment which is safely outside the realm of anything too controversial or personal. The climate is damp as well as changeable, and is usually under the
influence of depressions coming in one after another from the Atlantic. Long periods of sunny weather are rare; sunny and hot
summers, like the unprecedented heat wave of 1976, are long
remembered. Foreigners sometimes ask, "Did you have a summer
in Britain this year?" and the fact is that in 1979 and 1980, which
were wet and cloudy summers, the truthful answer would have to
be no. In 1981, after an extremely wet May and June, the depressions moved off north to Iceland and Britain basked in sunny
weather for all of July and August. That was exceptional: the year
before, the London correspondent of *Le Monde* had spoken of
Cornwall's "refrigerated" beaches.

But the crucial feature of the British climate is the lack of extremes, which may have something to teach us about British social
attitudes and the approach of the British to politics. Just as Medi-
terranean-type summers are very rare, so winters as harsh as those
of the American Midwest are unknown. Snow is not even normal
in the South of England; recent mild winters have rarely seen
snow settle for more than a few days anywhere except in high
areas in Scotland, though 1981 was an exception. A temperature
above 85° F (30° C) is rare except in a brilliant summer, and a
temperature below 15° F (−10° C) is also exceptional. The British climate is oceanic and temperate, not continental or given to
extremes. Mists are common on the coasts, especially in the early
morning and evening in winter, but the London fog is only a memory. Now that open coal fires are rare in private houses and industry uses gas or electricity rather than coal, the "pea-souper" is

non-existent, though non-smoggy fogs do occur, particularly in the English Channel, but no more in London than anywhere else in southern England.

This people, living on a well-endowed island with a changeable but basically mild climate, evolved a social and political structure that remains unique in Europe and in the world. Yet throughout the world—and not only because Marx did most of his work in England—the very name of Britain is synonymous with class. Britain is supposed to be riddled with archaic class differences and distinctions, and while superficially this may be true, there are important ways in which Britain is no more class-conscious than any other advanced industrial country, including the United States. One of the most perceptive modern writers on Britain, a Frenchman, Professor Jean Blondel, sees the absence of a peasant class, and the basic uniformity of the national British culture, as crucial factors absent in other European countries. "Class divisions," Blondel has written, "play a much greater part in the structure of British society simply because, elsewhere, local characteristics often unite people of all classes to an extent which is rarely attained in Britain." National class divisions are the main divisions of British society. It has, until the very recent past at least, been class, rather than geography or religion, that has been the main division in British politics.

Yet the classic division into workers, middle classes, and upper classes, with its Marxist overtones of exploiters and exploited, bears little resemblance to the reality of modern Britain. There is an upper class, with the monarch at its head; there are some very rich people and gentry; and there are people who would quite happily describe themselves as "middle-class" or "working-class." In habits and life-styles, titles and modes of address, the British class system is complicated, subtle, and gradated, but economic distinctions are far less important than in the nineteenth century. An aristocrat can be poor, but he remains, in bearing and manner and in the way people defer to him, an aristocrat; and the so-called working class—in economic terms—is scarcely different from many of the "middle class." Car-ownership, holidays abroad, and —especially among the young—life-styles and taste in music and clothes show very little distinction. Attitudes to education and ambitions do, however, vary a good deal, and the public (that is, private) schools remain a bastion of class distinction. Nevertheless, studies have shown that class mobility—measured, for example, by the number of children of manual workers who enter university—is far greater in Britain than in other European countries, and rather more than in the United States. But it is important to realize that much of the class game in Britain—and, as we have seen, class is the big divide in Britain—and much of the language of class politics, whether of the trade unions or of the upper classes, is pure charade.

THE HONOURS SYSTEM AND THE ARISTOCRACY

Foreigners, however, tend to take the class system at face value. Americans, for example, delight in the belief, carefully fostered in their history books, that Britain is a much more class-conscious and class-ridden society than is their own. Conveniently forgetting the aristocratic nature of the Founding Fathers of the Republic, they hold vehemently that in the United States a beneficent Almighty has created a society in which not only are all men legally equal, but also class distinctions have genuinely ceased to matter. Conversely, they seem to believe that many of Britain's problems, whether industrial, economic, or political, originate in a social

structure still dominated by class. Diverted, if not positively bemused, by the profusion of honours in Britain, by the knights,
baronets, barons, earls, and dukes, the K.C.M.G.s, the K.C.V.O.s,
the O.B.E.s and P.C.s, Americans tend, I fear, to be misled by
these trappings.

This is not the place to discuss class and social distinctions in
the United States. Suffice it to say that they exist and seem to me
to be deepening rather than diminishing. What they lack is the
public nature of many such distinctions in Britain. A senior career
ambassador in the British Foreign Service always becomes a
knight (or, if female, a dame). Thereafter, for life, he is Sir William Brown, known as "Sir William" to all the world, instead of
mere "Mr." In the United States, of course, all such distinctions
are eschewed. An American ambassador will never become "Sir
Joseph" or "Dame Pearl"—but he or she remains a permanent
"ambassador." The same is true of presidents, governors, judges,
senators, congressmen, and mayors. The title of the office thus
remains with the individual in the United States for life, whereas
in Britain it ceases with the tenure. There is perhaps little
difference in reality between retaining a knighthood for life and retaining the title of a long-abandoned office, and whether a man becomes Sir William or remains Ambassador Brown for life seems
to me to make little difference.

What is much more important is the extent to which class matters. What does it actually mean, and how significant in practice
are the distinctions to which a perception of class differences gives
rise?

If one were to ask a dozen Britons to define class, one would
get a dozen different answers. Accent, dress, style, education, job,
domicile, family, money, flair, power, a title, even the sport a person plays or enjoys, all these might figure somewhere in the answers. But class is, in fact, almost impossible to define save in
terms of the perception of the beholder.

Class is a quality attributed by others and not innate or even
acquired. It is how one is treated, rather than a set of qualities,
themselves quantifiable, that objectively justify the treatment.

The common thread appears to be that the perception of class
depends ultimately upon the belief in the mind of the beholder
that the object of his deference is a person who has a greater claim

to authority or superiority, is more used to power, and therefore is someone who should be approached with care and treated with caution. All the rest are indicators, but they are ones that most Britons recognize.

Accent is one such. There is still in Britain (despite all the efforts of the last fifty years) an accent and mode of speaking in which it is believed most powerful or "superior" people communicate with each other. Of course, there are exceptions, but the moment a person opens his mouth in Britain, certain common attitudes come into play. Perhaps the BBC has had something to do with it over the years; perhaps it is a common educational system through which many of our administrators and professionals have passed; perhaps it was the armed forces, in which the officer class tended to speak one way and the other ranks another; perhaps it was the Church, in which the parsons intoned in a certain way, or the theatre, or the movies, or now television—perhaps it was one or all of these influences. I frankly do not know whether any one can be said to be dominant, but whichever it was or is, the fact remains that in Britain, even today, the accent of authorized power still brings with it some of the deference that authority traditionally expected and received.

The accent must not, however, be too forced. It must be natural, not patently acquired as a deliberate act of self-advancement. It must not be over-gracious, or too excessive. It can, indeed, have regional undertones. A Scottish, Welsh, or Irish tinge is not only "permissible" but positively attractive, as it adds a touch of colour to an otherwise over-bland foundation. The voice per se can be imperfect, even defective—Churchill and Aneurin Bevan had great problems with sibilants and R's respectively. But what it must have in total is a quality that can be recognized as authority.

The phenomenon is perhaps due to the homogeneity of influence or power in Britain when compared with other countries, particularly the United States. We do tend to concentrate our power in London, and our institutions of government are national rather than regional in character. Not having states or a federal government, Britain has tended to be run as a unit and the accents of bureaucracy have been southern English rather than Scottish, Welsh, Yorkshire, or Somerset. Regional differences exist (indeed, conscious efforts are being made to nurture and preserve them), but at the level of governance there is neutralization. To be fair to the BBC, however, it now seems to be deliberately attempting, as a matter of policy, to import a regional flavour into the announcers' accents. The BBC Wales Service announcers sound different from those in Glasgow or Manchester, and certainly from those in Belfast. There is a distinctive colour added to the "norm" which makes such a voice recognizable as originating in a particular part of the U.K., but which nevertheless retains enough of the pattern to make it acceptable. Professor Higgins boasted that he could place any accent in Britain, and in the opening scene of *Pygmalion* amused himself and surprised Colonel Pickering by playing such a game. I suspect that a latter-day Higgins could still do the same.

The most obvious distinction in Britain, however, is an actual title. The list is sonorous and long and in strict order of precedence. After three Peers of the Blood Royal—the Prince of Wales, the Duke of Gloucester, and the Duke of Kent—and the two Archbishops (of Canterbury and York), there are 25 dukes, 30 marquesses, 160 earls and countesses, 105 viscounts, 40 bishops, and no fewer than 792 barons and baronesses. Thereafter come the baronets, knights, and dames.

The roll could almost come out of Henry V. There are Dukes of Norfolk, Somerset, Richmond, Grafton, Beaufort, St. Albans, Bedford, Devonshire, Marlborough, Rutland, Hamilton, Buccleuch, Argyll, Atholl, Montrose, Roxburghe, Portland, Manchester, Newcastle, Northumberland, Wellington, Sutherland, Westminster, Fife, and Edinburgh, and two Irish dukes—Leinster and Abercorn. The marquesses include Winchester, Salisbury, Bath, Exeter, Anglesey, and Reading. The earls have Shrewsbury, Devon, Westmorland, Essex, Warwick, Cawdor, Liverpool, Balfour, Oxford and Asquith, Lloyd George of Dwyfor, Baldwin of Bewdley, Attlee, and finally the most recent creation, the Earl of Snowdon (Anthony Armstrong-Jones). The viscounts and barons are similarly grandiose.

It is said that the English love a lord, and certainly there are enough of them to go round, but apart from the honour due to the possessor of a name famous in English history, such as Wellington or Marlborough, the relevance of the hereditary peerage to actual life in contemporary Britain is small. The introduction of life peerages in 1958 has, however, been an important development. Before then all peerages were hereditary and a son succeeded to the title automatically on the death of his father. In 1958 Parliament passed an act authorizing the creation of peerages for life that cannot be transmitted. The act also permitted the creation of life peeresses, a new departure.

The result has been the transformation of the House of Lords, the second chamber of the British Parliament. Life peerages have meant that men and women who have or have had a prominent career in public life can now sit in the House of Lords for their own lifetime. Thus the Lords now have a larger part to play in British life than for many years past. Under our system, any Act of Parliament has to pass through both the Commons and the Lords, who have a power to delay final enactment. When the House of Lords consisted solely of hereditary peers, the proceedings there received less respect and consideration. Now the debates are more respected because of the quality of the new arrivals. A body containing such persons as economist Barbara Wootton, Methodist churchman Donald Soper, Kenneth Clark, and Laurence Olivier, in addition to a host of ex-Cabinet ministers, former ambassadors, trade union leaders, and industrialists, is one that deserves respect. There is no subject on which there is not at least one expert sitting there. Whether the subject is swine-fever in the Highlands, or the independence of St. Helena, at least one noble lord or lady will have farmed in Northern Scotland, and one will have served in St. Helena in some capacity or another. Indeed, the title "Lord" is itself becoming somewhat misleading. For life peers it is a working status rather than a class indicator. Perhaps "Senator" would now be a better title, since the functions are not entirely dissimilar from, for example, those of the Senate in the Australian Parliament. There is also a case for distinguishing the working Lords from the hundreds of hereditary peers who rarely attend save on the few occasions when the Conservative Party decides to whip in its "backwoodsmen." If they all attended at once, then the Conservative majority would be immense, but out of more than 1,150 peers in all, only about 150 are in any sense regular attenders, and they are mainly life peers rather than hereditary ones. This has meant that debates and votes have been more evenly balanced between the two sides. There is, too, a healthy sense of self-preservation in the reluctance of the Conservative Party to use its massive majority. Were it to do so, the chances are that a future Labour government would seek to reduce the powers of the Lords still further, or as a minimum would seek to remove the power of the hereditary element. The resulting constitutional crisis of a "Lords versus the People" nature is one that the Conservative Party would hardly wish to face in the last quarter of this century. It could not even win that argument in 1910, when a Liberal government against intense Conservative opposition successfully fought an election to curb the powers of a House of Lords that had rejected some of the government's key legislation. The precedent is still in the minds of Tory Party managers (and Labour's too).

Thus the nature of the peerage has changed, and while the hereditary element may still demand some regard in political terms because of its size, it is the life peers who now receive more attention. There is a case in any system of government for having available to the country a body composed of elder statesmen, for whom the excitement of office has been replaced by more objective considerations. The story used to be told of the noble earl who dreamt that he was addressing the House of Lords, and woke up to find that he was. It is not entirely apposite today, though the tendency towards extreme courtesy that still characterizes their deliberations sometimes makes the Lords' debates more soporific to listen to than to read. But at least they are now worth reading.

While it gives one the advantage of membership of the Upper House of Parliament, being a lord does carry with it certain liabilities. Along with clergymen and lunatics, a peer has no vote in a parliamentary election. Nor can he stand for membership of the House of Commons. To take a peerage, therefore, effectively cuts one off from the topmost rungs of the political ladder. It is now inconceivable that a prime minister could be in the Lords rather than the Commons. That issue was settled as far back as 1923, when Stanley Baldwin, a commoner, became Prime Minister in preference to Lord Curzon. The most senior ministers in Britain have to be MPs elected by the people and therefore subject to rejection at the next election, and the appointment of Lord Carrington as Foreign Secretary in Mrs. Thatcher's government in 1979 was quite exceptional. The dilemma in trying to reform the

House of Lords is simple to state. There are advantages in having a second chamber of government: it makes for stability and gives an opportunity for review. The difficulty is that if it is to have more power, then it should have a democratic base, but to make the House of Lords elective would destroy the whole basis of the peerage itself. So far Britain has not been able to resolve this problem of how to make a permanent second chamber more effective without stepping over the lines of the legitimate demands of democratic accountability and recall.

Below the peers come the baronets and knights—approximately 3,500 of them. They look the same but are not. A baronet is a hereditary knight, distinguished by the use of the letters *Bt.* after his name and the fact that he can pass his title on to his son. Otherwise he is the same as any other knight, is addressed as Sir William Brown, and does not sit in the House of Lords. A baronetcy is not good enough for that. You have to be at least a baron to qualify.

Among the knights the orders of chivalry are many and diverse. The most senior are the Order of the Garter and the Order of the Thistle, the latter being Scottish. There is only one class of each order: a Knight of the Garter—K.G.; and a Knight of the Thistle—K.T. Moreover, there can be no more than twenty-six members of the Order of the Garter, and it is within the personal gift of the monarch.

The remaining orders of chivalry still used are the Order of the Bath, the Order of St. Michael and St. George, the Royal Victorian Order, and the Order of the British Empire, the appropriate lettering for a knight commander of each order being K.C.B., K.C.M.G., K.C.V.O., and K.B.E. As a simple working rule, any man in Britain with a *K.* after his name is a knight and entitled to use the prefix "Sir," and any woman with a *D.* becomes "Dame." Knights and dames are equal in this order of precedence. Mr. William Brown becomes Sir William Brown, addressed thereafter as Sir William, even in situations where Christian name terms would not normally exist.

Below the *K.*s are the other classes of the orders, the companions (C.B., C.M.G.) or commanders (C.V.O., C.B.E.). So far so good. But there are further complications. Above the *K.*s there is one additional class, the "Knight Grand Cross," and the holder, although a knight, has the magic letter *K*. replaced with a *G*. (for Grand). The full order for the Order of the Bath thus runs:

> G.C.B. Knight Grand Cross of the Order of the Bath
> K.C.B. Knight Commander of the Order of the Bath
> (if a man), or
> D.C.B. Dame Commander of the Order of the Bath
> (if a woman)
> C.B. Companion of the Order of the Bath

The top two are knights; the C.B. is still only a "Mr." Similar rules apply to the other orders. That of St. Michael and St. George runs G.C.M.G., K.C.M.G. or D.C.M.G., and C.M.G. The Royal Victorian Order and the Order of the British Empire each have extra rungs on the ladder below that of Commander: the former has an M.V.O.—Member of the Royal Victorian Order—and the latter an O.B.E.—Officer of the Order of the British Empire—and an M.B.E.—Member of the Order of the British Empire.

The ladders therefore run:

> G.C.V.O., K.C.V.O. or D.C.V.O., C.V.O., M.V.O.
> G.B.E., K.B.E. or D.B.E., C.B.E., O.B.E., M.B.E.

Overwhelmingly, these orders are now awarded to public servants, military, diplomatic, or home civil service. The Order of St. Michael and St. George, for example, is very much a Foreign Office preserve. Originally established in 1818 for Malta and the British Ionian Islands, it has somehow become an appropriate honour for our diplomats. A serving diplomat can expect to climb from C.M.G. to K.C.M.G. and even to G.C.M.G. if he is very, very senior, giving rise to the in-house joke: "Call Me God. Kindly Call Me God. God Calls Me God."

Finally there are the knights bachelors, "Sirs," who belong to no order of chivalry and have no letters after their name, but who cease to be "Mr." and become "Sir William." These titles are given to industrialists, bankers, newly created High Court judges, some (but fewer these days) politicians, persons eminent because they are generally perceived to be so, and those notable in the arts or music—Geraint Evans, the opera singer, and the composers

William Walton and Michael Tippett, to name a few. It is a useful means of honouring those citizens who it is believed deserve a public mark of public favour. Rarely is an honour actually refused, save on the grounds that the putative recipient should perhaps have been offered something better, or by Labour politicians anxious not to prejudice their proletarian credentials. An honour is a relatively harmless way of being noticed, and provided the whole system is not taken too seriously either by those honoured or by the rest of us, it will almost certainly survive.

Something, however, must be done about the women. They now sit in the House of Lords as "Ladies," and the orders of chivalry are open to them. They can hardly become knights, since by tradition knights have always been male. They have therefore logically, if a trifle ungallantly, become dames. A female knight is a dame, and a sillier sentence than that I have rarely penned. She cannot be a "Lady" since that title designates the wife of a peer, a peeress in her own right, the wife of a knight, or the daughter of a duke, marquess, or earl. But to call her a "dame" is surely the invention of a misogynist and to transform Miss Janet Baker into Dame Janet is a translation to ugliness. I fear, however, that the title is now too well established to be susceptible to change. Dames they are and dames they are likely to remain.

All honours in Britain stem, in theory, from the Queen. In practice, they almost all stem from the Prime Minister. Discreet enquiries are made of the recipient whether the proposed honour would be acceptable. If it is, the name appears in one of the two annual honours lists, one on New Year's Day and the other on the Queen's official birthday at the beginning of June. Thereafter Mr. Brown becomes Sir William, and perhaps more important even than that, Mrs. Brown becomes Lady Brown. If there are letters to go with the honour, they appear with the recipient's letters for degrees, medals, etc., after the name. The person honoured is addressed differently thereafter, though it is perhaps anomalous that while the wife of a knight becomes a lady, the husband of a dame remains a mister. Moreover, the recipient is usually very pleased. A knighthood is not only an honour, but usually a delight, and this is still recognized in those political circles responsible for bestowing the award. I do not suppose there is a very great difference between awarding a man an honour for his services to a political party in Britain and making an ambassador of a major contributor to the party war chest in the United States. Either way he gets a title for life.

EDUCATION AND CLASS: THE PUBLIC SCHOOLS

"Public schools" in Britain are in fact private schools to which access is generally denied to the public as such, save on payment of fees, or via competitive scholarships. Only about 8 per cent of British children actually attend public schools, and of the public schools only nine—Eton, Harrow, Rugby, Winchester, Westminster, Charterhouse, Merchant Taylors', Shrewsbury, and St. Paul's —belong to the élite inner circle of Clarendon schools—so named because a Royal Commission under Lord Clarendon investigated them in 1864. The subject of the public schools remains one of the hottest potatoes in British politics: Should they be swept away? Do parents not have a right to educate their children as they choose? The debate is interminable and runs along predictable lines. Yet the fact is that the public schools, far from being a mere expression or support of an existing class system, *are* the class system. Where you went to school is, in Britain, an important indicator of class; the public schools were places where, in the past, new members of the shopkeeping or merchant classes could introduce their sons to the upper classes. They helped to mould the governing classes as an adaptable and changing force.

Still today there are, educationally speaking, two Britains, one private, the other state-run. The educational experience of the 8 per cent who have gone through the private system is totally different from the experience of the other 92 per cent. Traditionally, the child (usually male) of upper-middle-class parents was normally educated wholly in the private sector from his very early years. From a single-sex preparatory school to which he would be sent at seven, to his public school, then to university, the carefully bred offspring of rich and powerful parentage would spend most of his time away from home and family. It was a brutal, if not barbaric, system. For a boy to be sent to a single-sex boarding school at seven, away from his parents and the warmth of his family background, may have encouraged resilience, but it did little for the psyche. To pass then to another single-sex boarding school at eleven or twelve and remain there until thrust into an unfamiliar world at eighteen could often be a prolonged trauma. The agony of a sensitive boy surrounded by five hundred exuberant male striplings living in a highly competitive environment can be imagined.

Girls, until the mid-nineteenth century, tended to be educated more genteelly at home, but the growth of schools for "young ladies" such as Cheltenham and Roedean meant that for many their education mirrored that of their brothers. Boarding schools for girls never became quite so popular as those for boys, nor could they ever have the history and tradition of a Winchester or an Eton, founded respectively in the thirteenth and fourteenth centuries. But for many girls the same process applied: an early rupture from the family, a degree of regimentation unheard of in the United States, and a conformism that made them readily identifiable.

For years that was the educational fate of the children of the "Establishment." They grew up deliberately segregated, insulated against the infections of the world outside their narrow male (or female) preserves, highly competitive and physical, the boys, particularly, obsessed with sporting success. The public schools produced an élite capable of loyalty, service, and self-reliance—strong virtues for an imperial nation, but singularly ill balanced if unmatched by a comprehension of the different outside world.

Most of the boys' public schools were founded in the nineteenth century, to cater for the military and administrative demands of the Empire, and for such demands the public school virtues were doubtless admirable. Self-reliance was certainly a quality needed by a solitary young district officer in Africa, or a political officer on the North-West Frontier in India. If that was their only function, however, one would have expected the public schools to disappear as the Empire was decolonized. This has not happened. The independent schools in Britain flourish, and their influence seems to remain.

What is still important about the public schools today is not merely that they are élitist and exclusive, it is that they confer practical advantages on the children who attend them because of the length of their parents' purse. Not only is the system élitist, but it produces an élite not necessarily originating in ability. Of all children in Britain in school at the age of sixteen between 8 and 9 per cent attend public schools. The percentage of public school leavers going to a university is 15 per cent, and of those going to Oxford or Cambridge, 32 per cent. Fifty-five per cent of our generals, admirals, and air chief marshals attended a public school, as did nearly 70 per cent of the directors of our major companies, 75 per cent of our bishops, 80 per cent of judges and Q.C.s (Queen's counsel—leading barristers, or advocates), and 77 per cent of the directors of the Bank of England.

Twenty per cent of Labour MPs and 75 per cent of Conservative MPs went to public school, including most of Margaret Thatcher's ministers (though not Mrs. Thatcher herself), and Michael Foot and Tony Benn of the Labour Party leadership. These are extraordinary figures for a small number of schools and 8 per cent of the school population. They indicate perhaps more clearly than any other set of statistics the narrowness of the educational

and social base of many of our national institutions. The reverse
side of the equation is frankly appalling in its implication. If 80
per cent of our judges and Q.C.s are drawn from only 8 per cent
of the school population, then either the parents of that 80 per
cent were extraordinarily far-sighted in perceiving the legal talents
in their offspring and in sending them to similar schools, or the
remaining percentage, of those at other schools, have been disregarded in legal promotion. The second is the more likely propo-
sition. The waste of national talent seems to have been prodigious.
We have just not made use of what is available if these figures
mean what they seem to imply.

This is not to argue that public schools are not good schools per
se. Most of them are, and some are indeed extremely good if one
accepts the premise that sending children away to boarding school
is socially or personally desirable. There is now a far greater emphasis on the arts, less on games and the "classics" (Latin and
Greek), and more effort is being devoted to science, mathematics,
and engineering. Many schools are now beginning to be co-educa-
tional—which removes at least some of the sexual insulation of a
single-sex boarding school. Eton is arguably the best school in
Britain, but mainly because of the freedom it gives to the eccentric
or the unusual. The temples of national conformity (which is what
the public schools used to be) are, at their best, now becoming
educational refuges for the unorthodox. The "interested" child,
who would find it hard to accept the disciplines and rules of a
more orthodox public school, seems at Eton to be able to develop
in his own direction and at his own pace. This can be done because of the high quality of the staff and the low pupil/teacher
ratio, far lower than in a state school. What parents get for their
money by sending a child to one of the better public schools
is quite simply a better educational opportunity for the child, and
the chance of quicker social and economic advancement in the future. The old-school tie is no longer the discriminating factor that
it once was, but it can still help, just as the old-boy or old-
regiment net does, or any other cosiness of that sort. It will not get
one a job these days, but it will almost certainly guarantee an in-
terview. It will not get a brief for an incompetent barrister, but it
will help him to get a good pupillage (legal clerkship) where he
can demonstrate his competence or otherwise. It will not make a

doctor, but it is still a fact that 65 per cent of the physicians and surgeons at the London teaching hospitals and on the General Medical Council went to a public school.

Few men nowadays actually wear an old-school tie, but many parents still believe that it could be an asset to have one hanging up in their son's closet, ready if need be. In a sense, it is a convenient point of identification, and the chances are that among one's schoolfellows are now some recognizable successes.

There are, fortunately, some signs that these attitudes are beginning to change. While the public schools are still full, some of the products now seem to find the exclusiveness of their education an embarrassment rather than an advantage. This is particularly true in the theatre, music, and the arts. While there is still an admired stereotype of the public school boy—clean, well scrubbed, disciplined, moral (where girls are concerned)—it is a stereotype that is beginning to be more attractive to parents than to the children themselves. A kind of reversal may be taking place, in which a public school education may be a positive disadvantage, to be concealed and certainly not to be flaunted. In the high reaches of the bureaucracy this is not yet so, but in journalism, the media, the arts, applied science, particularly the higher technologies, the old-school tie is no longer the power it was. Much of this is, of course, due to the social changes that have taken place since the war. Britain is much less of a class society than it was, and too-open identification with educational exclusiveness tends to set one apart too much from the rest of us. The trend is, however, recent and we must just wait and see how it develops.

I spent four years myself at one of England's public schools, Cheltenham College in Gloucestershire. My parents having taken the decision that I should go (though there was precious little money to play with—but I had fortunately won a scholarship, which helped considerably with the fees), I went to a single-sex boarding school for the first time at the age of fourteen, rather older than most. It was a bizarre experience. Coming as I did from the mining valleys of South Wales, it was a considerable trauma to find myself suddenly thrust into the alien world of the English upper middle class. My accent was different, my background quite dissimilar, my roots were definitely not upper-bourgeois. I had not been away from home before, nor could I play cricket. Moreover, many of the rules of the school, written and unwritten, struck me as quite absurd. As a new boy, I could enter my boarding house only through the back door, and not by the much more convenient side entrance, a restriction that seemed to me ludicrous. From having my own bedroom, I suddenly found myself in a dormitory with twenty-three other boys, being told when to sleep, eat, get up, dress, wash, bath, play, work, and even think. It was, I think, the recognition that from then on I was going to be regimented that was the hardest to accept, but like almost all other boys similarly incarcerated before me, I learnt to adapt to the system and even use it. One sat in a certain fixed order, dressed in the same way, with a white shirt and black tie on Sundays, when, well scrubbed and shining, we paraded formally in chapel. The regime was muscularly Christian—chapel every morning, games most afternoons, and a cold shower to start the day. It was a little daunting at first.

Did I enjoy it? Not exactly. It was not the sort of experience one actually enjoys at the time. In retrospect, I remember the more pleasant times and suppress the others. Fortunately I played a reasonable game of Rugby football and was sufficiently large to deter bullying, but for some of my contemporaries it was clearly agony. I think, too, that it heightened rather than lessened my class-consciousness, though not in the way that was perhaps intended. Far from joining "them," I think it made me more aware of being part of the "us." The contrast between the secure world of an English public school and the mining town I went home to was marked. Cheltenham made me a member of the Labour Party, though that was, I am sure, accidental. The unpleasant truth was that Cheltenham did instil a sense of difference into its pupils. I doubt whether this was deliberate, but segregation is bound to breed a sense of separateness. If this happened to me, I think it happened to many others, too, of my generation and may well be still happening today.

One should not, however, confuse class with conformism. There is a difference. Conformism exists (and far too much of it) in Britain today. We have a great capacity for making the non-conformer feel awkward, small, or out of place. If he does not know the rules or flouts them too overtly, ways will be found of letting him know that he has transgressed and that his transgressions have been noticed. But if he becomes successful, then transgression becomes mere eccentricity and all is forgiven. What I have never understood is why the trivia have been allowed to become so important. Does it really matter if one wants to wear brown shoes with a blue suit or drink red wine with fish? Of course it does not, but the extraordinary fact is that so many people think it does.

In my own profession of the law the unwritten laws are strong. One tended to dress a certain way—white shirt, stiff collar, and a vested suit. One large advocate appearing without a vest before a somewhat pompous judge was told, "Mr. X, I'm afraid I cannot see you." "I'm sorry Your Lordship's eyesight is so poor today," was the response.

One was supposed to conform in one's clothes, behaviour, and decorum—unless and until one was brilliantly successful. The most successful libel advocate at the bar could and did marry three times and be divorced twice. The most highly paid civil lawyer when I first went to the bar spent many a happy evening with his clerk at London's dog racing tracks. But they were both successful and spectacularly so. What in lesser mortals would have been serious examples of forensic instability, in them became acceptably eccentric. Conformity may be the protection of the average, but by definition that is what most of us are.

In a very real sense, however, a title, one's education, accent, or conformity are only the trappings. If there existed in England one recognizable class that set artistic or social standards for the rest of us, that would have importance, but such a group does not exist. The state and the large corporations are now the major patrons of the arts. Covent Garden exists on a massive government grant. The Arts Council, a public body, is responsible for ensuring that £80 million a year is spent on promoting the arts in Britain, in their widest sense, and there is a Minister for the Arts who is a member of the government itself.

Moral preaching is now firmly left to the philosophers and the churches. Indeed, if the nineteenth-century aristocracy was anything to go by, what has happened is that the permissiveness of late Victorian and Edwardian country house living has been democratically extended to the population as a whole. It would be a very bold and foolish person indeed who would claim that any one class in Britain today was either more or less moral than any other. The effect of the press, films, radio, and television extends to all, and the media seem to have a far greater influence on the way we behave towards each other than does any one group of our population. The self-appointed moral guardian of the nation is a Mrs. Mary Whitehouse. She has taken it upon herself to campaign vocally and vigorously against films or television programmes that she finds morally offensive. Whatever else she is, she is certainly impossible to categorize in any class terms, being a Birmingham housewife, and recognizable verbally as such. One of her strongest supporters, however, is the Earl of Longford, a Catholic peer of boundless generosity towards his fellow men. This unlikely combination has attempted to apply their standards of morality by public agitation and complaint to an increasingly liberal Britain. Fortunately they have not met with too much success, though they are now regarded with affectionate respect for having tried.

Nor is there one recognizably church-going class. Abstention from religious worship seems just as common among the aristocracy as it is among the rest of us. In some regions, church-going is still more usual—Wales, Scotland, and parts of the North of England remain areas where attending a place of worship is the norm rather than the exception. But even here attendances are declining. Taking the two countries as a whole, the United States is much more given to formal worship than is the United Kingdom. Forty per cent of the American population go to church, as compared to 14 per cent in Britain.

Of course, there are groups of people who set standards in literature, the arts, music, sport, fashion, or indeed any other facet of our national life. What no longer exists in Britain is one class of people who are recognized as the standard-setters to be emulated by all others. Increasingly, the innovators in our society cut totally across the traditional class barriers, whether they are the Beatles, Mary Quant, Peter Hall, or Henry Moore. The enormous relative increase in personal incomes in this century has meant in turn that the followers of the pace-setters are no longer drawn from one class of the population, for mass consumption has meant mass standards. Whether the objects concerned are records or motor cars, the standards in the end are those that people will accept. This is not an argument for crude commercialism. It is a recognition that standards in Britain for a whole host of issues now tend to take the mass of our people into account to a far greater extent than ever before. Well-designed, cheaper housing and furniture, mass communications, and greater mobility have transformed the life of the average Briton to a degree unimaginable even twenty-five years ago. It is the popular nature of these developments that is important, not their exclusivity. They cannot be attributed to the views or opinions of any one class in our society. There have been mass movements in which the innovators have come from all classes, not one, but why, then, is class-consciousness important in Britain today? We are still too much of a deferential society in which the accepted structure of things is important. There is a consciousness of class-division in Britain that still persists even if we find those divisions almost impossible to define. We have fortunately moved a long way from the nineteenth-century hymn that congregations sang approvingly:

> *The rich man in his castle,*
> *The poor man at his gate,*
> *God made them high and lowly*
> *And ordered their estate.*

But order in Britain is important. Perhaps we became too insular and stratification became too firm. We developed quietly over the centuries a social order based on firm economic distinctions. The traditional one of a land-owning aristocracy and a land-renting peasantry did not survive for long. By the eighteenth century the new mercantile classes had demanded and received their share of the power, and in the nineteenth century the industrial working class did the same. The result is that today the old distinctions are disappearing. Economic class no longer matters so much in Britain. Mobility upwards and outwards is now common enough for there to be no one section of our population permanently at the bottom of the heap. The availability of grants for students has meant that any child of ability, whatever his or her background, can go to a university. Once the young person emerges, it is difficult to categorize the result. What class is the university lecturer who is himself the son of a South Wales miner? Whatever his category by job and position, he is clearly not working-class in the functional or historical sense of the term. By origins and early upbringing he may, however, have been precisely that, and indeed may well still consciously identify with his roots.

It is not that all the distinctions have disappeared in Britain (would that they had), it is that the old categories have become invalid. The pigeon-holes are just not appropriate any more.

The one instance where they may be still damaging, however, is —as we have seen—in the decline of the size of our industrial base. Less of the intellectual stream of our society is prepared to go into manufacturing industry as a career. Its members tend to become lawyers, accountants, journalists, civil servants, advertising executives, teachers, and television and radio producers. Not enough of them seriously consider the possibility of engineering, manufacturing industry, or even old-fashioned entrepreneurial capitalism. The trend has been an unfortunate one, which is only now beginning to be taken seriously with the belated recognition that the standard of living of our people depends in the end on the export performance of the private sector of British industry. The problems of enlarging that base, and of making it more competitive and efficient, are some of the most urgent facing the country. One of our difficulties here seems to be the class-consciousness of our society itself.

Class-consciousness in Britain does reveal itself in more than one's accent or the way in which one is treated by a policeman or a shop assistant. It is still true that certain occupations are "acceptable" and certain others are not. Unfortunately, given the nature of a twentieth-century industrial society, it is frequently the "acceptable" ones that are non-productive and the "unacceptable" ones that are. It is also unfortunately true that the "acceptable" jobs are often those that are the most lucrative, interesting, and enjoyable. The higher reaches of the civil service, the legal profession, politics, teaching, advertising, or the media seem to be infinitely more agreeable than the joys of industrial management to many of our brightest graduates. With the recent opening of a number of schools of business administration this may be beginning to change, but it is a slow process. Moreover, our tax system has hardly encouraged money-making as an acceptable prime motive for human endeavour.

Perhaps these trends were inevitable given the fact that educational mobility is a modern innovation. Before this century the economic divisions were such that people could not easily move up the educational (and thus the social) ladder. One forgets that universal literacy is a relatively new achievement in the West, and that only in recent years have the industrialized countries had to cope with the problems of an educated, ambitious population, capable of physical mobility, with access to an abundant supply of consumer goods and sophisticated taste-buds stimulated daily by the press, radio, and television. Everyone now knows what the "good life" is like; or they at least know what our society tends to categorize as the "good life."

Against the background of these profound social developments in our society, it is hardly surprising that the "acceptable" occupations have become more acceptable and the less acceptable have tended to be shunned.

When I first started to practice law, the chambers that I joined had as its head a wily old lawyer who was renowned for his skill in drafting. He had never become a Queen's Counsel (a senior advocate), but his law was good and he had a high reputation for forensic guile. In his youth he had been a merchant seaman, but when he was twenty-five an aunt had died and left him £1,500. With that sum he educated himself, passed the necessary examinations, and then became a barrister. He once said to me, "Every day when I wake up, I give thanks that I no longer have to earn my living with my hands." And he was, of course, absolutely right. I suspect that the phrase the "dignity of labour" was invented by someone who had successfully managed to avoid it. Much of manual work is dirty, unpleasant, underpaid, and exhausting, and the sooner we can devise ways of getting such jobs done other than by the discomfort of our fellow human beings, the better I shall be pleased. If the day ever arrives when the last miner can leave the last pit, as coal can be won from the earth by other means, I shall regard it as a matter for rejoicing and not for regret.

Nor am I in the least surprised at the "drift from the land" into the cities. There have been a number of "socially realistic" books on Britain written recently in which people have talked into tape recorders and then been transcribed by their author listeners. One such was Ronald Blythe's *Akenfield,* a study of an East Anglican village, in the course of which the squire, the parson, the farmers, the innkeeper, the farm-workers, and others were all interviewed.

It was fascinating to see the extent to which the agricultural labourers hated the work they had to do. To have to get up at dawn
summer and winter, rain or shine, and help till someone else's
land, or tend another's beasts, is hard. The thought of a nice warm
factory in which they worked shifts in relative comfort was obviously much more appealing. The fact that the young people of the
village preferred the town with its amenities and enjoyments is not
at all surprising.

In the small Welsh mining town where I was brought up, the
ambition of every miner was to prevent his son's having to follow
him down a pit. For this he would sacrifice, scrimp, and save, to
give the next generation a better opportunity than he had had himself. The local school was good and the quality of teaching high.
There was pride if someone from the valley did well at a university or in his chosen profession. People tended to be judged more
by their achievements than by their origins—the origin, after all,
was a common one. There was little squirearchy, and the distinctions, such as they were, were intellectual and professional. The
doctor, the lawyer, and the teacher were respected, but so was the
miner who played the organ, the school caretaker who wrote poetry and was a prominent local bard, or the small grocer who
played a good bass fiddle. In many ways it approached a classless
society, or at least more of one than is to be found in the United
Kingdom as a whole, and the essence of it was education and mobility.

Education was indeed the great leveller, and the years immediately after the war were the first in which Britain's population as a
whole began to stir. Good college education ceased to be the pre-
rogative of the wealthy and became more available. It coincided
with a number of profound changes in our society at home and in
our position abroad. Emerging from the Second World War victorious but impoverished, Britain did seem determined to avoid the
more obvious absurdities of our pre-war society. The election of
the 1945 Labour government produced a conscious attack on privilege and class, which, although not entirely successful, has meant
that power in society has since been more diffuse. The country is
no longer governed solely by a small number of self-perpetuating
clubs. Power has been spread, or at least the clubs have been en-
larged and the membership made more accessible to all. The ex-

clusivity of Victorian politics, so accurately displayed in Trollope, no longer subsists, and Belloc's acid view on a general election fortunately no longer applies. He wrote:

> *The accursed power which stands on Privilege*
> *(And goes with Women, and Champagne and Bridge)*
> *Broke—and Democracy resumed her reign:*
> *(Which goes with Bridge, and Women and champagne).*

The present membership of the House of Commons is 635. It includes 103 lawyers, 52 journalists and authors, 74 teachers and lecturers, 77 managers and executives, 39 engineers, 28 trade union officials, and 16 miners. There has been a steady increase in the proportion of middle-class managers and professionals in the House of Commons (41 per cent of Labour and 78 per cent of Conservative MPs in 1951, as compared to 57 per cent and 79 per cent respectively in 1974); and while 37 per cent of Labour MPs were manual workers in 1951, only 28 per cent were in that category by 1974.

Whatever else these figures show, they do indicate that change is taking place in Britain, even if slowly. The great upsurge of national vitality that some looked for after the war has not taken place in a dramatic way. It has, rather, been a slower process of gradual incorporation in which class origins have ceased to be quite so relevant and educational achievement has become relatively more important. Britain is still governed by an élite, but the nature of this élite has changed in the last thirty years—and changed immeasurably for the better.

A FLABBY AND
CODDLED PEOPLE?

Eighty years ago, the average Briton, probably living huddled in a
tenement block in one of the major cities like London or Glasgow,
surrounded by poverty and disease, could expect to live to the age
of forty-eight. Today's modern Briton, living in a council house on
the edge of one of the major conurbations, can expect to live
to seventy (for men) or seventy-six (women). On many international comparisons, Britain's health record stands up well. Infant
mortality in Britain has declined dramatically since the beginning
of the century, and the rate is about the same as in the United
States, lower than in Germany, and higher than in France. Since

the National Health Service was set up by the Labour government after the Second World War, there has been a dramatic decline in the incidence of infectious diseases: tuberculosis and diphtheria, which were killers in Britain's cities at the beginning of the century, and which as recently as 1951 produced 50,000 and 826 cases respectively, have virtually disappeared as causes of death. As in the United States, cancer, heart attacks, and strokes are now the commonest causes of death in Britain.

What is the truth about "socialized medicine" in Britain? Some argue that we are trying to do too much for too many with too few resources, with the result that standards of medical care have declined; others, particularly Americans, see the National Health Service as the symbol of British self-indulgence.

The truth is that the provision in Britain of comprehensive medical care to all our population is no longer an object of political argument. No major party or political figure would nowadays advocate a return to the days of private medicine or the abolition of the health service as such. There are, of course, furious arguments on details—on whether or not we have the balance right between the NHS and the private medical sector, whether we should be spending more or less on hospital provision, on home services, or on dentistry, or whether prescription drugs should be more expensive. All these and many other similar disputes are quite common, but over the central principle that Britain needs and should retain a comprehensive nationally financed and administered health service there is quite simply no dispute at all. It is now part of the social fabric in Britain and should be regarded as having the same degree of persistence as do many of our other national institutions. How, then, does it actually work?

Any person in Britain who wishes to (almost all do) registers with a doctor in the area where he or she lives. You do this quite simply by going to the doctor of your choice and asking him (or her) to put your name on his list of registered patients. The choice of doctor is yours, just as the choice of patients is his. He can, if he wishes, refuse to accept you, and if you happen not to like the look of him, you can decide to go elsewhere. By and large there are enough general practitioners in Britain to go round, so that finding a doctor to accept you as a patient should not be too difficult. If it proves to be so, the local office of the Ministry of Health will help.

What is important, and contrary to much American belief, is the element of choice. The commonly held idea that in Britain one is allocated a doctor is simply not true.

Nor is it true that a doctor is paid a salary by the state. He is not. He receives a fixed amount each year for each patient on his list—a "capitation" fee. Whenever they consult him, he treats them. The treatment as such has therefore no direct effect on the doctor's remuneration. He does not earn more money for more treatment, or less for less. Since most doctors are conscientious in their work, this certainty is probably desirable rather than the opposite, though there is a double-edged element to the argument. Most doctors in Britain make house-calls, and again there is no charge to the patient. House-calls are accepted as part of the normal service that one's doctor is expected to render, which in turn the doctor expects to have to provide. If further treatment is needed, the doctor refers the patient to the local hospital where specialist attention, "in-patient" treatment, and surgery or any other specialist service are available, again free to the patient. Britain is thus quite a good place in which to be acutely ill. It is not quite such a good place to be chronically unwell or to need prolonged non-hospital treatment. The more lethal the disease or the more urgent the condition, the speedier is the treatment. However, waiting lists for non-severe ailments are far too long. In 1979, 600,000 people were waiting for admission to an NHS hospital.

The point also needs to be made that treatment, once one is in a hospital, is good. The nursing staff is skilled, and the specialists extremely competent. British doctors and nurses must be good—otherwise they would hardly be in such demand in the United States. Convalescent and recovery services are adequate, and the standard is as high as anywhere else I know.

Prescription drugs in Britain are provided virtually free. A charge of about $2.00 is made for each item on a prescription. A patient with a prescription from a doctor has only to take it to a pharmacy and pay his $2.00 per item, and then receives the drugs. Old-age pensioners, children, and people permanently disabled or on welfare (in England called, somewhat confusingly, "social security"; social security in the American sense is called an old-age pension) do not even have to pay that charge; they get medicines free.

It is always difficult, if not impossible, to compare medical costs in different countries. There are so many variables that the comparison is rarely entirely valid. In Britain, however, the NHS cost to the patient is certain. The patient will be rendered no bill as such and will not be called upon to pay anything at all (save for prescription drugs). An open-heart operation, involving consultation with a general practitioner (the family doctor), specialist treatment, hospitalization, a major operation (with perhaps a senior cardiac surgeon performing it), post-operative treatment, and finally convalescence—all this would be free. Not only would it be free, but the fact that it is so occasions neither comment nor interest. It is an accepted social benefit.

I am told that comparable treatment in a major New York hospital would run to tens of thousands of dollars. To any European, and particularly to anyone from Britain, the concept of having to find such an immense sum of money to pay for medical treatment, even for treatment as comprehensive as a major operation, is totally alien. It just would not be considered socially acceptable that medical care should be sold in this way, and at such a high price.

Dentistry and eye care are both provided in Britain in much the same way as other medical services. Again the patient picks the dentist or optician. The patient is examined, a course of treatment is decided upon and given, and a small sum is charged—at present a maximum of £10 for a course of dental treatment—when the treatment is completed or the glasses supplied. Of course, if someone wants gold fillings or exotic eyeglass frames, he or she pays for them, but normal treatment is extremely cheap and readily available.

There is, moreover, in the United States a widely held belief that the only treatment available in Britain is that which is provided by the state. Again, this is simply untrue. There are private doctors who do not practise under the National Health Service at all, there are National Health doctors who do some private practising, and there are some who do none. The choice is the doctor's.

The same is true of hospitals. There are many private hospitals and nursing homes in Britain, ranging from the small private local maternity home to the London Clinic or the newly built Wellington Hospital in London, which is run and staffed privately and for which high fees are paid. Harley Street and Wimpole Street, the traditional "doctors' area" of central London, are filled with private practitioners and specialists. Their consulting rooms are full of paying patients, many now from abroad. The advantage of private treatment is not that the treatment is medically superior to that of the NHS but that there is far less hassle in getting it. To someone whose time is money, the advantage of speed and convenience may be considered to be worth paying for. Private hospital treatment can be quicker, the food is probably better, and one can demand a room of one's own. But given these advantages, there is little difference in the actual treatment itself. Moreover, there are in Britain private health insurance schemes akin to Blue Cross and Blue Shield for those who want to insure themselves and their families against the cost of private medical bills. This is a boom industry (given the pressure on the NHS); by the end of 1979 nearly 3 million people were covered by private medical insurance schemes.

The health service was established in Britain in the late 1940s and the main political arguments were decided then. We decided, as a nation, that health care should be made available to all, irrespective of their means and their capacity to pay. We decided that there was something repugnant in the idea that the quality of medical treatment should be dependent on the income of the patient. It was at the time a courageous decision by a country that had just emerged victorious but impoverished from the Second World War. It was a decision that only a tiny and quite unrepresentative minority in Britain would now wish to reverse.

It is, I fear, impossible to give an adequate picture of the British social services in a few pages. The health service is comprehensive. We have a social security system that pays a modest pension to all our retired workers; men retire at sixty-five and women at sixty. There is an adequate but certainly not extravagant unemployment insurance scheme, and a residual welfare payments system for those in real need. No one in Britain today actually starves, though few grow fat on the benefits of the social services alone. Where we have succeeded, however, is in removing some of the fears in the minds of most people: the fear of illness without the means to pay for treatment, the fear of destitution in old age, the fear of poverty through unemployment. These claims are perceived as legitimate ones against the collective national income, and while largely self-financing (each person who works pays a weekly contribution from pay towards these benefits), the total cost of social security and the NHS, taken together was nearly £30 billion in 1979–80—about three times the amount the government spent on defence.

What is significant about the British attitude to the health and social services as a whole is indeed the fact that they are not considered to be in any way extraordinary. Of course there are some abuses—some are perhaps inevitable. But the system seems to work reasonably well and people do not appear to be taking an unfair advantage of the benefits available.

We have not cosseted our people to the point of stagnation, nor have we made indolence attractive, though this is a criticism one hears from time to time in the United States. I do not believe there are many people in Britain who would actually prefer not to work —all the evidence is against that belief. The longer these services are accepted as part of the normal pattern of our national life, the less temptation there is to take an unfair advantage or to claim an unfair share. The Labour Party in 1950 campaigned on the slogan "Fair shares for all." When challenged on it, Clement Attlee, the Labour leader, retorted, "Well, what do you want, then—unfair shares?" This concept of national fairness is one the British take seriously, even if they rarely articulate it. We do believe that society can and should be organized in such a way that the extremes of poverty and opulence should be removed. There is an obscenity in the contrast of extreme wealth and extreme deprivation within the one society. It makes for a country that is unstable as well as unhappy, particularly if the deprived feel little hope of being able to escape.

What is unquantifiable, however, is the economic price that Britain may have paid in order to create our present somewhat gentler society. I simply do not know, but then neither does anyone else, not even the economists. There is certainly an argument that our tax system may have borne too heavily and directly on middle management or the skilled industrial worker and this has had a disincentive effect. Precisely what effect this may have had on production or investment is, however, unknown and probably unknowable. Judging by Britain's overall post-war economic performance, when compared with that of our major industrial rivals, it may be that in the process of avoiding the extremes of opulence and poverty we have blunted some of the sharp cutting-edge of wealth creation. If so, it may be that in terms of the quality of the society we are producing, the price is one worth paying. Certainly it seems to have been one that the British people were prepared to accept.

THE ABSENCE OF REVOLUTION

By most standards other than that of crude commercialism, I am content that my country should be judged. Whether for the quality of life of its citizens, the social and international consciousness of its governments, or the intellectual vitality of its arts or media, I think Britain compares reasonably well with most other industrialized nations. If so, much of the credit is due to the longevity of our institutions and the compromise we have thereby evolved between the libertarian and the collectivist strands in our political, social, and economic thought and development.

The origins of the libertarian side of British politics are more ancient than those of the collectivist. The rights of the individual against the state have been asserted with varying success since the Magna Carta, signed by King John in 1215. They were probably most vivid in the seventeenth century during the Puritan and Parliamentary rebellion against the personal rule of Charles I. This led to our Civil War, the defeat of the Royalists, and the execution of the King himself. In 1649 Charles I stepped onto the scaffold from the Banqueting House in Whitehall, a building that can still be seen in the centre of London. Later, in 1688, the "bloodless revolution" saw a major transfer of power from King to Parliament.

The conflict between Parliament and King was over the extent to which a central government was entitled to rule without the consent of the elected representatives of the people. Though it was expressed in terms of the monarch versus the House of Commons, the dispute was in reality over fundamental principles of democratic government and particularly the power to raise revenues. If the King could tax without parliamentary assent, where did power really lie? It was precisely the same issue that surfaced in a later dispute between a British monarch—this time George III—and his American colonies. "No taxation without Parliament" and "no taxation without representation" are but separate facets of the same principle: that governments derive their authority from the people, and that without that authority the people are entitled, perhaps even bound, to resist.

Within the Parliamentary side during the Civil War there were inevitably differing views and different factions. While they were all opposed to the continuation of an absolute monarchy, they were not agreed on the nature of the system of government by which it should be replaced. Some, notably Cromwell, tended towards élitism, holding that the King's power should be reduced and Parliament's accordingly increased, but also believing universal suffrage to be undesirable. Others, notably a group known as the Levellers, believed that all men had the right to participate in the choice of the government of their country.

The Levellers were one of the most interesting of the groups that grew up on the Parliamentary side. They were a strange combination of radical reformers and theologians. There were two main strands to their thinking: one was the radical Calvinism of the Protestant Revolution; the other, the more optimistic view of the Renaissance and particularly the concept of a natural law to which all men, whether governors or governed, were subject. They also believed that all power lay in the people, who merely entrusted their elected representatives with as much of it as they chose to give for the sake of order, safety, and the convenience of the country as a whole. It was this concept which led to their characteristic ideal of a sovereign legislature, in which all power resided, subject to recall by the electors (and that at frequent intervals), and which was itself bound by certain unalterable, inalienable, and God-given fundamental laws.

In 1647 the Civil War in England between Parliament and King was continuing. The Puritan army had been successful but not yet decisively so. It must have been a strange army for the seventeenth century. There was a sense of individual equality that made it unique among the forces of that time. The soldiers themselves, and particularly their officers, were in many cases men deeply interested in the future course of the political institutions of their country. Many of the officers were Levellers. In October 1647 they drew up a document purporting to be on behalf of the army as a whole, known as "the first Agreement of the People." It is well worth examination, since what happened to the Levellers thereafter is significant in the development of our political institutions and thought.

The agreement was on behalf of a number of regiments of horse and of foot and was headed: "An agreement of the People for a firme and present peace, upon grounds of Common-Right." The prose of the document itself is magnificent and the sentiments noble. The preamble reads:

> Having by our late labours and hazards made it appeare to the world at how high a rate wee value our just freedome, and God having so far owned our cause, as to deliver the Enemies thereof into our hands: We do now hold our selves bound in mutual duty to each other, to take the best care we can for the future, to avoid both the danger of returning into a slavish condition, and the chargeable remedy of another war: for as it cannot be imagined that so many of our Country-men would have opposed us in this quarrel, if they had understood their owne good; so may we

safely promise to our selves, that when our Common Rights and
liberties shall be cleared, their endeavours will be disappointed,
that seek to make themselves our Masters. . . .

The main requirement in the agreement was for a sovereign
Parliament to be elected once every two years "upon the 1st
Thursday in every 2nd March" to begin to sit the "1st Thursday
in April" following and to continue till "the last day of Septem-
ber, then next ensuing and no longer."

It also established that the power of Parliament should be sovereign and "inferior only to those who chose them." It was to
have full powers save for five matters upon which it and no
successor could legislate.

Full religious freedom was guaranteed.

The right of conscription in time of war was denied: "The
matter of impressing and constraining any of us to serve in the
warres is against our freedom and therefore we do not allow it in
our representatives."

There was to be an indemnity for anything said or done "in ref-
erence to the late publike differences" (the Civil War), and this
clause was in turn followed by one eloquent in its simplicity but,
for the seventeenth century, awesome in its implication.

"That in all laws made, or to be made, every person may be
bound alike, and that no tenure, estate, charter, degree, birth or
place, do confer any exemption from the ordinary course of legal
proceedings whereunto others are subjected."

Finally there was an injunction that as the laws were equal, so
they ought to be good.

In this document the fundamentals of a pluralistic democracy
are expressed. Power belongs to the people, who exercise their
choice of representatives once every two years. Parliament is to
be sovereign, religious freedom is to be guaranteed, and the rule
of law is to be universal, even when applied to monarchs—and all
this only 27 years after the Pilgrim Fathers stepped ashore on
Plymouth Rock and no less than 129 years before the Declaration
of Independence.

The subsequent history of this movement is moving. It was not
attractive to those in power—particularly to the Puritan establishment itself. To the Parliamentary élite it smacked too much of

populism. The Levellers and the Parliamentary leaders, notably Cromwell and Ireton, accordingly met to debate these issues at the parish church of Putney on the outskirts of London (the church still stands just to the south of the present bridge over the Thames). The debate raged over three days in late October 1647. A Mr. William Clarke, who was fortunately present, took down the proceedings in shorthand and later transcribed them. Thereafter the records disappeared from view until 1891, when they were rediscovered and published—some 244 years after the debates themselves had taken place.

Argument was immediately joined between the libertarian and the property owner. Ireton, who was Cromwell's son-in-law, straightway challenged the whole concept of universal suffrage, arguing that only those who had a share in the community could be relied upon to cast their votes with the necessary degree of objectivity. The confrontation between the democrat and the élitist was thus raised at the outset.

Ireton and the Puritan establishment were answered by one of the Levellers, a Colonel Rainsborough, in a simple sentence profoundly moving in the innovation of its thought and the beauty of its language. He said:

> For really I think that the poorest he that is in England hath a life to live as the greatest he; and therefore truly Sir, I think it is clear that every man that is to live under a government ought first by his own consent to put himself under that Government, and I do think that the poorest man in England is not at all bound in a strict sense to that government that he hath not had a voice to put himself under.

In the spring of 1978 I quoted this statement to a somewhat mystified United Nations session on human rights in an attempt to show that Britain's concern with democracy went back a long way. I don't think it convinced the Russians, but it may have underlined the fact that democracy is not a new concept and that hope for equality existed in England centuries before Marx.

Unfortunately, the Levellers did not succeed as a political movement, though their ideas persisted. They were later crushed by the Parliamentary establishment as mutineers, and England proceeded to replace dictatorship by monarch with dictatorship by the Lord Protector Cromwell. Yet the failure is significant in itself. The Levellers did preach political democracy many years before it became fashionable. They did represent a recurring theme in British thinking over the centuries—one side of an argument over the nature and extent of participatory government that was not finally resolved until the twentieth century. As such, they expressed views and exemplified a feeling still important in Britain today, the belief that "the poorest he" has just as much right to a say in the way he is governed as the most powerful. It is a consistent strain which, though not always predominant (Britain has had its share of autocracies too), has nevertheless proved lasting.

The collectivist strand in British political thought is much more recent, arising as it does from the industrial revolution and its social effects on the working class in Britain. The impetus came from the rise of the trade unions in the nineteenth century. Forced to counter the more extreme effects of the first industrial revolution, the working class in England soon came to feel the need for political as well as industrial power. Unlike the labour movement in the United States, they were never content to see their role solely in terms of working conditions, pay, and industrial relations, perhaps because in their early days they were singularly unsuccessful in ameliorating the lot of their members. "Combinations," as they were known, were met by the government of the day with a mixture of coercion and rejection. Union organizers were arrested, charged, and imprisoned. Some were deported for little more than attempting to publicize the grievances of the ordinary man.

On February 24, 1834, George and James Loveless, Thomas and John Stanfield, James Hammett, and James Brine, six agricultural labourers from Tolpuddle in Dorset, were arrested and charged with the crime of having participated in the administration of an illegal oath. The oath concerned was that required for admission to a Friendly Society of Agricultural Labourers in Tolpuddle, which the six men perceived as the centre of a number of similar societies in Dorset and in due course as a possible affiliate of Britain's main union of the day, the Grand Consolidated Trades Union. The purpose of the society was to advance the wages and improve the conditions of work of agricultural workers in and around the town of Tolpuddle. Wages, which had been ten shillings a week in 1831, were first reduced to nine shillings and by the end of 1832 to eight shillings a week, a wage insufficient to maintain a man and his family. A contemporary song ran as follows:

> *Come all ye bold Britons, where'er you may be,*
> *I pray give attention and listen to me,*
> *There once was good times, but they've gone complete*
> *For a poor man lives now on Eight Shillings a week.*
>
> *Such times in old England there never was seen,*
> *As the present ones now, but much better have been,*
> *A poor man's condemned and looked on as thief,*
> *And compelled to work hard for Eight Shillings a week.*
>
> *The "Nobs of Old England" of shameful renown*
> *Are striving to crush the poor man to the ground,*
> *They'll beat down their wages and starve them complete*
> *And make them work hard for Eight Shillings a week.*
>
> *A poor man to labour (believe me 'tis so),*
> *To maintain his family is willing to go*
> *Either hedging or ditching, to plough or to reap,*
> *But how does he live on Eight Shillings a week?*

By 1833 wages had been reduced further to seven shillings, and then to six. The response of the men was to form their Friendly Society.

The six men were tried at Dorchester Assizes and convicted of administering an illegal oath on legal grounds that were, to say the least, doubtful, involving as they did recourse by the prosecution to the Mutiny Act of 1797, passed after the British fleet had mutinied at Spithead. Their sentences were the maximum provided by law: seven years' transportation to Australia. Fortunately the public reaction to this draconian punishment was intense. The men were later reprieved before the end of their sentences and allowed to return home, five of them later emigrating to Canada. The "Tolpuddle Martyrs" have become part of the folklore of British trade unionism, though derided sometimes in other quarters because of the name. Yet their cause was just, and their sacrifice great.

It was, moreover, no isolated instance. Throughout the nineteenth century the history of the trade unions in Britain is one of strife and disappointment. Reforms, when they came, were late and little. Factory conditions were unbelievable, and the opportunities of rectifying them depended on the actions of a Parliament in which the working class was barely represented at all. An occasional "radical," whether formally in either of the ruling Liberal or Conservative parties, could help and did. Josiah Wedgwood, Lord Shaftesbury, the Liberal leader William Gladstone, and even the Conservative Benjamin Disraeli, all tried within their limits and according to their lights, but by twentieth-century standards their limits were narrow and their lights were dim. The elegant paternalism of nineteenth-century politics was all very well, but what was believed to be lacking was direct parliamentary representation. Even after the suffrage was extended in 1866, the choice available to the country was still basically between two parties of virtually identical social and economic background. As Lady Bracknell says of the Liberals in Wilde's *Importance of Being Earnest,* "Oh, they count as Tories. They dine with us. Or come in the evening, at any rate."

Politically the country was polarized into the Conservative and Liberal parties—the Tories and the Whigs. The choice was, to say the least, limited. As W. S. Gilbert puts it in *Iolanthe:*

> *I often think it's comical*
> *How Nature always does contrive*
> *That every boy and every gal,*
> *That's born into the world alive,*
> *Is either a little Liberal,*
> *Or else a little Conservative!*

It was perhaps comical, but it contained more than a grain of truth.

Allied to the rise of trade unionism in Britain was another movement of profound significance, the Methodist Revival, and the rise of nonconformist dissent.

Wesley's evangelism produced in England far more than a mere heightened consciousness of sin. Quite apart from purging the Church of England of its more obvious venalities, the rise of the nonconformist "chapels" provided an educational and social stimulus to the newly emerging industrial working class. Before this, their educational opportunities had been slender indeed. The chapels tended to give the untapped energy of the new industrial working class a direction and a channel. The old saying that the Church of England was the Tory Party at prayer remained valid well into the nineteenth century. The land-owning aristocracy and those with pretensions to join it went to church. The labourers went to chapel. A unique blend of Christian egalitarianism began to develop, owing allegiance basically to no one political party. Christianity was perceived as leading to a more just and more equal society in which the apparently meek inherited the privately owned earth. That strange mystic William Blake in his poem *Jerusalem,* perhaps Britain's alternative national anthem, summed it up:

> *And did those feet in ancient time*
> *Walk upon England's mountains green?*
> *And was the holy Lamb of God*
> *On England's pleasant pastures seen?*
>
> *And did the Countenance Divine*
> *Shine forth upon our clouded hills?*
> *And was Jerusalem builded here*
> *Among these dark Satanic Mills?*
>
> *Bring me my Bow of burning gold!*
> *Bring me my Arrows of desire!*
> *Bring me my Spear! O clouds, unfold!*
> *Bring me my Chariot of fire!*
>
> *I will not cease from Mental Fight,*
> *Nor shall my Sword sleep in my hand,*
> *Till we have built Jerusalem*
> *In England's green and pleasant land.*

The message here is clear. Christianity leads (or at least should lead) to social and political action in the direction of greater equality and fairness. The deepest instinct of this movement was fundamentally religious, not political. It was not an economic ideology in which its adherents believed—it was a divinely inspired state of mankind.

Britain has, by and large, escaped Marxism in the continental European sense. Marxism has always been a non-British movement despite the fact that Marx wrote *Das Kapital* in the reading room of the British Museum. He is in fact buried in Highgate Cemetery in London, where stands a memorial bust of quite monumental tastelessness to which earnest delegations of East Europeans make occasional pilgrimage. That Marxism has never taken hold in Britain is partly due to the essential pragmatism of the British themselves, who are empirical in their approach and non-dogmatic in their answers. It is also due to the realization that Marxism as an analysis was hardly compatible with a belief in the importance of the individual and in the subordination of society to the individual, rather than vice versa. A Marxist form of government just could not fit with either the libertarian or the collectivist strands of our political development.

Collectivism in Britain came to be expressed not in terms of the "dictatorship of the proletariat" but more in the moral obligation for society as a whole to take a greater responsibility for the well-being of all its members. In turn, this led by a practical extension of the argument to the belief that our major industries should be publicly rather than privately owned—that what Aneurin Bevan once called "the commanding heights of the economy" should be in public, not private, hands.

These two concepts of individual liberty and collective responsibility have over the years come to be accepted not only by the Labour Party but by almost all the other political parties and leaders in Britain. They provide the ideological basis for much of our industrial and social development since the war. They are responsible both for nationalization and for the health service and welfare state.

Yet this is hardly surprising, given the character of the people. There was, and still is, a streak of stubborn individualism in the British. They tolerate eccentrics, even welcome them, despite the inevitable pressures that go with the complications of a twentieth-century industrialized democracy. The right to turn out a government, the belief that authority needs humbling from time to time for its own good, is deeply imbedded in the British psyche. There is also the view that the individual is entitled to believe that he knows what is good for himself. He may not always be able to achieve it, but at least he thinks he knows what he wants. Certainly he does not trust the government to know any better. One of the most successful political slogans of the post-war era was that of the Conservative Party in 1950–51. "Set the people free" was the battle-cry with which Churchill led them into an election. He demanded an end to rationing, to allocations, to form-filling, to being, as he claimed, overorganized. He struck a responsive chord, so responsive indeed that much the same appeal kept the Labour Party out of office for thirteen years from 1951 to 1964.

The British are still individuals, though sensible ones, who for the most part recognize the need for law and order, for a degree of conscious planning, and for an acceptable framework within which the nation can and should function. Moreover, they tend to see this in non-ideological terms, arguing that the common sense of the situation demands a degree of centralization, rather than that a degree of centralization is necessary to achieve a particular political and economic objective.

This practical approach to social organization is now common to all parties in Britain, save for the extremes on both left and right. The interesting thing about British politics since the Second World War is the extent of the national consensus and not its lack. In turn, this is why so much of the political argument in Britain is marginal and why the party spectra tend to overlap somewhat. Naturally, each party has its own altar of household gods, at which it is called upon to worship ritually, particularly at election time. The Conservative Party tries to portray free enterprise—but with a caring heart. The Labour Party has traditionally sold socialism, but not too much—and with a strong commitment to personal freedom. The Liberal Party talks of its past and free trade, while our newest party, the Social Democrats, talks of "breaking the mould of British politics" and a fresh start for the country free from the traditional party confrontations, which the Social Democrats regard as sterile.

The Wall Street Journal once wrote that there are two parties in

Britain: one is called Labour and is socialist; the other is called Conservative and is socialist too. It could just as easily have said there are two libertarian parties in Britain, one being called Conservative, and the other Labour.

The Queen,
Politics, and
Parliament

THE QUEEN
AND HER ROLE

In a hard-hitting book on the monarchy, *The Crown and the Establishment* (1962), Kingsley Martin wrote:

> Until the last quarter of the century Queen Victoria seemed likely to be the last British monarch; highly respectable Liberals, like John Bright, Sir Charles Dilke, Joseph Chamberlain, and John Morley, deprecated as unchivalrous anything like personal criticism of the Queen, but they were not prepared to hold that her scapegrace son Edward should succeed her.

Not only did Edward succeed Victoria; despite Edward's own tendency to speak of his son George (later George V) as "the last King of England," the monarchy is still going strong and is now possibly more popular than ever. Very few British people—and only one or two MPs—are republicans. When Charles, Prince of Wales, married Lady Diana Spencer in July 1981 a group of young republicans decided to take advantage of the public holiday to spend a day in France paying homage to France's republican institutions. But when they got there, they found that François Mitterrand, the newly elected socialist President of France, had gone to London to be at the wedding, and millions of republican Frenchmen spent the time glued to their televisions watching the royal wedding.

This may have, as Martin thought, something to do with the "television age," but it is also, paradoxically, a measure of Britain's decline in the world and of the humdrum nature of government and politics. An echo of past grandeur and a reminder of what is unchanging and unchallengeable in the British heritage, the British monarchy remains what Walter Bagehot called the "ceremonial" part of government, as opposed to the day-to-day business of actually fixing income-tax rates and working out potato policy in the European Community. Prime ministers are heads of government; the monarch is head of state. In the United States and France the two functions are combined, whereas in Britain the deference and respect that in those countries are directed to the office of President are reserved for the monarchy, and the Prime Minister is an ordinary mortal, probably, given the two-party system, hated by half the voters, and ensconced in the elegant but unpretentious No. 10 Downing Street, not in the huge and magnificent Buckingham Palace.

The fact that British kings and queens reign but do not rule was established long ago: the people possessed political power and elected their representatives, leaving the monarchy as a useful constitutional device and, as Martin put it, "the focus of national unity." But as sultans, emperors, and kings were swept away, many British people felt the monarchy to be an out-of-date anomaly, while to this day many foreigners cannot understand why we still have a monarch. The fact is that the behaviour of the monarchs themselves has been as responsible as anything else for their survival. Edward, Prince of Wales, was, while his mother Queen Victoria was alive, a notorious playboy and layabout, but when he became King he showed a wisdom and moderation that surprised everyone, meddled far less in the affairs of his ministers than his mother had, and trained his son George V to be a highly conscientious monarch whose popularity was unsurpassed. Today Her Majesty the Queen is an experienced and skilful head of state whose popularity is greater than ever.

Yet the British Royal Family is quite unlike other European royal families, such as the Dutch, Danish, or Swedish—or, now, the Spanish—not in its constitutional role, which is much the same, but in its life-style. While Scandinavian monarchs ride bicycles to work, the British royals have retained to a far greater extent their palaces, state coaches, courtiers, a royal yacht, and many of the trappings of traditional monarchy, including an aristocracy with titles and gradations. The Queen remains head of the Church of England and of the Commonwealth, and as the latter presides over the periodic meetings of the Commonwealth heads of government. Anthony Sampson summed up the situation:

> At the head of this unique institution is Her Most Excellent Majesty Elizabeth the Second, by the Grace of God, of the United Kingdom of Great Britain and Northern Ireland and of Her other Realms and Territories Queen, Head of the Commonwealth, Defender of the Faith, Sovereign of the British Orders of Knighthood. The Queen is the fortieth monarch since the Norman Conquest, descended among others from Charlemagne, Egbert King of Wessex, Rodrigo the Cid, and the Emperor Barbarossa.

If the Queen merely reigns but does not rule, who does the actual running of the country? Here the fiction is still maintained that the Queen is doing so: the government is "Her Majesty's Government" and her ministers are technically merely giving her advice—but she cannot constitutionally ignore it, so in fact they *are* the government. She is the head of the judiciary, an important part of the legislature, and the commander-in-chief of all the armed forces of the Crown. The Queen may not do any actual ruling; but without her, many functions of government could not be performed. She has to summon Parliament or dissolve it; without her signature no bill, even when properly passed by both Houses of Parliament, can pass into law; and, formally, all appointments of ministers, judges, ambassadors, and officers in the armed forces are made by her. Perhaps most important of all, it is the monarch who appoints the Prime Minister. Normally the Queen invites the leader of the majority party in the House of Commons—or the politician who can command a majority in the House—to form a government. When a prime minister dies or resigns unexpectedly, the Queen, after seeking advice, invites the person whom she thinks most likely to be able to form a government with Commons' backing to do so. This is the nearest the Queen is likely to get to actual power in a direct political sense. There have been occasions, as, for example, when Sir Anthony Eden resigned as Prime Minister in 1957, when the choice of a successor may be controversial within the ruling party.

Much of the residual role of the monarchy derives from the days when the monarch was a feudal lord who actually "owned" the country. In the days of William the Conqueror everything now undertaken by the "state" was undertaken, literally, by the servants of the King. Now only the language lives on: the mail is carried in vans bearing the title "Royal Mail" and even tax demands come in envelopes marked "On Her Majesty's Service." Where any other country would have the notion of "state property," the British have "Crown property." In the law courts it is formally the Crown, not the state, that prosecutes.

Thus the British have personified the state. This has some interesting consequences. A policeman or a soldier is serving his Queen, not the disembodied state, and when the Queen is as impressive a person as Queen Elizabeth, and a person as remote from the government or party politics as she, the notion of loyal service has a new relevance and meaning. A bureaucratic posting for a general or an ambassador is the "Queen's Command"—when put that way it is harder to ignore than a routine letter, containing the same message, from the personnel office. As a leading constitutional lawyer, Sir Ivor Jennings, put it, "it is a little easier to put aside our private interests in order to serve the Queen than it is to put them aside in order to serve the State."

The consequences of all this are profound, and not only for the unity of the country and the armed forces. The idea of serving the

Queen rather than the government legitimizes the whole idea of opposition. The theory would run something like this: "I am a patriot, but I oppose the government even though a majority of my fellow citizens voted it in. I genuinely believe that Her Majesty is ill served by her present ministers, and that her cause would be better served by policies diametrically opposed to those of her government." In other words, while in most countries of the world to criticize the government is treasonable, in Britain, provided you accept the monarchy, opposition is justifiable in terms of patriotism: Her Majesty's—in other words, the country's—cause is above that of mere transitory administrations and your opposition can be justified as an attempt to improve her situation. That is why, in Parliament, the Leader of Her Majesty's Loyal Opposition receives a special salary and a chauffeur-driven car to boot.

The complex relationship between the sovereign and her ministers and Commons is well illustrated by the whole question of who finances the monarchy. The approval of the House of Commons is formally necessary for most of the expenditures of the monarchy, whether for funds for the Queen's official engagements —the "Civil List"—or for the host of other costs, such as the royal yacht, the royal train, or the upkeep of the royal palaces, which come under the budgets of separate government departments. Although the Queen also has income called the Privy Purse—an inheritance that has helped finance monarchs since 1399—and private income from her estates and personal investments, the institution of the monarchy is largely financed from public funds. How much it all costs is not entirely clear, though the 1981 Civil List for the Queen is £3.25 million and for the whole of the Royal Family (the Queen included) is £4.25 million. There is, however, no problem about the House of Commons approving the Civil List or ministers authorizing expenditure on the Queen from their departmental budgets. Although from time to time an anti-royalist MP will attempt to stop or hold up approval of the Queen's money, there is never any problem. It is known that Her Majesty is extremely careful, in these times of mass unemployment, to keep increases in the Civil List to a bare minimum. There were nearly 3 million unemployed when, with all the pomp and ceremony that British tradition can muster, the Prince and Princess of Wales were married in St. Paul's Cathedral in July

1981. Yet the vast majority of Britons, if asked whether, at a time of economic recession, they approved public money being spent to the tune of £3 million on the Royal Family, would have replied, "It's cheap at the price." Things have, of course, changed since Victorian times, when the monarchy was proportionately much more expensive. Now, far from coming under increased scrutiny in hard times, the monarchy seems more valued as something that adds some colour to an otherwise dreary world.

ELECTIONS IN BRITAIN

At frequent but irregular intervals Britain is gripped by a short, intense bout of election fever. It is usually a relatively brief attack precisely because it is irregular. We do not have "fixed term" elections in Britain. Elections are held whenever the Prime Minister of the day considers it appropriate, and that in reality means when he or she thinks the party can win. The maximum length of time that can elapse without an election is five years, but within that period the decision on timing is one solely for the Prime Minister. We do not, therefore, have a long slow buildup to an election date known long in advance, nor can Members of Parliament ever be quite sure how long it will be before they have to face their electorate again. Towards the end of the fourth year of the five-year term,

politicians in Britain tend to get jittery. Nerves start fraying and
the political temperature begins to rise, but even then there is no
certainty about it, and much of the verbal sparring is in truth
shadow-boxing only. The press is full of rumours, and it is not
until the final announcement is made that rumour becomes fact
and uncertainty disappears. The election campaign itself starts
only when the Prime Minister announces that he or she has formally requested the Queen to dissolve Parliament.

This flexibility of the Parliamentary system, and the discretion
given to a sitting Prime Minister in the timing of an election, is
one of the most striking differences between our system of government and the American. President Reagan knows that he will not
have to face another election until November 1984. He knows
that his own position as President is secure until that date. No
British Prime Minister could ever make such a claim with such authority. In principle, a government can be defeated at any time on
a motion of no confidence, or censure, in the House of Commons.
If it were to lose such a vote, then the government would have to
resign and an election would ensue. Even for a government with
an overall majority in the House of Commons, the parliamentary
position is always difficult. For a minority government, or one vul-
nerable to a revolt by a section of its own party, the parliamentary
situation can be a nightmare.

Campaigning in Britain is totally different from the art of getting
elected in America. The campaigns are shorter, less expensive,
and more national in character. A voter does not have to register
as Labour or Conservative. Since there are no primaries, such a
registration would be superfluous.

Each fall a form is delivered to every household in Britain. The
householder has a legal obligation to fill it in, listing everyone over
eighteen resident in the house on a certain date. The form is then
returned to the local city or borough council offices, where a register of electors is then prepared. That register is public and freely
available to all, including the political parties.

When an election is called, the whole effort in any given constituency is devoted to two specific aims: first, identifying where your
vote is; and second, making sure that supporters actually do vote
on polling day. Teams of canvassers armed with the appropriate
section of the electoral register descend on those areas. The theo-

retical objective is to contact every voter and find out which way he or she intends voting on polling day. On election day itself there is quite an elaborate procedure to make sure that those who have promised to vote for you in fact do. Outside each polling station stand representatives of the major parties. As each elector emerges, he is asked for his polling number, which has been sent to him on an official card by the council in advance. The numbers are noted, the party committee rooms check off the numbers of those who have voted against those who promised to, and one should, in theory, then be able to see which of one's prospective supporters have not yet actually cast their vote.

The last four hours of election day are confused and hectic. The names of those who have not voted are given to teams of volunteer workers who then physically call on them. When I first came to the United States I was describing the process at a small midwestern university and could not understand the hilarity my description evoked. I later discovered why. The activity on the evening of polling day in Britain is called a knocking-up campaign and the volunteers are known as knockers-up.

The whole electoral process from canvassing to polling day invariably produces some humour. There was the woman who on election night said that she could not come today but would try and pop round tomorrow if her legs were a bit better.

Or the man who swore that he had voted yesterday and it was not legal for him to do it twice.

There are always the ones who say they thought it was next week, despite the saturation from television and the press.

And when it comes to canvassing, the stories are myriad. One of my all-time favourites was that of the candidate who knocked at a door and, when the man of the house appeared, introduced himself in the time-honoured way.

"Good morning, sir, my name is ———. I am the Labour candidate for this constituency. I hope we can rely on your vote on polling day."

Only to be met with the response: "Vote, oh, I never vote. It only encourages them."

Or the friend of mine who was a candidate at a by-election where race was an issue who introduced himself in the above manner to a lady whose name was Mrs. Kaslowsky, to be answered by her with the retort: "I am not voting Labour. You want to let the blacks in. I want to keep them out."

As he turned away, my friend had a thought and said to her, "Excuse me. You are Mrs. Kaslowsky?"

"Yes," she replied.

Thinking he now had her, he went on triumphantly, "You are British?"

"Yes."

"Is your husband Polish?"

"Yes."

"Was he one of those that came here after the war?"

"Yes," she replied.

"Should we have kept him out?" He delivered the *coup de grâce*.

"Yes, you bloody well should," she said and slammed the door.

The first election I fought was in South Kensington in London in 1959. It had the second-largest Conservative majority in England, and, alas, retained it despite all my efforts to the contrary. It was indeed so Conservative that when canvassing for Labour one did not actually reveal the party affiliation. Instead of saying, "Good morning, madam, my name is Ivor Richard, I am the Labour Candidate," I used to vary it to, "Good morning, madam, I am doing some canvassing for the election. I wonder if you would care to tell me which way you are thinking of voting on polling day?"

That way there was at least a fair chance of getting one's foot through the door.

One Sunday morning I knocked at the door of an apartment in one of the gentler Kensington squares to be greeted by an attractive lady in an elegant negligee. In answer to my opening gambit she said, "How nice. I have not had anyone round so far this election. Do come in and have a glass of sherry." Feeling I was at last among civilized electors, I was just stepping across the threshold when she turned, a thought obviously having just struck her, and said, "Of course, you are from the Conservative Party, aren't you?"

Feeling valour to be the better part of political discretion, I owned up and said, "Well, actually no. I am the Labour Candidate." Thereupon the door was slammed in my face. Somewhat daunted at such an abrupt change in my fortunes, I consoled myself with the thought of adversities yet to be overcome, and battles still to be won, when the door opened again with the most crushing blow of all.

"Excuse me. I do not want to be rude. It is just that we do not want your sort in the house."

Every candidate at every election has a fund of such incidents. The most unlikely people vote the most unlikely ways, and for the most unlikely reasons. One old man I knew always voted Conservative because he did not like "that there Lloyd George." My father always voted Liberal because he did like him, and the fact that Lloyd George ceased to be Prime Minister in 1922 and had died in 1945 was quite beside the point. My mother usually voted for the candidate she thought would come bottom of the poll because she did not want to see him totally humiliated.

Electioneering in Britain does occasionally have a bizarre attraction. In South Kensington we had little money and few supporters. In the end we managed to raise enough to fight the seat but the vote/money ratio was the lowest in England. Never in the field of political conflict had so much been spent by so few to so little result. Each vote cost us seven shillings, which in those days seemed a great deal of money. We had no permanent office but hired a room over a highly dubious café in Earls Court. As for meetings, they were confined to the open air. Twice a week I would stand on a soap-box opposite Earls Court tube station and hold forth to the assembled throng. We always had good crowds. The trouble was that none of them had a vote. They were either too young, Australian, New Zealand, South African, or tourists. They were lively, politically somewhat irreverent, but enormous fun. The ventilation was good, and while the standard of the politics was not particularly intellectual, it was all good practice.

The amount a candidate can spend on his election in Britain is very strictly limited. It is now approximately £2,500 per constituency. Nor can the limitation be evaded if the expenditure is made by the candidate's friends. The test is the object of the expenditure, not who does the spending, and if the legal limits are exceeded, then a successful candidate can in principle be ousted. No one can buy television and radio time. By law this is forbidden, and we are therefore spared the procession of earnest candidates

all assuring us that they really care. The appeal in Britain is much
simpler. I never tried to persuade the voters of Barons Court that
Ivor Richard was the only possible one for them, as he cared for
them and would look after them better than any other candidate.
The appeal was much simpler. "If you want a Labour government
in Westminster, then you need to vote for Ivor Richard in Barons
Court." The "pitch" was a national one, and, I am happy to say,
was successful for me three times until Barons Court was redis-
tributed out of existence and disappeared as a constituency in a
boundary revision in 1971.

The electoral process is thus far more institutionalized around
the party in Britain than in many other countries. The nomination
comes from the local party activists. The local party is a permanent institution fighting municipal and regional elections and remaining in being. The appeal to the electorate is as a party, national in character, and the result depends on how many MPs are
elected from which parties when the votes are all counted. The
scope for the independent in British politics is therefore minimal,
and the eccentric needs his party label and niche to flourish.

It is not really possible to compare the British and the American systems of government. They are frankly just different.

You have fixed-term elections. We do not.

You elect an executive. We do not.

You have a written Constitution. We do not.

You have formally "separated the powers." We have deliberately mixed them.

All our Members of Parliament are elected simultaneously.
Your legislators are not.

Members of Parliament do not have to reside in the constituency they represent. Your legislators do.

You have an intricate system of primary campaigns to select the
party candidates. We do not.

We have a permanent and functioning party structure between
elections. You do not.

The distinctions between our two constitutions are indeed great,
and the formal similarities are not obvious. We both have a pas-
sionate belief in the right of the people to throw out the government under which they have to live. Thus the fundamental principle of popular choice applies in both our countries. But the way in

which that choice is exercised, the manner in which the options are presented to the people, and the procedures by which that choice is translated into the transfer of actual power—all these differ greatly.

The most important single principle of British Government, indeed the one on which our whole system is based, is the supremacy of the House of Commons. There are 635 Members of Parliament, each one representing a single constituency. There is no double representation, as is the case in the Senate. Each individual represents one district, and in the chamber of the House of Commons is always referred to by his (or her) constituency. He would be called "the Hon. Member for Blankshire West" rather than "Mr. Brown." Most Members of Parliament belong to one of the two major parties, the Labour Party and the Conservative Party. There are some Liberals, some Social Democrats, a sprinkling of Scottish and Welsh Nationalists, the Ulstermen, and an occasional independent, but, despite the existence of these minorities, the real political battle in Britain has traditionally been between two giants. How this may be affected by the emergence of the Social Democratic Party is perhaps too early to say. This new party now has a fair sprinkling of MPs—27 in all—but whether it has yet broken the mould of British politics is something on which I would prefer to reserve judgement.

Moreover, since all the 635 Members of Parliament stand for election simultaneously, an election day in Britain is one when the whole country votes to choose a new House of Commons.

In almost every constituency there is a choice between a Labour candidate and a Conservative candidate, and next time a Liberal or Social Democrat as well. To these are perhaps added a Nationalist, in a few constituencies a Communist or an even more exotic fringe candidate, perhaps for the National Front (extreme right-wing) or the Workers Revolutionary Party (extreme left). The ballot paper itself is extremely simple, consisting only of a list of names with the party affiliation of the various candidates. There are no propositions put to the electorate, nor do they vote for anyone save for their choice as Member of Parliament for the district. Naturally the electorate votes for its municipal governments, but on other days, which are deliberately kept separate from parliamentary election day itself. The voting process itself is simple and

manual. There are no voting machines. The voter takes the ballot
paper into a curtained booth, marks a cross next to the name of
his (or her) choice, folds it, and deposits it in a sealed ballot box.
The whole is supervised by some usually benevolent policemen
and by two or three clerks employed by the local town or municipal council. Polling stations are numerous. The voter goes to the
one that is the station for his immediate home and gives his name
and address to the clerk, who checks it against the voters' list and
then hands him the ballot paper. He then votes. Polling stations
open at 7:00 A.M. and close at 10:00 P.M. Voting in a British parliamentary election is usually heavy—around 70–75 per cent—and
invariably takes place on a Thursday.

I have fought a number of parliamentary elections, some successful, others not, but each election day I find the process by
which power is either transferred or consolidated impressive and
moving. It is the total absence of pomp or pretension that is
awesome. The very ordinariness of the quiet line of people waiting
to cast their vote and thereby exercise their choice is a sure indica-
tion of how deep the democratic commitment is in Britain. When
one considers the immense power at the disposal of a government,
the calmness with which the electorate goes to the polls is remarkable. When one further considers that the calmness is genuine
calm, not apathy—else why should they vote at all?—then my respect for our institutions and the steadiness of our inhabitants further increases. Across the nation, from the great metropolitan
centres to rural Wales, the northern factory towns, or the Scottish
Highlands, the Ulster shipyards or the Birmingham automobile
plants, the process is the same: a quiet and considered judging by
the people of the performance and the promises of its leaders.

It is, moreover, a national judgement. Britain is a relatively
homogeneous country politically, and dissatisfaction with one
side or the other usually reflects itself in a uniform swing. It would
be unprecedented to find positive enthusiasm for a party in one
part of the country and distinct unpopularity in another. Of
course, there are some regional differences, but, overall, British
politics are much more national in character than in the United
States. Not only is this due to the difference in size of the two
countries, it is also inevitable, given the differences in their systems
of government.

LIFE IN THE HOUSE OF COMMONS

The government in Britain is formed from the party that wins the largest number of seats in the House of Commons, and the Prime Minister is the leader of that party. He or she is also one of the 635 MPs, as is the Leader of the Opposition (an official title). The process of counting the votes is extremely rapid. The polls close at 10:00 P.M. on election day. By midnight many results will be known. By 3:00 A.M. the result is usually clear. By noon on the Friday it will be obvious which party has won. The Queen then has to perform her constitutional duty of sending for the leader of the party that has won and requesting that person to

form a government. The party leader goes to Buckingham Palace
as leader, accepts her commission, moves straightaway into No.
10 Downing Street, and starts governing as Prime Minister. The
transfer of power, if there is a change of administration, is brutal
and quick. Three times in recent years has the incoming Prime
Minister moved into No. 10 through the front door while the outgoing leader was still upstairs packing. It is crude but effective. By
the Friday evening, power has been transferred and the new Prime
Minister is well on the way to forming a government. It is the
Prime Minister who appoints all the other ministers. By Saturday
the senior ministers will have been decided, and the Cabinet may
even have already met. Junior ministers will be appointed in the
course of the next few days, so that when the new Parliament
meets a week or two later the government is complete. The Prime
Minister then asks the House of Commons for approval of the
government, which, since by definition the Prime Minister's party
has a majority of MPs, is invariably given. The government is
then formed and off and running.

   I well remember the election of June 1970. At the time I was in
the Labour government as Minister for the Army, a post I ceased
to hold when we lost to the Conservatives. On the Friday I rang
my office when it was obvious that we were out and told them I
would come in to clear up on the following Monday. I asked for
the car to arrive at 10:00 A.M., only to be told that as unfortunately I was no longer a minister there was to be no ministerial
car, but that if I cared to drive myself in, they would make sure I
had somewhere to park. On the Monday when I had emptied my
desk and made my farewells, the final shaft which went home was:
"Do you mind leaving your pass, sir. We will give you a tempo-
rary permit to make sure you get out of the building." It was dis-
tinctly painful at the time, but, like having a tooth out, the extrac-
tion was less wearing than a nagging ache. It was, moreover, done
by the bureaucracy with a delicate feeling of regretful continuity—
regret that I was leaving, but a brisk pride in being able to effect
the transfer efficiently and well. A friend of mine who was also a
minister at the time was actually working in his office on the Friday afternoon. His private secretary entered at about four-thirty
and said, "I'm afraid I shall have to take the files away, sir; Mr.

Heath has just been summoned to the Palace." Unnecessarily brutal, perhaps, but therapeutic.

The great practical advantage of a quick transfer of power is, of course, continuity in government. In Britain the duck has hardly time to hobble, let alone get lame. I have never understood why it is that in the United States an election takes place in early November but the new administration does not actually assume office until mid-January. Nor am I impressed when American friends tell me that this is much quicker than it used to be. There is no other major Western country that so encourages governmental paralysis, and apart from the fact that this happens to be the American way, there seems little other justification for the practice.

The speed of transfer in Britain means that a government is installed within hours and therefore the business of the country can be carried on. Parliamentary approval comes a little later. The new House of Commons actually meets within about two weeks of the holding of a general election. By then the government will have crystallized some of its ideas into a programme of legislation and executive action. This programme becomes the "Queen's Speech," read when a new session of Parliament is formally opened by the monarch. The title "Queen's Speech" is, however, a total misnomer. It is in fact the government's speech, read for it by the Queen, in a ceremony of glittering obscurity at the state opening of Parliament. She drives in state to Westminster and sits on the throne in the House of Lords. The members of the House of Commons, meanwhile, sit in their chamber. An official called Black Rod, who is usually a retired admiral or general, is sent to summon the Commons to the chamber of the House of Lords. When he reaches the door of the House of Commons, it is slammed in his face, after which he has to hammer three times to gain admission. The symbolism derives from the time immediately preceding the English Civil War, when Charles I came into the House of Commons to arrest five Puritan Members of Parliament. Since then no reigning monarch has entered the chamber, and the Queen's personal messenger is similarly kept waiting until the House decides to admit him—which, of course, it always does.

Black Rod having been admitted to summon MPs to attend the Queen in the chamber of the Lords, they all then solemnly walk through the corridors and the central lobby, to the Bar of the

House of Lords. There they stand to listen to the Queen reading a speech written for her by the government. The speech over, the file returns to the Commons and the debate on the Queen's speech, or rather the government's programme, starts shortly thereafter.

I walked in this procession on a number of occasions and must admit that I felt it somewhat remote from the task of helping to govern a thriving modern industrial democracy. Once, however, I watched the ceremony from the gallery of the House of Lords. If it seemed strange looked at from the Commons end, it was even more bizarre from the other. Nothing seemed to happen. The Queen arrived and sat on the throne. She then stood up, Black Rod was despatched, and then she and the rest of us waited and waited. Eventually a crowd of MPs arrived at the entrance of the House of Lords, could not all get in, crowded around the Bar, were read to, and then dispersed—and not a word was said by any of them.

Clearly the government's programme for the next session of Parliament has to be promulgated, and one form of promulgation is, I suppose, as good as any other, but the whole procedure for opening Parliament owes more to the British attachment to the ceremonial than it does to the efficacy of government. But perhaps that is no bad thing. Flummery when confined to the inessentials can indeed be helpful. It becomes dangerous only when people start to take it seriously.

At the end of the debate on the Queen's speech, a debate which goes on for four or five days, the government has to face some major votes. If defeated in these votes, a government would have to resign, since it clearly would not have the confidence of the House of Commons. Without an expression of confidence it could not carry on, and if it attempted to, the Queen would be constitutionally justified in dismissing the Prime Minister and calling upon the Leader of the Opposition to form a government. Such a course of action would undoubtedly precipitate a general election. This has not happened in recent years in Britain, but something like it did happen in 1975 in Australia. The then Governor-General, Sir John Kerr, who was the Queen's representative in Australia and surrogate head of state, dismissed the Labour Prime Minister, Gough Whitlam, because he said the business of governing Australia could not be carried on. The last thing I would wish to do is to express an opinion on the accuracy or otherwise of the Governor-General's contention. It is sufficient to note, first, that the government (Labour) had a majority only in the lower house, and that the Liberal majority in the upper house, the Senate, was refusing to pass any major finance bills, with the danger that the country might run out of money; and second, it was remarkable how little challenge there was to the right of the Governor-General to dismiss a prime minister. His judgement was hotly contested, but hardly his right. His action was not challenged in the courts of Australia, though its wisdom was furiously and bitterly debated. The eventual result of Mr. Whitlam's dismissal was that the Leader of the Opposition was asked to form a government, could not, and then called for an election. At the election there was a change of government, the Labour Party going out and the Liberal Party coming in. The episode illustrated also the undeniable fact that the monarch or her constitutional equivalent, a governor-general, possesses, in extremis, constitutional powers of very great importance. This power of dismissal and of dissolution of Parliament is very rarely exercised save on the constitutional advice of a prime minister, but it exists and can, as the Australian precedent shows, be used with devastating political effect.

In more normal times, however, the right of dissolution is exercised on the advice of the Prime Minister of the day, and in asking the Queen for a dissolution of Parliament and therefore a general election, the strength of the government in the House of Commons is of extreme importance. It is on the floor of the House that power in Britain finally resides, and it is to that assembly that governments are directly responsible. They have to account for their stewardship openly and publicly to a body a very considerable part of which is openly and publicly opposed. As an exercise in accountability it can at times be very impressive. Since the executive sits in the legislature, the ministers are all known personally and weighed accordingly. Unlike the situation in the United States, there is only one ladder to political success in Britain, the House of Commons. It is quite impossible for a relatively unknown yet charismatic individual to become Prime Minister. Since the Prime Minister is the leader of the party with the largest number of MPs, any aspirant to the highest office in the land must first get himself elected leader of the party. Members of Parliament play a major role in that election. In the Conservative Party they alone pick the leader. In the Labour Party that power is now shared with the trade unions and local constituency parties. Any such election therefore contains an element of choice by colleagues of another colleague. They will have seen each other for years, have watched and weighed parliamentary and ministerial performance, have assessed them as individuals over a period of time. Whatever else the process is, it is at least revealing. The Commons is somewhat like a goldfish bowl, too small for comfort and not large enough for concealment. It has, moreover, the same slightly magnifying effect, which tends to produce gentle distortion when viewed from outside or above. But despite this political parallax, it does mean that the goldfish tend to know each other well.

On each side, therefore, the leader of the party is the open choice of his (or her) parliamentary colleagues. Having become leader, the person's primary function is to lead the party to an election victory. With success, all else will be forgiven and forgotten in the early heady days of power. With failure, all will be magnified and intensified to the point sometimes of open rebellion. Of course, each party handles its affairs somewhat differently. The Labour Party is often in vocal rebellion against its leaders, but nothing much actually happens. The Conservative Party is much more avowedly loyal until one day one notices the blood trickling gently from under a committee room door. The Conservatives are indeed much better plotters than we Labourites are, having learnt better over the years the virtues of silence and discretion in committing an ignoble political act.

It is again the paramountcy of the House of Commons and of MPs that is underlined by the position of the leaders of the major parties. So long as the parliamentary party backs its leader, he or she can survive. When that support begins to fade, then there will certainly be serious trouble, and what consolidates that support is either electoral success or the hope of future gain.

The House of Commons is, however, primarily a deliberative and legislative assembly. How, then, does it work in practice?

It is perhaps easier at times to define what the House is not, rather than what it is. It is not primarily a check on the power of the executive in the way that Congress is constitutionally ordered. Since the executive sits there, and since the very origin of its power is its parliamentary majority, the situation could hardly be otherwise. We do not have a detailed committee system as does the United States. We do not have the seniority rules that are so important there. Parliament, it is true, is the body to which and in which the government is held accountable, but one reason for this is the existence of a permanent opposition, organized and structured to challenge ministers in a highly sophisticated way. The opposition is indeed a "shadow" government in waiting. Each minister has his opposition shadow whose function it is to harry, probe, question, and if at all possible unhorse his opponent. The system is somewhat gladiatorial, if unevenly so. Behind a minister is the whole power of the civil service. The shadow minister has only the research department of his party machine.

But the contest is fundamental to the working of our parliamentary democracy. The House of Commons is, essentially, the arena in which the confrontation takes place between the "in" party, which has won the election, and the "out" party, which has lost. It is a truism to say that the function of the government is to govern and the function of the opposition is to oppose, but in my experience the British system works best when the government is firm and the opposition is intense. Then the confrontation is sharp and Parliament functions with vigour as a reflection of the broad national division into the great parties of state. That division focuses on the two despatch boxes facing each other across the floor of the House of Commons, from which ministers and their opposition shadows speak.

The House is for a newcomer a desperately difficult place in which to learn to speak. There are no desks to lean on, and the very geography of the chamber is itself confrontational. It is not semicircular but oblong. The government sits on the right of the Speaker and the opposition on the left. The seats themselves are rising rows of green leather benches, so that to speak from one of the back benches is a physical, as well as a psychological, ordeal. You must hold your notes in your hands, there is little leg-room, and because of the rake of the rows of seats there is a distinct feeling that one is about to overbalance. Moreover, the acoustics are odd—perfect, but odd. The speaker's voice is amplified, the others are not, giving a slightly disjointed and unnatural sound.

When you get up to speak, therefore, what you actually see are the faces of your opponents and the backs of the heads of your own side. Nor are the faces particularly friendly. If your party is in power, the opposition believe their party should be on your side of the House, and if your party is in opposition, they believe (with cause) that you are a threat to their remaining where they are. Either way they are not particularly anxious to listen, and the first and major problem is to get a hearing. It is not important that they should like you, indeed it is probably better if they do not, but they do have to respect you at least sufficiently to feel that they have to listen to what you have to say.

The House is, moreover, quite extraordinarily ill mannered. People shout, heckle, roar, interrupt, bay, laugh, mutter, walk in and out, stand talking at the Bar, ignore the speaker, in short do whatever they think proper to put the speaker off. It does, however, happen to everyone. Any MP worth his salt has been through this annealing process and therefore knows its value. The only exception is a maiden speech, which by tradition is heard in silence and always greeted with fulsome congratulations, but this occurs once only, and thereafter the maiden is deemed to have grown up.

To speak as a minister or a "shadow" is in some ways easier. You perform from the front bench, speaking from the despatch box, so there is somewhere to put your notes and even a glass of water. On the other hand, you are actually nearer to the opposition and are deprived of the view of even the backs of your supporters' heads. Support is expressed verbally with a chorus of "hear hear," which en masse sounds very strange but is wonderfully inspiriting. The worst treatment of all is silence. From your own supporters it means disappointment, and from the other side it signifies contempt.

My own maiden speech was quite unforgettable—at least to me—and was made in a debate on the immigration of blacks from the Caribbean and of Asians into the United Kingdom. It proved painful, but mercifully short. There is a convention in the House of Commons that a maiden speech should be non-controversial. The new member is, after all, introducing himself to the

House for the first time. He is supposed to describe his constituency and say something nice about his predecessor, particularly if he has just beaten him. Unfortunately, this was something I forgot, though I thought I was well prepared. By the time I sat down, I felt my parliamentary career was destined to be both brief and inglorious, and was somewhat surprised to discover that the speech had gone reasonably well.

Once I lost my parliamentary virginity, the second speech was easier. Fridays are quiet in the Commons, usually given over to private members' bills, or to debating relatively uncontroversial issues. Since I was a London member, I took to going in regularly on Fridays and speaking quite often. After a while I got the feel of the place, the atmosphere became less strange, and I could relax. But it was a difficult process, and one wearing to the psyche. The result of this process is, however, a debating chamber that genuinely debates and a Parliament in which skill in oral argument is not only prized but essential. I am not claiming for one moment that the House of Commons "gets it right" more often than any other system. I claim merely that the argument is better expressed. The "debates" are more real because speakers are chosen from each side in turn, and because the rules of procedure do not allow speeches to be read. In the words of Erskine May, who wrote the Bible of Parliamentary procedure, however, "copious notes are allowed," and this is particularly true for ministers or opposition spokesmen who are speaking not merely for themselves but also for their party, or indeed for the nation.

One effect of the way in which the House of Commons works has been the development to what some would claim to be an extreme extent of party discipline. Each party now has a number of whips, selected on a regional basis, whose function it is to ensure that their side polls its required strength, and in the case of the government, to guarantee that it is not defeated. The Chief Whip sits in on meetings of the Cabinet, though he is not technically a full member. His function there is to advise the government on the likelihood or otherwise of there being serious trouble in the coming week.

The whipping machinery is simple. Each week on Thursday there arrives by special messenger at each MP's address a document setting out the business of the House for the following week. Each item of business is underscored with one, two, or three black

lines. If the number of lines is one, there is little chance of a vote
on that item, so unless interested, you do not actually need to turn
up. If two, then there will be a vote, but pairing with an opposition MP is allowed. Obviously, if two MPs, one from the governing party and one from the opposition, agree to absent themselves
from a vote, the government's majority will remain unchanged.
Pairing is simply the procedure by which such absences are arranged. If the number of lines is three, then, short of death in the
family, urgent affairs of state, or unavoidable detention elsewhere,
such as by fog at Heathrow Airport, you have to attend and vote.
Excuses are not accepted and an MP can be away only with the
Chief Whip's permission. Although I have never actually seen one,
I imagine the Tory "whip" is much the same as the Labour. The
system can operate only if two essentials are observed: first, that
each side broadly knows the other's intentions; and second, that
one can rely on the other side's pair. In my experience both these
were generally fulfilled. Each week the whips on each side meet
and discuss the business for the following week. These are the
much-referred-to but anonymous "usual channels." The opposition having indicated its strength of feeling on a particular issue,
each side makes its dispositions accordingly. As for pairing, this is
very much a personal matter for the individual member. Like almost all other MPs, I had a regular pair. Each week we would
meet and sort out when we needed to be away the following week.
Never in ten years did either of us have cause to regret the ar-
rangement. Once paired, one remained paired come hell or high
water, and to break a pair was recognized as the ultimate parliamentary sin. The procedure was, I suppose, extraordinarily ad
hoc, but it worked and still does.

The sanctions that a party can use against a rebellious member
are imprecise and on the whole ineffective. In theory, a member
who persistently disregarded the whip and voted against his party
on a regular basis could be deprived of membership in the parliamentary party and expelled. But this sanction is theoretical in the
extreme. I know of no instance where a difficult MP was expelled.
Indeed, in the Labour Party trouble with the whips is frequently a
passport to popularity with the party rank and file in the country,
since Labour rebels inside Parliament and constituency Labour
activists outside all tend to be on the left of the party spectrum,

and therefore at odds with the parliamentary leadership. The sanction was far more the opinion of one's colleagues than anything more formal, and it was quite impossible to ignore that collective opinion unless one's ego was large and massively insensitive or the cause of the revolt was so deeply felt as to be insulating. There was also the feeling that attacking one's own government in the end only comforted the enemy, and we were, after all, there to attack them, not each other. Of course, people had different views, and each party is inevitably a coalition of opinions and interests, sometimes even overlapping each other. But provided the different strands of opinion could make themselves heard, and could feel (as they were entitled to feel) that their views were being considered even if not accepted in high places, then the coalitions survived and the parties remained relatively intact.

The House of Commons in Britain is therefore essentially a confrontation, and its procedures are, if anything, designed to sharpen, not blunt, that. There are some signs that, with the recent live broadcasting of some of the proceedings of Parliament, the electorate may be passing a more critical eye or ear over the party battle. People have been slightly shocked at the vigour of the House. Serious matters perhaps demand a more serious approach, but parliamentary time is the main weapon at the disposal of an opposition and to hold up government business is generally regarded as a victory. Decorum is always much more in the interests of a government than of an opposition. A prime minister can always attempt to play the "Father of the Nation" role, aloof from the party dogfights, his mind concentrated on higher matters of state, while he leaves the hatchet-work to his minions. For some reason in Britain the elder statesman has always seemed more acceptable than the younger statesman, which may account for the air of quite insupportable gravitas that some younger politicians adopt. For a prime minister to attempt this role is understandable. For a leader of the opposition to allow him to get away with it would be unforgivable. He has to be brought down to political earth, if necessary by being roughed up a little in the House.

The one thing a minister cannot do in Britain is avoid the House of Commons. He has to appear, answer the questions asked, parry the supplementary questions that may then arise, and explain his policies in public. For a prime minister this means that twice a week, on Tuesday and Thursday afternoons, he or she has to stand at the despatch box and expose himself to opposition probing. The kind of constitutional isolation possible in the United States, as when President Nixon avoided publicity in 1973 and 1974, is just not possible in our system of government. A prime minister may try and avoid answering, but appear in the House he must, and nowadays appear on national radio too.

The advantages of a parliamentary system of government may be in its qualities of public accountability, or at least visibility. The disadvantages may be in the importance that we attach to parliamentary performance. It certainly does not follow that the best speechmakers make the best administrators, but the House of Commons is a good testing ground in the main political art—that of verbal communication and rapid thought. It also produces wit, sometimes of a very high order, but one should be careful in judging Britain not to confuse verbal felicity with a lack of seriousness. The British are good at concealing earnestness under a façade of facile indifference. Why this should be so, I really do not know. I do not justify the trait—I merely report.

The instances of quick parliamentary wit in Britain are legion. One can only pick one's own favourites, conscious that the choice will undoubtedly seem restrictive and unfair to everyone else.

There is the famous exchange between Wilkes and the Earl of Sandwich, who during a heated debate once remarked that Wilkes would die either upon the gallows or of the pox.

"That depends, my Lord, on whether I embrace Your Lordship's principles or Your Lordship's mistress," came the retort.

On another occasion, while Wilkes was campaigning, a heckler shouted, "I would rather vote for the devil than John Wilkes."

"Ah, and if your friend is not standing?" Wilkes replied.

Then there was the incomparable David Lloyd George, whose gift for invective was only equalled by his readiness of wit. A colleague once said to him when he was Prime Minister that "if you treated me half as badly as you treat Curzon [the Foreign Secretary] I'd resign tomorrow morning." Back came Lloyd George's reply: "Oh, but he does resign, but there are two messengers at the Foreign Office. One has a limp; he comes with the resignation. The other was a champion runner; he always catches him up."

During the Irish negotiations he once described their progress as: "Negotiating with De Valera is like trying to pick up mercury with a fork."

His great friend Winston Churchill was one of the most gifted practitioners of the English language that the House of Commons has known.

In 1948 he said: "Trying to maintain good relations with the Communists is like wooing a crocodile. You do not know whether to tickle it under the chin, or beat it over the head. When it opens its mouth you cannot tell whether it is trying to smile or preparing to eat you up."

In 1947 the following exchange took place with the then Labour Leader of the House of Commons, Herbert Morrison, known in British parliamentary terminology as Lord President of the Council.

Churchill: Here I see the hand of the master craftsman the Lord President.
Morrison: The Right Honourable Gentleman has promoted me.
Churchill: Craft is common both to skill and deceit.

The two Harolds—Wilson and Macmillan, both Prime Ministers —had their sparkle. In 1958, in the course of a debate, the former said of the latter: "Words for the Right Honourable Gentleman are like the false trail laid in a paper chase to cover up the way he is really going. It is when he has just been attacking the social services that he most likes to quote Disraeli. I always thought Disraeli was one of his heroes until he went to Hawarden this year and made a speech about Gladstone. The Right Honourable Gentleman is the only statesman of this century to claim with characteristic modesty to embody all that is best in both Disraeli and Gladstone. In fact, of course, he is wrong. He has inherited the streak of charlatanry in Disraeli without his vision, and the self-righteousness of Gladstone without his dedication to principle."

Macmillan once replied to an alleged claim by Wilson that when at school his family had not been able to afford to buy him any boots. "If Harold Wilson ever went to school without any boots it was merely because he was too big for them."

Another Wilson gem was a comment he made when Macmillan

had returned from a visit abroad and been greeted by his Deputy Prime Minister, R. A. Butler. "Talk about splits in the Labour Party! Every time Mr. Macmillan comes back from abroad, Mr. Butler goes to the airport and grips him warmly by the throat."

One of the finest debaters I heard in the House of Commons was the late Iain Macleod. Once when replying to Harold Wilson he said: "The speech which the Right Honourable Gentleman the member for Huyton has just delivered was, as always, witty, cogent and polished [pause] and polished [pause] and polished [laughter]. He paid me the great compliment of saying that to this situation and to this debate I had brought a fresh mind. I wish that he would bring a fresh speech."

This remark caught an echo of the comment on a ministerial speech made by Richard Brinsley Sheridan in the early nineteenth century. "It contained a great deal both of what was new and what was true, but unfortunately what was new was not true, and what was true was not new."

Aneurin Bevan was one of the great natural orators of this century. His gift for impromptu phrase-making was prodigious. "Righteous people terrify me. Virtue is its own punishment." "Stand not too near the rich man lest he destroy thee—and not too far away lest he forget thee." On the Allied invasion of Italy in 1943: "Indeed, I am bound to say, if the House will forgive the metaphor, that the Allied High Command have approached the Italian mainland like an old man approaching a young bride, fascinated, sluggish, and apprehensive."

Of Churchill he once said: "He refers to a defeat as a disaster as though it came from God, but to a victory as though it came from himself."

Finally, as a piece of controlled invective, it is hard to better his comments on the abdication of King Edward VIII.

The gladiators of the parliamentary arena faced each other across the table adorned by the mace, symbol of the authority which was supposed to be in issue. The trembling accents of the Speaker fell into a well-awed silence as he read the Royal message. Surely never have sentiments so meagre been arrayed in language so ennobled by great usage and cautioned by awful deeds. A mean wine in a goblet of old gold. Here indeed was the past mimed by the ignoble present. "History repeats itself," said Marx, "first as a tragedy, second as farce." And here was farce. The pathetic can never be epic, and there was bathos affecting to speak in accents of the heroic. The Prime Minister [Stanley Baldwin], who has a natural gift for the counterfeit, surpassed himself. He spoke of a pilot who had guided the ship of State safely to harbour through stormy seas, past jagged rocks, and in the teeth of buffeting winds. The winds, indeed, were boudoir hysteria, the rocks threatened to wreck only his own career, and the official Opposition had not blown even a zephyr across his path. But what of that? He was fighting one of the great tourneys of history and he laid about him dauntlessly with his wooden sword. . . . The Labour Party missed a great opportunity. . . . Against the cant and hypocrisy of the Court scandals, the Parliamentary Labour Party should have limned its own message. . . . But from beginning to end of the monarchical crisis it revealed one grave defect. The Labour Party has too much reverence.

The tradition of hard-hitting verbal debate in Parliament is long and honourable, and if it seems today that there are few forensic giants left, I am by no means sure that this impression is any more than the reverence one age feels for its predecessors. Buried in Hansard are many examples, and while few could compete with Churchill, Lloyd George, Bevan, Wilson, or Macmillan, it is still true that a good performance in the House can have an effect on policy, not in terms of votes cast there and then either for or against a measure, but in disclosing the vulnerability or otherwise of an individual or his party.

GOVERNMENT
AND THE CIVIL SERVICE

In eighteenth-century Britain, it was said that, whatever party was in office, the Whigs were in power. In the nineteenth and early twentieth centuries, people spoke, particularly in the Labour movement, about the Tories' stranglehold on power. But in the latter part of the twentieth century, the civil service has replaced the landed gentry as the favourite *bête noire* of those who believe that the will of governments is thwarted by the permanent establishment. Indeed, in some quarters the civil service has become the politicians' scapegoat, a ready explanation for all of the catalogue of failures that have seemed to dog the country in the years since World War II.

Civil service bashing is now the favourite sport of politicians out of office. The memoirs of Richard Crossman, a Cabinet minister in the 1966–70 Labour government of Harold Wilson, caused a sensation: after his death in 1972, three volumes of diaries, detailing his life as a senior minister, took the lid off a world which, until then, had been totally unknown to the general public. Crossman said that on his first day in ministerial office he felt himself to be "a person who is suddenly certified a lunatic and put safely into this great vast room, cut off from real life and surrounded by male and female trained nurses and attendants." Another former minister in the same government, Barbara Castle, described how the departmental machine took over her life and dominated her engagement diary: she wrote that, simply to have some private conversation with political supporters, she had to "lie like a trooper" to the department about her private engagements. Tony Benn, the leading left-winger in the Labour Party, believes that the civil service has been responsible for getting ministers to water down their policies and forget their commitments to their supporters; "there has been a massive shift," Benn has written, "of power to ministers and officials and away from Parliament." The journal *The Economist* went so far in May 1980 as to write: "The constitutional model has collapsed. The minister no longer proposes, while the official disposes; the official more often opposes, and the minister then runs away."

There is no "spoils system" in British Government, and apart from ministers, very few civil service posts are filled by political nominees. This is a major difference between the two countries: in the United States, after he had been elected President but before taking office, Ronald Reagan set up a special unit to screen and sort out applications and nominations for the thousands of government posts which, in the American system, change with the government. In the United States the theory is that all posts with a policy-making content need to be filled by political appointees, while those posts which are essentially administrative can be filled under a merit system. Presidents' cronies get ambassadorships; generous contributors to party funds are generously rewarded. All the major policy posts in the State Department come up for review by an incoming president. In Britain things could hardly be more different. I was one of only two politically appointed ambassadors in the last Labour government (the other being Peter Jay in Washington). If you exclude Jay's successor Sir Nicholas Henderson (who is a career diplomat appointed politically because he is past the standard civil service retiring age of sixty) the Thatcher government has made no political appointments to ambassadorships at all. Political appointments in a department include a Cabinet minister (usually a "Secretary of State") and two or three ministers of state, plus a couple of "parliamentary under-secretaries." These are almost invariably Members of Parliament or members of the House of Lords and therefore are democratically accountable. So-called administrative heads of departments—called permanent secretaries or, in the Home Office and Foreign and Commonwealth Office, permanent under-secretaries—are all career officials. There are about twenty Cabinet ministers, and they work with about 500,000 civil servants, including about 40 of permanent under-secretary rank, about 150 deputy secretaries, and about 560 under-secretaries.

It is these senior officials who are said by their detractors to wield so much power. They are the top grade of civil servant—the administrative class—which recruits a handful of graduates a year straight from university and has the occasional recruit promoted from the other civil service classes, the clerical class and the executive class. The clerical class are people who have left school at sixteen; the executives (who include many of the people the public look on as civil servants, such as immigration officers at the ports and airports) are normally holders of the General Certificate of Education at the Advanced Level, the exam taken by school-leavers at about age eighteen; while the administrative class is formed of graduates with good degrees. For years, criticism has centred on the alleged "Oxbridge" and generalist bias of the civil service at administrative level, and it is true that a large proportion of administrative-class civil servants are graduates of the universities of Oxford or Cambridge, and many of them have graduated in English literature, Latin and Greek, or history. The same goes for the Foreign Office—though efforts have been made in recent years to promote more diplomats recruited into the executive class to higher positions. But most senior British civil servants are graduates of Oxford or Cambridge, and most senior career diplomats went to public schools, too.

The advantages of a strong permanent civil service are clear to Americans, who tend to see the disadvantages of a system with more patronage and political cronyism built into it: the administration is consistent and well co-ordinated. The Foreign Office, in particular, is greatly admired, not only for the quality of its officials, but also because of the flow of information and the co-ordination of ambassadors' diplomatic activities throughout the world. It is not unknown, when a head of state or foreign minister is received in London, for the British ambassador to get a full report in the country concerned while the foreign ministry of the visitor is ignorant of what has transpired in London.

The Wilson government in the 1960s set up a major commission of enquiry under Lord Fulton to look at the civil service. Its recommendations included the recruitment of non-civil servants into ministers' offices (which was implemented by the recruitment of one or two political advisers by senior ministers in the 1970s); the use of more expertise in the civil service (instead of, as at present, having a scientific civil service whose members are kept out of policy questions and simply considered as technical experts); and the merging of the administrative and executive classes into one class called the "administration group." This last proposal is being implemented gradually.

Criticism of the civil service has tended to come from the Labour Party, both on grounds of class and because it is alleged that senior officials have too much power, but the Conservative government of Mrs. Thatcher has been known to have criticisms of the civil service, though of a rather different nature. Mrs. Thatcher's government clearly believes the civil service to be over-paid, too secure in its job tenure, and overprivileged in such matters as the index-linked inflation-proof pension. She has successfully fought strikes of various groups of officials seeking to—as she would say—obtain excessive salary increases. But above all the Thatcher team believes the Treasury to be profoundly sceptical about government economic and monetary policy, seeing it as made up of Keynesians opposed to monetarism.

As with the trade unions, the debate about the civil service in Britain is like the question of the chicken and the egg. Which came first, trade union militancy or wage inflation? Did civil service power increase because ministers' policies were not to the liking of officials, or because ministers themselves did not know what they wanted? Who really holds power in government is a common subject of discussion between ministers and officials. Ministers are transitory, lack detailed knowledge of the subjects with which they deal, and deal with so many subjects that it is simply not possible for them to control every detail of a department's work. Civil servants are permanent, know the details of policies, and have a time-scale which may go beyond that of the government in power, but they never appear in public and always give the impression that they are serving the minister loyally. Sometimes it seems that the politicians and the officials have made a deal: the ministers, though transitory, will get the glory if things go well, but may have to carry the can if things go badly; the officials will do their best, producing good ideas as well as making the occasional disastrous mistake, provided they maintain their anonymity and security of tenure. But many ministers and many officials agree that civil servants like nothing so much as a strong minister who knows what he wants to do; trouble arises when a weak minister does not give clear instructions to the department and the politics of bureaucratic caution fill the vacuum.

Mrs. Thatcher has tried to reduce the number of civil servants, though her measures are often criticized as bookkeeping (such as sacking office cleaners and replacing them by outside contractors) or as "hiving off" by transferring functions from government departments to semi-independent commissions or boards. But the Conservative government claims to have reduced the civil service to its lowest numbers since the war. Jokes about the tea-drinking civil service are common, and statistics are quoted showing that 30,000 civilians now work for the Navy, for example, compared with 4,300 in 1914 when it ruled the waves. A highly successful television series called "Yes, Minister" satirized the whole question of minister–civil servant relations. A typical exchange ran like this:

Minister, reviewing policy after his first few months: Well, Humphry, how are our plans going for keeping down the number of civil servants?

Sir Humphry, Permanent Secretary of the Ministry of Admin-

istrative Co-ordination: Well, Minister, we have 400 more staff
than when you came in.

Minister: But that's ridiculous. You know the Cabinet agreed
to look at every single civil service job to see if it was necessary.

Sir Humphry: Of course, Minister. But, you see, we had to set
up a special unit to look carefully at jobs and check up on
waste—

Minister: . . . Yes, I know, the bureaucratic Watch Dog.

Sir Humphry: Quite, Minister, but in order to do that job we
had to take on 400 extra staff. It will, of course, be some time before their work begins to take effect.

Perhaps this is an example of the British sense of humour, the
ability to laugh at ourselves, but, as is often the case with the British sense of humour, it is disguising a highly serious and rather
sensitive topic. There has been an increasing feeling in recent
years that the civil service, being permanent, has its own policies,
and that ministers, being transitory, get converted to the civil service view of things: the theory, of course, holding that civil servants will serve any government to the best of their ability,
both—as has happened in the recent past—conscientiously nation-
alizing the steel industry for the Labour government one year and
cheerfully denationalizing it five years later. Politicians on both
sides have tended, therefore, to think that the civil service, far
from being non-political, in fact espouses a centrist viewpoint,
pulling left- and right-wing ministers alike back into the centre
ground.

If this is the case, it is easy to see how it came about. Each of
the two major political parties in Britain, the Labour and the Conservative, has a fairly broad spectrum of views in its ranks. Labour covers the ground from hard-line to pragmatic socialism,
with a few old-fashioned liberals on its right wing. The Conservatives have their "liberal" wing (which means liberal on issues
like race relations and capital punishment, and Keynesian rather
than doctrinaire free-market in economics), its monetarists and
free-market wing (which includes Mrs. Thatcher and her supporters), and, on the far right, a motley band of traditionalists,
male chauvinists, and racists. There are people in the Labour
Party whose views are not far from those of the Communist Party,
and, on the extreme right of the Tory Party there is a sprinkling of

racists and near-fascists. But both parties tend, in government, to be led from the centre; Mrs. Thatcher, who leads from the right of her party, is rather an exception. Ministers tend to come from the centre of both parties, and in sensitive areas such as defence and Northern Ireland policy, particularly where the armed forces and the lives of British soldiers are at stake, an effort is made—by the *politicians*—to maintain as far as possible a bipartisan policy.

The idea that there is a "permanent centre" may have some basis in fact, but this permanent centre is definitely not the creation of the civil service. The politicians in successive governments have looked for areas of consensus and have even, in some cases, taken account of the attitude of the opposition when framing policy. Continuity of government is only possible when what one government does is not immediately demolished by its successor: governments need to accept what has been done and build on it. A supreme example is the National Health Service, as we have seen. When it was set up by the post-war Labour government it was almost revolutionary, a major change in British society. But the Conservatives, when they returned to power under the leadership of Sir Winston Churchill in 1951, did not dispute what was already on the statute book and functioning.

In recent years this convention has been breaking down. Both the Conservatives, in embracing "Thatcherism" or monetarism, and a section of the Labour Party, in pursuing changes in party procedure designed to make elected politicians accountable to party activists, have apparently come to the conclusion that radical changes of direction are needed. The parties seem to have concluded that traditional ways of governing the country have not worked because the policies the parties have put forward have been watered down or destroyed by the machine. The policies themselves are very simple, often slogans rather than clear prescriptions for policy, but they are what the party activists believe: more socialism or more private enterprise. But political leaders have tended, not to question the validity of what the activists want, but to claim that past attempts to put the activists' policies into practice were unsuccessful because they were not properly applied. Mrs. Thatcher's hard-line economics are almost identical to those of the previous Tory government of Edward Heath, which collapsed in 1974. Mr. Heath has now virtually disavowed those

policies, but Mrs. Thatcher has convinced Tories that the problem
is that *real* Tory policies were never applied. On the Labour side,
Tony Benn does the same: he is extremely vague about how he
would do the things he promises, but instead promises the party
activists that the procedural changes he is proposing will, if implemented in full, ensure that never again will Labour ministers
sell out to the establishment and the vested interests.

While debates go on in the political parties about abstruse and
esoteric subjects—the Conservatives getting very excited about
monetarism and M3 (an indicator of the money supply that no
one has ever been able to explain) while Labour activists are consumed in arguments about methods of election of the party leader
—someone has to run the country. Vast areas of policy and day-
to-day government hardly seem to interest the party activists, or,
indeed, some of the politicians who make it to the top of the ladder and a minister's office. Tories want to reintroduce a spirit of
genuine free enterprise, Socialists to end privilege; but as far as re-
forming the prison system or improving the service nationalized
industries give their consumers are concerned, few political pas-
sions are aroused. The civil service, cautiously and taking care to
avoid identification with either major party, therefore gets quietly
on with its job—administration. Rethinking hardly ever occurs, because the politicians are distracted by the concerns of the activists,
and the officials are careful not to exceed their limited mandate.

The fact is that, with very few political appointments in the civil
service, and only councillors elected locally, civil servants and
local government officers in Britain have much more influence
than in the United States. Mayors are not even full-time, but
merely one of the council members elected to serve as mayor, normally for a year. At the local level, the size of administrations has
greatly increased since the 1970s, both in terms of the areas they
serve and in terms of the numbers of officials they employ, but
there are very few members of the public who would claim that
they have had a noticeably better service from their local authority
as a result. The tendency has been for government to set up a unit,
or appoint an official, when a problem occurs, so that units, direc-
torates, and co-ordinating bodies have proliferated in British local
government. It was the Conservatives in the early seventies who
established the larger local authorities, and Labour in the second

half of the seventies who agreed to the explosion of local bureaucracy. Today many would argue that local government has grown remote and ineffective.

The result is that Britain, in some eyes, is administered rather than governed. Vast areas of government, local and national, go on virtually unaffected—except in broad general ways such as the allocation of overall resources—by any change in politicians. There are those (as we shall see in the next section) who blame the electoral system, claiming that it produces polarized government by parties dominated by narrow dogmatists; and there are those who see the bureaucrats, not as "Your Obedient Servant," but as Public Enemy No. 1. Basically, a nineteenth-century political system, with ministers still recruited to run departments which are enormously more complicated than they were then, is maintained. Ministers work extremely hard and do what they can to run the country, but inevitably the permanent administration has spread into many areas which it is physically impossible for the politicians to supervise properly. And the politicians, don't forget, are MPs appointed as ministers, not necessarily experts in the field covered by the ministry. Indeed, prime ministers have a knack of appointing ministers expert in one field, say social security, to another ministry, perhaps agriculture, because the conventional wisdom is that the politician brings judgement, the civil service the expertise.

If the "executive" in Britain consists of this uneasy alliance of elected ministers and unelected civil service officials, does the legislature provide a check? Ministers are accountable to Parliament, both in debates and at Question Time, when they can be probed by MPs personally on the working of their departments. But whereas in the United States a senior official in an incoming administration—for example, Assistant Secretary Chester Crocker at the State Department—may have to wait weeks for Senate confirmation of his appointment, his equivalent at the British Foreign Office will be a career officer, appointed by the permanent under-secretary, and unchanged when a new government comes in. He will not receive any attention from Parliament or the mass media—indeed, most people, including Members of Parliament, would not know him.

Major international negotiations over the future of Britain's nuclear deterrent, which culminated in July 1980 with the news that Mrs. Thatcher's government had entered into an agreement with President Carter's administration to buy 100 Trident missiles from the United States at a cost of £1 billion, were mainly conducted, not by ministers, but by an official, Mr. Quinlan, working, of course, to a Cabinet brief. For the first time, however, a major decision in defence matters was well explained to the public in a detailed information document. The House of Commons Defence Committee held its own hearings on the whole subject and produced a report entitled *Strategic Nuclear Weapons Policy,* which analyzed the government's position. Some observers contrasted this situation with the fact that the post-war Labour government had developed the atomic bomb without informing the House of Commons, tucking the estimates away in hidden corners of the defence budget.

There is, as yet, nothing in the British system to match the powerful Senate committees in the United States, but since 1979 there have been select committees "shadowing" all the major departments of state, with the power to examine ministers and officials if the minister agrees. These committees have already begun looking at detailed areas of government working. Norman St. John-Stevas, MP, who was Leader of the House (i.e., majority leader) when the reforms were introduced, said that they had "altered the whole balance of power between Westminster and Whitehall." But some observers still feel that the executive is too powerful in the British system, and that the presence of Cabinet ministers in the House, supported as they are by members of their own party who, in many cases, are hoping to obtain office themselves, means that, although the government is elected, once it is, it has an immense amount of power provided it can maintain a Commons majority. The Conservative Lord Chancellor Lord Hailsham even went so far as to refer to the system as "elective dictatorship." He said that, however, when he was in opposition. One has to admit that, as a senior minister in Mrs. Thatcher's government, he has shown little sign of wanting to change things.

CRACKS IN THE TWO-PARTY SYSTEM?

One reason why the Conservative and Labour parties contain such a broad coalition of viewpoints, embracing near-communist to near-fascist, is that people wanting political power have realized that, without the support of one of the two major parties, they stand little chance of getting elected. Much of the blame lies with the electoral system, which is by single-member constituencies on a first-past-the-post basis. The government is then formed by the party that has the majority of individuals in the House elected. This means that in working-class areas Labour MPs tend to be elected; in the suburbs and in prosperous rural areas, Tories. But a party that has medium support across the country, but is not concentrated in any particular type of constituency, such as the Liberal Party, is likely to get far fewer seats than its share of the votes would indicate. The Liberals' hopes of changing the electoral system to one of proportional representation to benefit themselves have foundered in the past because both the large parties, for obvious reasons, are content with the first-past-the-post system.

Yet there have been distinct signs that the two-party hold on Britain is breaking up. Until recently as much as 85 per cent of the British electorate remained faithful to its party political allegiance, and the Gilbert and Sullivan refrain was basically correct. Very small shifts of opinion won and lost elections; there was an uncommitted centre that swung either way, and whose votes the party machines fought for, and there were those who would support only one party but might not vote at all if they were not happy with their traditional party. Actual political "shopping around"—studying party programmes and leaders and deciding who would get the voter's support—was rare; in fact, party programmes, or manifestos, were hardly read by anybody.

This system had certain advantages. Although the parties were generally considered to be left (Labour) and right (Conservative), the basic support was class-based rather than doctrinaire or ideological. There were many Labour working-class supporters whose attitudes on social and racial matters were illiberal, and many supporters of the so-called right-wing Conservative Party who wanted a strong welfare state and a good state-supported school system. The Conservatives, though in image the party of the upper classes, had to appeal to many of the working class simply in order to get a majority of the votes. Parties were broad coalitions: Labour sometimes did "right-wing" things, such as acting against non-white immigration in the 1960s, while the Conservatives on occasion emerged as strong supporters of the state sector.

For a variety of reasons, this picture now seems to be changing. In the 1979 general election, the Labour Party's vote was down to the level of the 1931 election. Candidates representing minor parties had begun to be successful in by-elections in the 1970s, and in particular many voters in Scotland and Wales had appeared to turn their backs on the traditional parties to give their support to Scottish and Welsh Nationalists. The number of "floating voters" is now far more than the traditional 15 per cent and may even be as high as 30 per cent of the electorate. Part of the reason lies in the breakdown of traditional class patterns of living, changes (as we have seen) out of manufacturing jobs into the service sector, and the increasing tendency of the British to live in suburbs, away from the tightly knit working-class communities of the past. In the 1974 elections neither party had a clear majority, and the Wilson/Callaghan governments were kept in power by Liberal, Nationalist, and Ulster votes. The Callaghan government only fell in March 1979 after the minority parties had withdrawn their support by failing to oppose a censure motion on the government's economic policy.

Mrs. Thatcher's government was, however, returned to power in May 1979 with a healthy overall majority of over forty seats. It may have seemed that this marked a return to the old set-up, but in fact a close look at Mrs. Thatcher's support in the 1979 election only confirms that things are not what they used to be. The Conservatives *appeared* to do well, partly because of the electoral system and partly because Labour did so badly. But in reality the Conservatives managed to obtain only 44 per cent of the votes (33 per cent of the electorate), while Labour took 37 per cent of the votes, or 28 per cent of the electorate. Much of the Thatcher election campaign was aimed at skilled workers, and above all at the prosperous communities in newish suburbs in southern England. Many new and expanding towns around London have wavered in their political allegiance, former Labour voters from the inner-London areas being perhaps one of the most typical examples of the "floating voter" in British politics. Mrs. Thatcher's strategists knew that, if they were to take power in 1979, they had to win over precisely such voters. In fact these voters were extremely unhappy with the Callaghan government because of wage restraint and found Mrs. Thatcher's emphasis on the free market much to their taste. The Thatcher appeal was carefully couched to win over such people, arguing against wage restraints and portraying trade unions as creators of inflation and stiflers of initiative. Those who were skilled and worked hard should be given a free rein— "the sky's the limit." The strategy was spectacularly successful, and Tory candidates swept to power in constituencies all round

London, especially in the new towns and on the sides of the Thames estuary, where huge and unexpected pro-Conservative swings occurred. At least in the South of England, an important segment of past Labour voters had switched its allegiance.

But that was not the end of the story. Another crucial part of the Thatcher government's economic policy involved getting the money supply under control, which in turn involved cutting government expenditure. All sorts of government spending programmes, from subsidies to commuter railway services to road repairs, were slashed. Yet the Conservatives' new clientele was quintessentially the section of the population that had benefited most from post-war prosperity and the setting up of the welfare state. They were people who were ambitious for their children and therefore wanted higher, not lower, standards in state education. They were not habitually supporters of private medicine (though that situation may be changing), and they used many of the services, such as the commuter railways, that were having their government support removed. There are now clear signs that many traditional Labour voters who switched allegiance in the 1979 election and dislike left-wing policies are now disenchanted with the Conservatives too. There may, however, be some regional variations. It appears that in the North of England and especially in Wales and Scotland Labour support is holding up, but in most of England—where most of the British electors live—there seems to be a distinct disenchantment with both of the two traditional parties. Elections, especially by-elections, are much less predictable than they used to be.

This change in the support of the voters for the major British political parties has been accompanied by important changes in the parties themselves. The seemingly intractable nature of Britain's economic difficulties, and the failure (as some have seen it) of traditional pragmatic policies based on an alliance between civil servants and ministers, have led individuals in both parties to put forward the view that what is needed is more politics and more, rather than less, ideology. Mrs. Thatcher is an atypical Tory leader: she is the daughter of a grocer, for a start, as well as being a woman, but she is also much more ideological than any of her predecessors, and has, ever since she became Prime Minister, shown an unshakeable faith in monetarist economics. Her statements of faith in her particular band of politics and economics have led some of her colleagues to nickname her TINA—after one of her commonest expressions, "There Is No Alternative" (to her own policies).

Exactly parallel processes had occurred in the Labour Party. After the 1979 defeat, many party activists felt that the Callaghan government, which had of course been dependent in the House of Commons on minority party support, had been insufficiently socialist in its approach. No one suggested in detail what being more socialist meant: for the party faithful "socialism" came to be more and more associated with nuclear disarmament, import controls, and leaving the European Common Market. But Tony Benn (the son of Lord Stansgate, a minister in the "National" government of Prime Minister Ramsay MacDonald in the 1930s), who had served in all the Wilson and Callaghan governments, worked hard on the activist base. What was at fault, he declared, was the way the party allowed its ministers, once in office, to forget the party's commitments to socialism. A radical change in the Labour Party's constitutional arrangements in order to strengthen activist control over Labour governments was, he believed, immediately necessary. This campaign had the effect of galvanizing a certain type of Labour Party activist into action, and the "Campaign for Labour Party Democracy" was formed to push for reforms in the way the party leader was elected, the way future Members of Parliament were chosen as candidates by the constituency parties, and so on. Policy was hardly discussed; the Benn bandwagon swept along on the belief that the promised land could be reached by the manipulation of procedure.

This "Bennite" campaign had the effect of enraging most of Benn's former colleagues in government, who felt that his whole approach was based on a questioning of their good faith as ministers and party supporters. In the House of Commons, fewer than 20 of the 270-odd Labour MPs were close associates and supporters of Benn, and many Labour MPs regarded Benn's campaign as an attempt to use the extra-parliamentary Labour Party as a spring-board to take power and impose control over elected Members of Parliament. James Callaghan and party leaders were unable to agree on the proposed reforms, and a special weekend conference was held to discuss them. This ended in agreement to establish an "electoral college" system for electing the leader and deputy leader of the Labour Party—a major change from past practice. Instead of the leader's being chosen by Labour Members of Parliament, the new arrangements were to allow a proportion of votes to come from other component parts of the Labour Party, meaning, basically, the trade unions and the constituency Labour parties. At a special party conference held in January 1981 all the new arrangements were approved, and an allocation of votes in the electoral college was made: the trade unions would have 40 per cent of the electoral college, and Labour MPs and constituency Labour parties 30 per cent each. This was a blow not only to the "moderates" or right wing of the Labour Party, but also to the moderate-left leadership, which had favoured a formula giving MPs the preponderant voice.

Ever since the 1980 party conference, which had passed resolutions favouring nuclear disarmament and withdrawal from the European Common Market, some leading members, such as Shirley Williams, a member of the party's National Executive Committee, had become increasingly unhappy at the way the party seemed to be heading. David Owen and William Rodgers, who, with Mrs. Williams, had also been senior members of the Callaghan administration, held talks with her and with Roy Jenkins, another former Labour Cabinet minister who had left the Wilson administration in 1976 to take up the post of President of the Commission of the European Communities. Soon after the special conference, they set up a "Council for Social Democracy" to push for their type of policies within the Labour Party. These were, basically, one member, one vote rather than delegate democracy, and what they considered to be a more realistic line on foreign policy. The success of the "council" was phenomenal: by the end of March its members were out of the Labour Party, and the council had been transformed into the Social Democratic Party. Thirteen Labour MPs and one Tory MP joined up, along with thousands of individuals throughout the country. Roy Jenkins contested a by-election in a traditionally working-class Labour area in the North of England in July, and very nearly won it; both he and Mrs. Williams succeeded in re-entering Parliament in 1981; and Roy Jenkins has since been elected leader of the Social Democratic Party. Additionally, many local council by-elections

—including some in rock-solid Labour areas—fell to the Social Democrats. Meanwhile Benn decided to put the Labour Party's new electoral machinery to the test by challenging Denis Healey for the post of deputy leader, so that, during the summer of 1981, as the Social Democrats built up their strength in the constituencies, the Labour Party seemed locked in a devisive and debilitating contest over the deputy leadership.

There seemed little doubt that, on their own, even despite the all-time low in the popularity of the Labour and Tory parties, the Social Democrats would stand little chance of taking power. But an alliance with the Liberal Party was an alluring prospect: it would provide an opportunity for voters who had given up hope on the old parties to vote against them, not in a futile protest vote, but with a very real prospect of power. By the autumn of 1981 the Social Democrats and Liberals had agreed to set up just such an alliance, but obvious problems lay ahead. In particular, hard bargaining would be necessary over which party contested which parliamentary constituency; and the Social Democrats had agreed on principles but had still to elect a leader and agree on more detailed policies. The Liberal leader, David Steel, was able to end the 1981 Liberal Party conference, for the first time in fifty years, by credibly exhorting his followers to return to their constituencies and "prepare for government!"

There is not total agreement between Social Democrats and Liberals on everything, but on one point the alliance seems clear: it will demand, as the price of its support for any other group in the House of Commons, immediate legislation to change the electoral system to one of proportional representation. This means that if, as seems likely, no party has an overall majority in the next House of Commons, the price for either the Labour or the Conservative Party to enjoy support in the House is likely to be a commitment to proportional representation. If Liberals and Social Democrats together form a government, they are committed to giving priority to a change in the electoral system. If they do not form a government but manage to get the electoral system changed as the price of their support for a minority administration, they would stand a better chance of coming to power in a future administration formed from MPs elected under the proportional representation system.

The prospects for the alliance seem unclear at present. Their initial success was blunted somewhat by what became known in Britain as "the Falklands factor," the popularity that accrued to Mrs. Thatcher and her government because of the war with Argentina. As the memories of the war fade and as 3 million unemployed again become a major factor of political consciousness, the prospects for the alliance will probably improve. Whether they have "broken the mould" of British politics remains to be seen. They certainly seem to have cracked it a bit, though the permanence of their breakthrough remains to be established. Much may indeed depend on the extent to which the Labour Party can pull itself together and regain some credibility as a possible alternative government. At the time of writing the only possible verdict on the Social Democratic/Liberal alliance is not proven. The test will, of course, come at the next election.

A change to proportional representation would have a dramatic effect. Governments would tend to be coalitions, as in the Netherlands or Italy, and the hold of the two large parties would be broken. There might be more regional or ethnic-based members—so far no black MP has appeared in the House of Commons. It would upset a balance of power which is reflected in public and semi-public bodies throughout the system. Above all, it would make the "socialism" of Labour Party activists or the doctrinaire free-market policies of the right wing of the Conservative Party much more difficult to implement. Whether or not the Social Democrats take off, a period of instability in British politics seems certain, if only because traditional party allegiances are fading and, as the old parties become seemingly more ideological, the process seems likely to continue.

Law, Order, and the Defence of the Realm

THE LAW, LAWYERS, AND THE COURTS

The Law is the true embodiment
Of everything that's excellent.
It has no kind of fault or flaw,
And I, my Lords, embody the Law.

These sentiments are those of the Lord Chancellor in Gilbert and
Sullivan's light opera *Iolanthe,* but they remain, roughly speaking,
a fair summary of the attitude of most British lawyers towards the
profession they practise. Like so much in Britain, the law has simply "grown." Besides legislation, there is the ancient common law,

and now, with Britain a member of the European Community, Community law has been grafted onto that. Yet everything keeps functioning, even though the legal systems and the terminology and the courts are still different in England and Wales, Scotland, and Northern Ireland. There is no overall philosophy or great unifying concept in British law, no written constitution, and no codified common law.

There are those, more perhaps on the right but with some support on the left, who believe that the time has come for the power of Parliament to be circumscribed, or at least checked, by a new written bill of rights. They fear an extremist government, either because it would confiscate private property or because it might turn against racial minorities. But so far no British government has felt it necessary to bring in a written constitution or a bill of rights. There is a strong resistance to formalizing anything. It is thought to be a hallmark of Latin formalism and floridity to express general constitutional principles, and English people tend to think of Latin-American or even the Soviet constitutions rather than that of the United States when the subject is raised. Better, they feel, not to aim for the sky but to work things out pragmatically as best you can. Thus the only constitutional principle on which Britain functions is that what Parliament has enacted will be and is the law of the land. It is then for the judges to interpret the will of Parliament as expressed in a statute. What we lack, and lack willingly, is any instrument against which the constitutionality or otherwise of an act of Parliament may be judged and, if found wanting, may be judicially declared invalid.

This means that government is quicker and more certain. Once the parliamentary processes have been completed by the Queen's signature being attached to a bill, the law has been duly enacted and is constitutional and enforceable. The system also makes for statutory moderation. The absence of a bill of rights analogous to that in the United States is unimportant only so long as basic rights are not being unduly infringed. If they were, or if there were a serious danger to that effect, then some such protection would undoubtedly be enacted. As it is, Parliament is extremely conscious of the limits of public opinion, and while in theory a government could govern in defiance of the general mood of the country, in practice it could do so only for a severely limited period. The formal constitutional protections may be limited in English or Scottish law, but the informal parliamentary defences are virtually impregnable.

One reason for this is the nature of parliamentary government in itself. We do not elect an executive head for a certain term of four years and then find it necessary to hedge his power around with legal and constitutional safeguards. We demand that the Prime Minister and Cabinet are themselves Members of Parliament. We demand, too, that a government retains the support of the House of Commons. If it is defeated on a major issue, then the government has to resign and a new election has to be held. Moreover, there are 635 Members of Parliament, and a government that sought dictatorial powers over the British people would first have to convince a majority of that 635 to vote for such powers.

The essential point is the pre-eminence of Parliament as the supreme seat of constitutional and legal power in the British system of government. In Britain the powers are not separated; on the contrary, they are concentrated. The executive sits in the legislature and retains power so long as it can command the support of that legislature—but no longer. The head of state is symbolic, and the judiciary is at best a peripheral check only.

To an American this mixture would doubtless seem messy, even deeply offensive to the Jeffersonian soul. The Founding Fathers of the United States were concerned to diminish what they believed to be the danger of tyrannical abuse of power by the executive. They felt that the legislature should be a separate check, and the judicial branch should hold the balance by weighing the government's actions and the legislature's laws against a written Constitution. We have preferred to mix the two branches of direct government, reserving ultimate power to the elected representatives of the people, namely, the House of Commons.

But if we have denied constitutional power to our judges, we have nevertheless insulated them with great ceremony. Ritual plays almost as large a part in British public affairs as it does in the daily life of a Japanese tea-drinker, and nowhere is this more true than in our legal system. It is indeed almost incomprehensible to one brought up in the more logical atmosphere of North

America, since the organization of the profession in Britain is bizarre, and legal education somewhat more so.

There are two main categories of practising lawyers in England: solicitors and barristers. Solicitors are much closer to the picture of an American attorney than are barristers. They can and do form themselves into partnerships. They draft documents, contracts, wills, and so on; they buy and sell property at fees that some (but not they themselves) consider exorbitantly high. They advise corporations on their legal problems and handle the financial details of divorce suits. In short, they behave in much the same way as lawyers do in the United States. There are, however, far fewer of them in Britain than in America—approximately 20,000 in England and Wales to serve 45 million people, compared to approximately 550,000 in the United States to serve 226 million.

A solicitor can also appear in the lowest criminal and civil courts. He can defend you on a speeding charge, or dispute a relatively small bill. What he cannot do is speak for you in any of the senior courts in the land, and it is here that the differences between the systems become apparent.

The position in Scotland and Northern Ireland is broadly similar to that in England and Wales. The legal profession is divided into the same two parts, though in Scotland a barrister is called an advocate. Otherwise the Scottish and English legal systems work broadly in parallel. The rules of law may differ somewhat, but the structure and organization of the profession remain the same.

While there are 20,000 solicitors in England and Wales, there are only approximately 2,500 practising barristers. Their training is different, their profession is organized quite separately, and their function is quite distinct. They are, in short, specialists, and specialist advocates at that. It is the barrister who wears the wig, cross-examines the witnesses, addresses the jury, argues with the judge, and conducts the appeal. He has the exclusive right of audience in all the senior courts of the land, whether civil or criminal. Every advocate who appears at the "Old Bailey," or, to give it its proper name, the Central Criminal Court for the County of London, has to be a member of the Bar, i.e., a barrister-at-law. Otherwise, there is no right of audience.

Not only does the barrister wear the wig; the colour of the wig he (or she) wears is also important. The newer and whiter the wig, the more junior the barrister. A wig is never changed voluntarily but is worn on the same head throughout a working life, even when it becomes decrepit and moulting. Wigs are made from horsehair (though I understand nylon is now being used as a substitute), are hot and uncomfortable in summer, and after a few decades of continuous use are insanitary in the extreme. My own wig after twenty years was turning brown in parts, had lost three curls, and was held together by binding tape only. Yet I could not in all conscience change it, having bought it when first called to the Bar in 1955. It was even then second-hand, and has so far served me well through twenty-three murders, sundry rapes and other crimes, the longest fraud case in British legal history, and the train robbery trial. One becomes attached to it as to an old family pet. While personally I would have a ceremonial wig-burning in Lincoln's Inn Fields, since I do regard the uniform as arcane and a little theatrical, if I were to toss my faithful adjunct into the flames I would feel a slight pang.

To wear with the wig there goes a stiff white butterfly collar, a pair of white starched bands of the sort Methodist preachers were attached to years ago, and a cotton gown. Thus attired, one is entitled to argue the gravest points of law or defend the most villainous of criminals.

Whence comes the complexity, you may say? Ah! but it does not end there, for within the Bar there is yet another division: between those who are Queen's Counsel, and those who are not. A Queen's Counsel, otherwise known as a silk, or a leader, is a barrister whose practice is large and sufficiently influential for him to apply to the Lord Chancellor to be designated a Queen's Counsel. If so designated (and each year approximately one-third of those who apply succeed), then he (or she) can duly appear in court as such, but invariably together with another barrister who receives a fee approximately two-thirds of the one the Queen's Counsel gets. In other words, the client has to hire two barristers, the Queen's Counsel and his junior, sometimes unkindly likened to the plumber and the plumber's mate. Of the two so hired, it is usually only the Queen's Counsel who actually does the talking. Why, you may ask, is this necessary? Why indeed! Senior judges are appointed almost exclusively from the ranks of practising Queen's

Counsels, rarely from juniors, so that the judiciary in England knows one another well, some would say far too well. There is a cosiness about the system which, while it keeps standards up, tends to exclude the radical or the nonconformist. There is a sameness about the British judiciary, which, while incorruptible, is somewhat overbland.

A Queen's Counsel is called a silk for the simplest of reasons: his gown is of a different cut and is literally made of silk. He is also permitted, indeed compelled, to sit in a row in front of his junior—hence the term *leader*. In everyday work his wig is the same as a junior's, but on ceremonial occasions, which fortunately are rare, the Englishman's innate taste for the ceremonial has full play. A Queen's Counsel is then an awesome sight. A full-bottomed wig *à la* Hogarth, lace ruffles and neck-piece, an eighteenth-century frock-coat, knee-breeches, black shoes with silver buckles and black silk stockings (two pairs, as the hairs poke through just one). Why this costume has survived so long is explicable only by the fact that an Englishman's love of personal adornment is not confined to members of the legal profession. Soldiers, sailors, clergy, peers, even diplomats, have over the years indulged this national whim to the full, and still do so. It perhaps helps to explain why the English revival in fashion both for women and for men has proved striking and colourful, if self-pretentious.

Each October, when the legal year starts, a ceremonial service of judges and lawyers is held in Westminster Abbey. Then the law in all its panoply is on parade in earnest. The Lord Chancellor in his gold and black robes, the Lord Chief Justice and his fellow judges in scarlet and ermine, the Queen's Counsel in their full regalia—all attend to be prayed over. After the service they walk solemnly and in procession across Parliament Square to the House of Lords for what is euphemistically known as the Lord Chancellor's breakfast. Although it has echoes of legal trenchermen of the past, the breakfast is now reduced in practice to a glass of sherry and a biscuit or two. The ceremony, not the reality, is the message here. It is a strange British trait that serious men of sober mien can take this dressing-up so earnestly. Not only is that surprising, but it is an even stranger national characteristic that everyone else takes it seriously too. In a unique way, pomp has become part of our national cement.

Apart from the difference in his dress, a barrister and a solicitor are quite distinct in other fundamental respects. Clients cannot go to a barrister direct; they have first to approach a solicitor, who then in turn hires or "briefs" the barrister. In litigation, the solicitor interviews the witnesses and takes their statements. A barrister is not entitled to do that unless the witness is either the client or a medical or technical expert. Quite why this should be so I have never been able to fathom. There is obviously a belief, extraordinarily offensive on analysis, that the barrister would somehow or other persuade a lay witness to speak other than the truth, though why this does not apply equally, and perhaps with even greater force, to the solicitor as well is beyond me. Any correspondence to be written on the client's behalf is done by the solicitor, and not by counsel. Eventually, when the solicitor has collected the evidence, interviewed the witnesses and taken their statements, and gone over the case with the client, the whole is tied neatly with red tape and becomes the "brief for trial." It is then delivered to the barrister to argue the case in court. He can be consulted at any stage, but only in an advisory capacity on the strategy to be pursued, on any enquiries that should be made, the plea that should be entered if it is a criminal case, or the drafting of the formal pretrial documents if it is a civil one, but in essence—and this is the chief distinction between the British and the American systems—the barrister is a specialist, brought in mainly for one purpose, the trial, and the skill he sells is therefore a specialized one, namely, his advocacy.

Britain is indeed well served by advocates. Whether it is always as well served by its lawyers as a whole is perhaps more debatable. Moreover, since each barrister has by definition a distinctive proficiency in his art and no two advocates can be the same, it follows that the client is buying the particular skill of a particular person. There are therefore no partnerships permitted at the English Bar, and each barrister is a separate entity, with his own practice. For convenience, a number may share office accommodation known as "chambers," a clerk who fixes their fees, telephones, stationery, and so on, but each still has a separate and individual practice which is treated as such by H.M. Commissioners of Inland Revenue. In my own chambers there are now around twenty barristers, sharing a senior and two junior clerks, an address in the Temple, and a common telephone number. Despite this, the clerk is clerk to each one individually and collects from each a percentage of his (or her) earnings.

Because of the smallness of the profession and the fact that one tends to appear in the same courts day in, day out, any barrister who has practised for a number of years will almost certainly know his opponent—and the judge. They all have their idiosyncrasies, likes and dislikes, strategies and stratagems. One soon learns those that have to be watched and those that can be relied upon to "play the game" according to the rules, both those written and, perhaps more important, those unwritten. For in essence much of English litigation or trial work is a game or at least a contest. We have elevated the adversary system into an ideology of argumentation and the articulate into an art form. It makes sometimes for sparkling trials when two giants are matched before a judge of substance. It can occasionally produce the opposite—an over-comfortable approach, which may preserve good relations between the protagonists but which may not always produce justice for the client. The contest is played out according to firm and fixed rules of what evidence is or is not admissible to be placed in front of the jury.

The judge's function is to be an impartial referee and to make sure that the rules are obeyed. This function he exercises vigorously, and woe betide the barrister who breaks the rules knowingly and deliberately. It is not a case of breaking them if you can get away with it. There are no "objection sustained" or "objection overruled" in an Old Bailey trial. Counsel are expected to behave in a way that makes judicial interventions unnecessary. Everything takes place, therefore, within an accepted framework, between advocates who usually know each other and before a judge who knows them both. It can make for verbal fireworks, particularly given the nature of Her Majesty's judges, and the independence of the barristers who practise in front of them.

It is, moreover, all done orally—even on appeal. We do not, for example, ever submit a written brief in the American sense, in which the argument is first reduced to writing and only amplified orally. A time limit on speeches such as the U.S. Supreme Court has would be impossible in Britain. The court just would not know enough about the case. The law is explained to the court as

the argument proceeds, and a list of twenty or more previously decided precedents is by no means rare in the Court of Appeal. By
the etiquette of the profession, one is requested to furnish a list of
the cases to be cited to the court and to the other side, but this is
more for the convenience of the ushers than for the necessity of
the judges.

We are in truth a very verbal country in which wit and felicity
in the use of language are highly prized—perhaps too much so. But
it would be a foolish observer who would assume that the wit is
everything and the substance is secondary. The art of enclosing a
serious point in a well-turned and attractive phrase is one practised a great deal in Britain. Moreover, the speaker who knows
this art and his own powers as a practitioner, and who understands his audience, whether judicial or political, derives confidence from it. It could, for example, only have been in Britain
that a Queen's Counsel, opening an appeal from a much-appealed
judge, could look at the three judges hearing it and say, "My
lords, this is an appeal from a decision of Mr. Justice X—but
I hasten to add, my lords, there are other grounds." Or where
Counsel, exasperated after a tedious afternoon spent wrestling
with a difficult judge, could say, "I really would be obliged, my
lord, if your lordship would turn this matter over in what your
lordship is pleased to call your lordship's mind." Or again the famous retort to one judge by F. E. Smith (later Lord Birkenhead
and a future Lord Chancellor), "Your lordship is right and I am
wrong—as your lordship usually is."

Since the two branches of the profession differ so fundamentally, it is perhaps inevitable that the education and training
for each also varies. It is assumed when a solicitor obtains his licence to practise that it means precisely that: that he is qualified
to engage in the business of being a practising solicitor. When a
barrister is called to the Bar, the assumption is somewhat different. It is that he now has a sufficient smattering of law and is
thus qualified to start his real education, the business of learning
how to be an advocate. To do this he becomes a pupil—attaches
himself to a busy junior, reads his master's papers, and follows
him around from court to court, listening and absorbing. He will
try his hand at drafting pleadings in civil actions, or at drawing up
an indictment in a criminal case. He will learn to take a quick and

near-verbatim note of what is being said by his master, the judge, and the witnesses. He is allowed to sit in on his master's conferences and helps look up the law. He is, in effect, an apprentice learning his trade by the example of an older and more experienced practitioner. At the end of this year of "pupillage" our newly called barrister may, if he is lucky, and if the clerk thinks him worth a try, get the opportunity of standing up in court himself and addressing a judge. It is a terrifying moment, and one which remains in his memory throughout his career.

My first case was a brief to appear in an adoption case before the Tottenham magistrates court. The adopting parents were a childless Jewish couple, and the child was the result of a liaison between a Chinese seaman and an Irish mother. There had been some technical problem over proving the mother's consent, and I was briefed to appear. The theory must have been that a barrister, however new, would have some effect on the magistrates. By the time I got to court I knew all about the history of adoption, how to prove, or at least imply, consent, and the circumstances in which the court could refuse to grant the application. What I was not prepared for was that I actually had to do it myself, and the attack of nerves that went with the gradually dawning realization of that fact. One's mouth goes dry, the limbs tremble, and there really is a sinking feeling in the pit of the stomach. I wondered why on earth I had put myself voluntarily in a situation where I was clearly about to make a complete fool of myself. The clients were anxious, but happily convinced that I knew much more about courts than I in fact did. For the agony of that afternoon I was paid the princely sum of £2.4s.6d.–two guineas (£2.2s.0d.) for me and 2s.6d. (or two shillings and sixpence) for my clerk. Somehow we got through it and the adoption duly took place. Many years later I walked into a tailor's shop in London. The owner looked at me and said, "Mr. Richard. How nice to see you again. It is many years since you appeared for me." He then produced a photograph of a fifteen-year-old girl, obviously part-Chinese. It was my first client. I had totally forgotten his face, but well remembered the case.

To study law in Britain means an undergraduate degree course at a university, and not a post-graduate one as in the United States. Indeed, a law degree is not absolutely necessary to become a solicitor, though it is desirable. One can become an articled clerk in a solicitor's office at eighteen, serve six years learning the trade, pass the examinations, and be admitted as a solicitor. As for the Bar, there are really only two compulsory requirements: the Bar examinations and membership of one of the four Inns of Court. These are the Inner Temple, the Middle Temple, Lincoln's Inn, and Gray's Inn. To be called, an applicant must have "kept" at least twelve terms at his chosen inn. He does this by eating six dinners in the hall of that inn each term; there are four terms each year. The food and wine are tolerable, the company congenial, and the halls themselves are ancient (if mainly restored), save for the Inner Temple, whose hall was totally destroyed in an air raid in 1941. Middle Temple Hall is a superb example of Elizabethan architecture, with a screen and a hammer-beam roof as good as any in England. *Twelfth Night* was first performed there in the presence of Queen Elizabeth I in 1601 and the hall itself, though damaged in World War II, has not changed much since. There is in a very real sense a consciousness of centuries of continuity. But the inns are not relics; they are working institutions within which all barristers in London have their chambers. Foolish indeed is the tourist in London who neglects them. They typify that strange blend of reverence for history and scepticism at tradition for tradition's sake which is uniquely British. We are conscious of our background, but find no difficulty in accommodating it to the present.

The same is true of the law itself and the way in which it is practised. Standards are high; one has to be able to trust one's opponent, and the judge must be able to trust both. There is a duty overriding all others—even the duty to one's client—not to mislead the court. Lawyers, both solicitors and barristers, are considered "officers of the court," and their delinquencies are treated accordingly, though disbarment is rare. A barrister never handles his client's money, and since his primary relationship is with the solicitor, it is to the latter that he looks to pay his fees. If the client lets the solicitor down, the barrister is nonetheless entitled to be paid. The rules of both professions prohibit any kind of advertising, and contingency fees are forbidden. In criminal cases, plea bargaining is banned. Standards of probity and honesty are therefore kept up by a series of pressures, some overt but many simply understood. A "shady" barrister is on the whole unlikely to prosper for long. He will almost certainly be known as such throughout the Temple and by the judges, who will tend to be predisposed against him. Since they want their clients to win their cases rather than lose them, few solicitors would wish to brief a counsel against whom judges are predisposed, unless the solicitors are somewhat doubtful themselves, and fortunately very few are. A practice thus founded is likely to be short, not very successful, and nonlucrative. Anyone aspiring to become a judge is inevitably jealous of his professional reputation and anxious to maintain it. Judges are appointed directly by the Lord Chancellor, who inevitably and rightly makes sweeping enquiries about the competence and reputation of possible candidates. One result of all this is that the practice of criminal law in Britain is as respectable as any other branch.

Criminal justice is, moreover, quicker under our system. Without a federal system to prolong appeals, it is rare that a person will spend more than six months after conviction until the final disposal of the appeal, unless there is something quite exceptional about the criminal or the crime. In the Train Robbery trial the crime took place in August 1963, the defendants were convicted after a full trial by April 1964, and the appeals had been disposed of by the summer; and this was a case in which there were thirteen accused, the amount involved was £3.5 million, the trial had taken nine weeks, and the sentences of thirty years' imprisonment were virtually unprecedented.

It is also true in Britain that people can be properly represented whether rich or poor. Our legal aid scheme is comprehensive and practical, perhaps because it is administered by the lawyers themselves, not by a government department. Someone charged with an offence goes to a solicitor, who applies for legal aid on his (or her) behalf. His means and income are investigated, and if he qualifies (and most do) he is then granted a legal aid certificate. Once that is granted, he is represented in exactly the same way as if he were not "on legal aid." The solicitor prepares the case; the barrister is briefed and appears in the usual way. The only difference is that the bill is submitted at the end of the day to a public authority and not to a private individual. A deduction of 10 per cent is made from it to cover the costs of administering the scheme and the cheque then comes through the post in the normal way. This means that the most senior counsel will appear in cases in which the client is legally aided, and will receive much the same fee (less the 10 per cent) as if the client had been paying privately.

While there is not exactly a tariff, a scale of fees is pretty well accepted as standard. A senior Queen's Counsel, for example, in a large, complicated case could well receive about £1,000 as his brief fee, and then a "refresher" of approximately £200 a day for each day after the first that the case continues. The junior will get about two-thirds of that amount. The busiest, most expensive barristers can expect to earn around £70,000 to £100,000 a year— a large sum by British standards.

But if he does hope to rise to the summit of the legal ladder, an ambitious Queen's Counsel will aspire to the Bench—to become a High Court judge, known as Mr. Justice Blank and with a knighthood to accompany it. He then becomes one of a rare breed of men—one of Her Majesty's Judges of the Supreme Court of Judicature.

Each age assumes that the previous one contained all the legal giants, yet each in turn produces its own. It would, I think, be inappropriate (and unwise if I ever hoped to return to practice) to comment too freely on the present occupants of the High Court Bench. At best they are a mixed lot indeed. Their great strength is that they are unelected, appointed by the Lord Chancellor, with security of tenure until they are seventy-five and removable only by a motion passed by a two-thirds majority in each of the two Houses of Parliament. They are thus totally independent of the government of the day. Conversely, they are extremely powerful in their own court, and unless their idiosyncracies become over-apparent they survive. If things get too bad, a quiet word from the Lord Chancellor is usually but not invariably enough to induce them to retire. If reversed too often on appeal because their law was wrong, or they talked too much, or even fell asleep too regularly and noisily, their state of health would soon diplomatically necessitate their giving up the burdens of their judicial office. And some do talk too much despite their best intentions. It is usually then necessary to allow them to run on, hoping the whole while that eventually they will run down. As they get older, some get deafer and their law can get rusty.

Since they have all been experienced practitioners themselves, they do tend to feel a strong sense of *déjà vu* and a great temptation to participate in the conduct of the case they are trying. To have to listen to someone else cross-examining inexpertly is agony to the expert on the Bench. He cannot leave; he cannot take the case over; he can ask the occasional questions or make the occasional point, but by and large he has to sit and suffer. To intervene too much usually prolongs the agony, since counsel will then feel that he has to cover the extra points made by the judge. He has to ensure that the case is tried fairly, and if there is a jury it is his duty to make certain that the issues are put clearly and equitably. Talking too much is the ultimate judicial sin, and it is this that usually provokes the fiercest clashes between judge and barrister.

F. E. Smith for some years had had great difficulty with one judge, Mr. Justice Willis. Things finally came to a head in a case where F.E. was appearing for an insurance company being sued as the insurers of a driver by a small boy who had been injured in an accident. The boy was brought into court, whereupon the following exchange took place:

Judge: Poor little fellow. Put him on a chair so that we can all see him.

Smith: Perhaps your lordship would like him passed around the jury box.

Judge: That is a most improper observation, Mr. Smith.

Smith: It was provoked, my lord, by a most improper suggestion.

Judge: May I remind you, Mr. Smith, of the saying of the great Bacon that "youth and discretion are ill-wedded companions."

Smith: And may I remind you, my lord, of the saying of the great Bacon that "a much talking judge is like an ill-tuned cymbal."

Judge: Mr. Smith, what do you think I am on this Bench for?

Smith: My lord, it is not for me to question the inscrutable ways of a divine providence.

This type of confrontation, though rarely so elegant or literary, is repeated at intervals throughout one's professional career.

There is something mystically disturbing about the effect that becoming a judge can have on a person. It is usually quite impossible to tell until he gets there how a particular individual will actually behave. The reticent barrister becomes talkative, the gentle counsel turns harsh and vengeful. The man who was the terror of the courts becomes a quiet and compassionate judge. The only generalization that one can make is that it is unsafe to generalize. The truth is that people's real natures emerge when they are placed in the position of judging their fellow human beings. Their true inclinations and views then have a relatively free rein. If someone is a suppressed bully by instinct, then young counsel are in for a hard time, for they are present and obvious victims. Most are worried, if not actually frightened, and if the judge's reputation is well known, that of course makes it worse. If someone is innately helpful or kind, then it will emerge. One can conceal one's true nature while in practice, but not on the Bench. It is the nature of the judge's power that reveals. In his own court he has great and almost unchallengeable authority. Most do not abuse it, and behave well. Most have a strong sense of their function, seeing themselves as part of a necessary process of law and order, and not as an opportunity to indulge their own personalities. Few are consciously unfair, and all, I think, genuinely believe that in their court at least justice is done, even if it is in fact done painfully, garrulously, and tediously. By and large we are well served by our judges, and in my experience their conduct of cases is generally fair and reasonable.

What one should not expect from British judges, however, is social reform. The freedoms of Britain were not won in the courts of the land. They were by and large won in Parliament, and part of the function of the courts is to see that they are now preserved. Unlike the case of the U.S. Supreme Court, our judges have a severely judicial function, not a political one, and great innovative movements for national change do not originate in Britain with the legal judgements of the courts of law. In this respect, at any rate, we have kept the political and the judicial powers separate.

The personalities of H.M. judges over the years have, to say the least, been varied. From the sadistic and venal to the gentle and reformist, they have left their collective mark on the British character. We are at heart a law-abiding people. Not only do we obey the law with less apparent difficulty than in the United States, we tend to admire or at least respect those who are responsible for seeing that the law is administered. It is still regarded as a learned and honourable profession. In the House of Commons, for example, a Queen's Counsel is always referred to as "the honourable and learned member for ———." All Members of Parliament are "honourable," but some are more "learned" than others.

As a nation, we expect that our legal processes should be speedy, that justice should be done insofar as it ever can be done, and, moreover, that it should be seen to be done in public. We expect that a man's trial should be fair, that he will be properly represented, and his case fully put. We expect that our judges will behave equitably and honestly in the conduct of cases. We do not demand that our judges should be superhuman, dealing justice with the wisdom of Solon or the precision of Solomon, but they should not be dehumanized either. We expect the legal profession to live up to its function: that of providing the essential framework of order and certainty within which 55 million people can order their affairs, conduct their daily lives, and live in decency and freedom. In the process we have produced a profession of integrity and preservation, if one that is conservative in instinct and narrow in origin. It is perhaps no small achievement and to the credit of the British. It is also one revealing of much of their national character—conservative and slow to feel the need for change, but innovative when convinced; anxious to preserve the standards of independence and conduct that have been developed over generations; somewhat arcane in their procedures and with a fine eye for the form as well as the substance; unwilling to be overgoverned and suspicious of too much executive power; articulate and polished in the use of that rich and noble instrument the English language, yet slightly distrustful when felicity veers into the glib; and finally, essentially practical and pragmatic in their use of their institutions.

CHRISTIAN BELIEF
AND MORALITY

Ever since King Henry VIII assumed the title of Supreme Head of the Church of England in 1534, the Church of England has had a curious relationship with the state. Basically, the Church and the state have over the years come to an understanding. The Church is self-governing, though all clergy swear an oath of allegiance to the Crown, but the sovereign, who must be a member of the Church of England and who appoints archbishops, bishops, and deans, in turn swears to uphold the Church. Despite the peculiar relationship between Church and state, the Church of England is not state-"owned" or state-subsidized, and it pays its way through the donations of the faithful and its large income from investments. At the same time, the Church of England, though an established church and very much part of the English heritage, is by no means the religion of all of the British people. Indeed, if the political system of the British over the years has generally been based on a two-party system, then for a very long time the British have preferred pluralism in religion. Britain is not a country like Italy or Israel where the majority of the population may be assumed to be—at least formally—of one religion.

Again, strangely, for a country with a more or less official religion, there is no religious bar to any public appointment—except for the post of Lord Chancellor, who must be an Anglican, or member of the Church of England (and for some other posts, such as ambassador to the Vatican, which are by tradition filled by practising members of the Church of England). The BBC broadcasts a certain number of religious services each Sunday, but there is no longer any assumption, as there used to be until relatively recently, that the whole of the population is made up of active church-goers. Indeed, many people in British public life make it clear that they are agnostic or have no religious belief. Church-going has little social duty attached to it as in the United States. It is probably true to say that the majority of people in British public life—politicians, civil servants, show business people, and lawyers —are atheists or agnostics, though there is little evidence one way or the other. On the other hand, there is a large category of what some clergymen call "four-wheeler Christians"—those whose journeys to church are made either by pram, or baby carriage (as infants to be baptized), by wedding limousine, or by funeral hearse. Most of the British probably avail themselves of the rites of the Church at these crucial times (more for funerals than for baptisms or weddings) but do not actively practise as Christians on a more regular basis.

But this is not to say that there is not an active religious life in Britain. A survey conducted in 1979 showed that about a seventh of the adult population attended church at least once a month, including about 1.25 million each in the Anglican and Roman Catholic churches. In the 1960s it looked as though church-going in Britain was on a steep downward slope, and there is still, for the two largest churches, a slightly downward trend (stronger now for the Roman Catholics than for the Anglicans) but other indicators, such as the number of men coming forward for the Anglican priesthood, show an upward trend. About 300 men entered the Church in 1978 and about the same number in 1979, but now the average seems to be between 400 and 450 a year. A writer in the *Church of England Yearbook* for 1981 commented: "The mood of the Church and of Christian people in England is strangely confident, at a time when the political, economic and social prospect at home is bleak and when storm-clouds gather in central and eastern Europe and in the Middle East." According to the 1979 survey, however, the really amazing increase was in the membership of the independent evangelical churches such as the Baptists or Methodists, with a spectacular 23 per cent increase between 1975 and 1979. Much of this increase was accounted for by the increase in church-going by Britain's black population, but the evidence overall appears to show that there is something of a spiritual revival among the people of Britain.

Some cynics think that the Church of England is now stronger and more confident, if smaller, than before, because it has become more religious than it ever was. Traditionally the Church of England has been seen as the "Tory Party at prayer," the Church of the gentry and the upper-middle classes, the official religion of the armed forces and the public schools. (Incidentally, the Church of England provides the official religion for most of the older and traditional public, i.e., private, schools, while state schools are merely enjoined by the legislature to provide a non-denominational act of worship; Anglicanism is *not* the religion of ordinary state schools.) In addition, Anglican chaplains work in state institutions like hospitals and prisons. In the nineteenth century and before in England and Wales, the middle and upper classes generally went to church, while the working classes usually went to chapel. The Methodist, Baptist, and Congregational chapels were where the poorer classes met to practise their religion and to feel solidarity and togetherness—the type of feeling symbolized by the fervor and emotion that the Welsh put into their hymn-singing. The Labour Party and the rise of Methodism were intimately bound up together, with Methodism, in Harold Wilson's famous phrase, being more important to its make-up than Marxism. As Blondel puts it: "The nonconformist chapels of the eighteenth and

nineteenth centuries operated against the established hierarchy
and they came to be based on social values which emphasized, not
hierarchy, but equality or perhaps more specifically fraternity and
solidarity." The social system was, of course, based on hierarchy,
but those who lived within the system could reject it and espouse
other values—while remaining part of the society—through their
membership of the dissenting Protestant churches. At that time,
the Church of England was, therefore, the other side of the religious coin, representing hierarchy and embracing the values of the
landed gentry and the aristocracy. It was in a very real sense Tory.
But all that has changed.

It has changed for two reasons: first, the Church of England is
now down to the minority of "faithful" and many of its old privi-
leges have gone; and second, there now exists a world-wide Anglican communion that vastly outnumbers its base at "home" in
England. It is no longer the case that the Church is seen as a career for the younger sons of the gentry, providing a handsome vic-
arage or rectory alongside the home of the squire and an assured
role in country society. The Church was, perhaps, slow to adapt to
urban society. While the villages all have churches, in terms of
population, it is in the towns that priests are needed and where
the life of the Church should be based. There was, too, a time
when bishops were well paid and ranked with senior army officers
and high civil servants. Today, in 1982, an Anglican bishop is paid
£9,875 a year, which is a quarter of the pay of a general or a
High Court judge and about what a thirty-year-old senior administrator in the civil service would be earning. Vicars and rectors are
paid much less; few earn more than a bus-driver or a postman
would earn without overtime. The grand old country rectories have
nearly all been sold off and now provide much-prized addresses
for those who have made their money by more secular pursuits. To
be an Anglican priest requires devotion to the faith, and not a desire to rise up the social ladder. Possibly because of the religious
education some public schools give, perhaps a higher proportion
than might be expected of Anglican priests were public school
boys, but it is now frankly nonsense to speak of the Church of
England as if it were the conscience of present-day Conservatism.

The other major change that has come over the Anglican
Church in recent years is its expansion overseas, which in some

ways has dwarfed its presence at home. There are just under 2 million members of the Church of England in Britain (which includes the Episcopal Church in Scotland and the Church in Wales). There are, however, a further 65 million scattered throughout the world, though there is no disciplined overall control in the Anglican Church as there is, for example, in the Roman Catholic Church. There are the Lambeth conferences held every ten years that bring the bishops of the 400-plus Anglican dioceses throughout the world to Britain for a meeting, but it was only after the 1968 conference that some sort of loosely co-ordinating body for the Church, the Anglican Consultative Council, was set up. The council, like the Lambeth Conference itself, has no legislative role, but it, too, has great prestige and is listened to attentively. Although there are strong branches of the Anglican communion in the United States and Canada (where it is called the Episcopal Church) the Anglican Church is now a predominantly third-world church. In some areas, such as Namibia, its bishops and priests have been active in political causes, and on questions like race relations and apartheid the Anglican Church is no longer silent. It has also taken positions, at home, on such subjects as the trade unions and Northern Ireland, and recently on nuclear disarmament.

Some people have therefore concluded that the Church is seeking a political role for itself rather than concentrating on its spiritual or pastoral function. Very often those who criticize the Church are not themselves regular church-goers but, rather, people who would like to see the Church preserve itself in the way they sentimentally remember the Church of their childhood. The appearance in 1980 of a new, or "alternative," version of the Book of Common Prayer provoked another major storm. Eminent literati wrote to *The Times* decrying the language of the new prayer book, calling on the Church to reject it and to maintain the seventeenth-century version.

The Book of Common Prayer does contain some of the finest prose in the English language. Take, for example, the Collect for the Fifteenth Sunday after Trinity:

Keep, we beseech thee, O Lord, thy Church with thy perpetual mercy: and, because the frailty of man without thee cannot but fall, keep us ever by thy help from all things hurtful, and lead us to all things profitable to our salvation; through Jesus Christ our Lord.

or this prayer from the Litany:

O God, merciful Father, that despisest not the sighing of a contrite heart, nor the desire of such as be sorrowful; Mercifully assist our prayers that we make before thee in all our troubles and adversities, whensoever they oppress us; and graciously hear us, that those evils, which the craft and subtilty of the devil or man worketh against us, be brought to nought; and by the providence of thy goodness they may be dispersed; that we thy servants, being hurt by no persecutions, may evermore give thanks unto thee in thy holy Church; through Jesus Christ our Lord.

Many of those who wanted to keep the ancient forms looked on the Church as the custodian of something special in the British heritage. There is also the great heritage of English church music, the music, in particular, of the great Tudor composers like William Byrd and Orlando Gibbons, which could, if the Church were nothing else, remain as a monument to past glories. The Church, however, has to combine its role as a custodian of English traditions, whether of language, of music, or of cathedral architecture, with its continuing role as spiritual leader of the nation. The decline of the Church and its retreat into greater spirituality may mean that it is doing just that; its apparent occasional straying into the field of politics may show that it has something to say these days and is no longer merely a pillar of the establishment. The final step in this process—which may not be far away—would be the ending of the Church's formal position as an established church.

Were that to happen, the question "Is Britain a Christian country?" would be more difficult to answer. The position of the Roman Catholic Church, too, would change. As it is, the Roman Catholic Church claims more members than does the Church of England, though the figures for church attendance are about the same for the two. Nevertheless, there are some in the Roman Catholic Church, like the priest who wrote in the *Clergy Review* in 1980 that Britain was a "Catholic country," who would expect the large membership of the Roman Catholic Church to be recognized more openly in the country. With the successful visit of the Pope in 1982, the Roman Catholic Church could well be on the way to regaining something of the position it lost in 1534.

The Roman Catholic Church ceased to be recognized in Britain in the sixteenth century, but was "restored" in 1850 and now has six provinces, each under an archbishop, in Britain. Some Anglicans still claim that their Church is the "holy apostolick church"—in other words the Catholic, or universal, Church in Britain, the inheritor of the Church and its traditions following the Reformation of the sixteenth century. Talks periodically go on about unity, and the Church of England maintains an "Anglican Centre" in Rome where scholars and priests on either side study and reflect on the different traditions. The primacy of the Pope, the role of the Virgin Mary and of the saints, and the doctrine of Transubstantiation cause Anglicans most difficulties, while married priests and a more liberal doctrine on birth control and divorce make the Anglican Church difficult for the Vatican to accept.

While Roman Catholics were virtually persecuted in Britain until the nineteenth century—until 1829 they had to live more than five miles from any town, and non-Anglicans have been allowed to teach at Oxford and Cambridge only since 1871—there now seems to be a growing view that Roman Catholics occupy a disproportionately influential position in British life. There was a time recently when the Secretary to the Cabinet was Sir John Hunt, husband of the sister of the Cardinal Archbishop of Westminster, Basil Hume, and such key members of the Establishment as the editor of *The Times* and the Permanent Under-Secretary at the Foreign Office were practising Catholics; and there have been many Roman Catholic novelists, from Graham Greene and Evelyn Waugh to Piers Paul Read. According to the Catholic Year-Book, there were thirty-nine Roman Catholic MPs in 1981. It is absurd to suggest that Roman Catholics are some sort of secret society in Britain, but they have certainly made a distinctive contribution to British life in recent years. There was a time when ancient noble families and the descendants of Irish labourers constituted the majority of Catholics in Britain, and there were few middle-class Catholics. Now there is a distinctively middle-class Catholic community; indeed, the appointment of Cardinal Hume as Archbishop of Westminster in 1976 was a move that for the first time brought an English priest rather than an Irish- or otherwise immigrant-descended priest to be the head of the Catholic Church in Britain. The Roman Catholic Church in Britain, like the Anglican Church but with a totally different historic tradition, represents today a significant minority of the population.

In addition to the Church of England and Catholicism, there is a considerable body of nonconformity in Britain. The Church of Scotland, the established church north of the Border, is Presbyterian. Methodists, Baptists, Congregationalists, Quakers, and just about every other Christian sect (including the Mormons) flourish in contemporary society. Many indeed, including the Shakers, started in Britain before moving West.

Apart from the practising Protestants (including Anglicans) and the practising Roman Catholics in Britain, there are about 410,000 Jews—and, as a largely new phenomenon of the recent immigration—thousands of Eastern Orthodox Christians, Muslims, Sikhs, Hindus, and Buddhists. The Jewish community dates from the Norman Conquest but was not formally organized until the seventeenth century. In 1760 the Jewish community formed the Board of Deputies of British Jews, which remains the principal vehicle for the transmission of Jewish concerns and preoccupations to the government. A very high proportion of British Jews live in major conurbations such as London, Manchester, Leeds, and Glasgow, and few in the rural areas.

If Britain is, in trendy parlance, a multi-faith society (despite the existence of an official church), it is interesting to see how many people marry through their church, chapel, or temple, and how many do so through the official "registry office" (for civil marriages). In fact the number of marriages solemnized in registry offices is now just about 50 per cent—except in Northern Ireland, where 90 per cent of marriages still take place in church. Divorces are more frequent in Great Britain than in Northern Ireland, and are more common everywhere than they used to be, but there is a clear trend towards secularization even, or perhaps above all, for the "four-wheeler" Christians. On the other hand, membership of some church-related groups, such as the Cub Scouts, is on the increase. This is for religion in Britain, as for so much else, a time when generalizations about the future are hazardous.

Earlier on in this book I mentioned a typical modern Briton. What would his religious outlook be? The typical young Briton, according to surveys, does have some sort of a belief in God but is unlikely to be an assiduous attender at church. He was probably baptized; he may have been a Cub Scout or joined a Scout troop attached to the local church. He may, on the other hand, have joined a church choir as a young boy and have experienced the great heritage of Anglican church music. There is a 50 per cent chance that he will get married in church. It will probably depend on his school, family, or fiancée. If he has a religious mother, the question is whether, later in life, he will return to become a regular member of a congregation.

A PERMISSIVE SOCIETY?

Although Christian worship has declined greatly in Britain, Christian morality has remained more acceptable. As A. J. P. Taylor commented, speaking of Britain in the inter-war years, "The commercial and financial system rested securely on sanctity of contract. England was one of the few countries where those liable to income tax could be relied upon to reveal their correct incomes, as near as made no difference." Many agnostic Britons will still say that they are Christian as far as personal morality, rather than actual religious beliefs, are concerned. The policing of Britain has, traditionally at least, counted on the support of a strong law-abiding majority, and in general the British state does not have to cope with what in France is known as *incivisme*—the refusal to co-operate with the authorities, pay taxes honestly, or co-operate with the police except on pain of physical violence or arrest. Of course, things have changed, and it is a common theme of readers' letters to Conservative newspapers that there has been "a general falling-off in standards"—but statistics can be interpreted in various ways, and Britain remains on the whole law-abiding.

In particular, attitudes to divorce have changed notably over the years. It was not until the twenties that divorced people sat in Cabinets or were promoted to the peerage; now the Queen's sister, Princess Margaret, is herself divorced; the parents of the Princess of Wales, the former Lady Diana Spencer, are divorced; and Mr. Denis Thatcher, the husband of the Prime Minister, is a divorcé. A third of all marriages in Britain now involve at least one partner who has been married before—indeed, the divorce rate in Britain has shot up in the last twenty years, from about 27,000 a year in 1961 to 147,000 in 1979. Twenty years ago Britain had one of the lowest divorce rates in Europe; now it has one of the highest, though divorce is still not as frequent as in the United States or Sweden.

Together with the virtual revolution in attitudes to marriage and divorce, the last few years have seen a marked increase in unmarried couples living together, not always as a prelude to marriage. The government's *General Household Survey* reported in late 1981 that 3 per cent of women aged between eighteen and forty-nine in their sample survey were living with men they were not legally married to, nearly all of them being under thirty-five and in paid work. The rise of the career woman and the ready availability of male and female birth control methods have brought about this change; attitudes, too, have evolved. "Living together" is now much more common, and the gossip columns of the newspapers—which used to be highly moralistic in tone—now regularly report on the "live-in" boy-friends and girl-friends of the stars.

Attitudes to illegitimacy have also changed. While contraception is widely practised, *planned* births outside marriage seem to be increasing. Many illegitimate births used to occur to single women; now births to parents living together but not married, who both recognize the baby, are more common. The Abortion Act, passed by Harold Wilson's Labour government in 1967, allowed

abortion where two doctors certified that the continuance of preg-
nancy would harm the mother or the child or her other children,
or where they were certain that the baby was likely to suffer from
serious abnormalities. The number of abortions has gone up dramatically since then. In the ten years from 1969 to 1979 the total
number more than doubled, from 50,000 to 119,000. There has
been great disquiet about the act, particularly in some Catholic
circles, and a lobby called the "Right to Life" campaign has raised
the issue of unwanted pregnancies in the newspapers. It is also alleged that many of the abortions have been carried out on foreign
women, often at great profit to specially established abortion
clinics; some of the right-to-life campaigners dubbed London the
"abortion capital of Europe." Typically, the Abortion Act does
not apply to Northern Ireland: in sexual mores, as in religious
faith and church-going, the people of Northern Ireland do not fit
easily into the general British pattern.

Attitudes to homosexuality have also undergone a revolution in
recent years, following the passing, in 1967, of a law which said
that homosexual acts between consenting male adults over the age
of twenty-one and committed in private were no longer unlawful.
There are no laws against lesbianism, although in the armed forces
(where the 1967 Act does not apply) women can be charged with
committing "disgraceful conduct of an indecent or unnatural
kind." The police still have considerable discretion in handling homosexual questions: for example, a homosexual party could be
technically unlawful under certain circumstances. Much depends
on the local chief constable. "Gay" groups claim that the police in
some areas harass them, but it seems to be the case that gays have
greater confidence in themselves and in their organizations than
ever before. It is no longer taboo for a public personage to confess
the nature of his or her sexual orientation: in one highly publicized case in the late 1970s, a woman Labour MP (who was not
subsequently re-elected), Maureen Colquhoun, left her husband to
live with another woman. The fact that Ms. Colquhoun was not
re-elected might indicate that the general public is not yet ready
for lesbian MPs, but the fact that she felt able to explain her position fully, and the newspapers were able to print the story in full
detail, would seem to indicate that the media, at least, feel less
inhibited than they used to about discussing such matters publicly.

Is Britain, then, a liberal country? There can be no doubt that the legal reforms, largely brought in by the Wilson government in the 1964–70 period, have transformed the climate affecting homosexuality, and public attitudes on questions like divorce and abortion have also changed. Things have changed, too, since the publishers of D. H. Lawrence's novel *Lady Chatterley's Lover* were in court twenty years ago on an obscenity charge. It was then that the prosecuting barrister asked the jury to consider whether *Lady Chatterley's Lover* was the type of book they would "allow their wives or servants to read." But how "permissive" is Britain? The basic live-and-let-live spirit that pervades the country also affects sex: provided you do what you do with privacy and discretion, you are unlikely to be frowned on. Yet so many popular British newspapers subsist on a diet of sub-pornography and divorce scandals that one is forced to wonder whether there is some need that newspapers like the *News of the World* cater for.

The *News of the World* is the largest-circulation newspaper in Britain. It appears on Sundays and specializes in titillating stories of a sexy type: they often seem to involve misconduct by priests, vicars, or nuns, and stories of the "air-stewardess speaks of the saucy captain" type. Every Sunday, half of adult Britain devours such material, traditionally in bed while the children are sent to Sunday school. The daily newspaper *The Sun* similarly contains news of the sexual follies of starlets, and it was the first newspaper to present topless photographs of women for its readers' titillation. Is there an instinctive prudery in Britain that such material serves to expurgate? It is often remarked, too, that the most squalid details of divorce cases and sex scandals are to be found, not in *The Sun* but in the arch-conservative *Daily Telegraph,* often accompanied by an enjoinder that such things should really be banned.

In fact, it appears to be the case that the ordinary Briton *is* somewhat prudish and puritanical. The average working-class male swears a great deal—a regular adjective is likely to be "fucking"—but many tend to believe that certain things should not be done or said "in front of the ladies," though this may now be changing somewhat. He may make himself out, in male company, to be a tearaway, a devil with the girls, but when confronted with female company may be at a loss for words. There is still an underlying sense of guilt where sex is concerned in Britain, a feeling summed up by the use of the word "naughty" as a synonym of "indecent." And alongside the progressiveness of the legislators and the liberalism of the commentators, there is a deep underlying current of unease about the "permissive society." Some people—in every generation—are likely to be frightened of youth, and to regard the young as morally degenerate and sexually promiscuous, but in Britain of late such sentiments have been organized politically in an articulate and increasingly influential way.

Some years ago there was a Festival of Light organized by antipornography campaigners including Mrs. Mary Whitehouse and the eccentric Roman Catholic peer and former Labour minister Lord Longford. Mrs. Whitehouse, as we have seen, is a housewife whose National Listeners and Viewers Association (whose membership is little known) is a scourge of BBC producers and a vigilant guard against what it considers to be indecency or pornography in films, books, and the mass media. Since the law relating to obscene publications is unclear, Mrs. Whitehouse, Lord Longford, and their supporters aim to change the climate of opinion so that there is a clearer—and therefore more restrictive—definition of obscenity. The 1959 Act is marvellously vague in defining obscenity. It says that an article is obscene if

> taken as a whole, it is such as to deprave and corrupt persons who are likely, having regard to all the relevant circumstances, to read, see or hear the matter contained in it.

What exactly "deprave and corrupt" means is not spelled out.

The late Lord Justice Salmon, in 1968, went a little further and defined corruption as to induce or promote

> erotic desires of a heterosexual nature
> homosexual or other perversions
> drug-taking
> brutal violence.

The National Council of Civil Liberties, in its handbook on civil liberty in Britain, comments that the obscenity laws are designed to "punish the promotion of activities which in themselves may be both lawful and normal, and yet are equated with 'depravity.'"

There is certainly a major difference of opinion between those, like Lord Longford, who hold that "obscene material" can induce crime and lead to rape and violence, and those who maintain that, on the contrary, such material is cathartic and induces nothing worse than fantasies and escapism.

Whether "pornography" is in a different category from obscenity is not clear either. There is a clear revulsion in Britain against pornography featuring children, although, again, it is not clear whether those who use such material then go on to commit violent acts on children. The trial in 1981 of a number of men involved in the so-called paedophile Exchange raised this issue, but the revulsion of the press and public was unanimous. It is, however, probably true to say that the tide is turning: there seems to be a less liberal and less tolerant attitude generally to such matters than a few years ago. After an era in which censorship in the theatre was abolished and freedom in fact was used to such an extent that it merged into licence, the pendulum is swinging back. In the absence of a clear moral consensus in modern society, it is to the courts that society looks for a lead, yet it is by no means clear that the courts are capable of responding. Legislation in this field is vague, and judges in Britain are not in the habit of laying down general principles of a moral nature.

In one field, relatively liberal recommendations by a government committee have never been turned into legislation. In 1969 a government report strongly criticized the law against the use or sale of marijuana, but the revised law continued to make marijuana as illegal as other drugs. In 1979 there were 2,809 people registered as addicts to hard drugs, mainly heroin, in the United Kingdom, but barbiturates remained the major cause of drug problems, though perhaps less publicized. Those campaigning for the legalization of cannabis point out that barbiturates are a common cause of death (through deliberate overdose), while, they say, marijuana is not addictive and does not kill in itself. The attitude of the general public to drug-taking is difficult to gauge, but this seems to be an issue that does not fire public opinion either way. Few politicians have been prepared to argue for the legalization of marijuana, so the law remains unchanged. Cigarette-smoking continues to decline, most particularly among the professional classes. Only 25 per cent of professional men were smoking in 1978, but over 60 per cent of unskilled male manual workers smoked. It is now quite possible to go to a middle-class dinner party in Britain at which no ashtray will be needed. But among the fashionable young, it does seem that marijuana-smoking remains popular.

Alcohol consumption in Britain appears to be on the increase. Indeed, surveys of household expenditure over the past ten years or so show alcohol as one of the items on which the British have been spending more and more of their income. Beer—and more recently lager—continues to be the favourite drink of the British, but wine has increased steadily in popularity for years, a demand that now seems to be levelling off. In Britain there are "licensing laws": alcohol may be served only with a meal in restaurants or in "public houses" ("pubs"). Their hours of opening are fixed by a local licensing committee, and pubs normally open for a few hours in the morning until mid-afternoon, and again in the evening until 10:30 or 11 P.M. Yet although some people would like to see a lifting of restrictions on drinking hours, the population as a whole seems to accept them.

The picture that emerges, therefore, is of a people who know how to enjoy themselves but who, for reasons that perhaps have to do with their puritanical past, seem to feel subconsciously guilty about overtly manifesting too much sensual enjoyment. There is therefore a relatively high level of alcohol consumption, but a tight control of the drinking hours; considerable freedom to buy and sell pornography, but a strong and active voluntary movement to curb excesses in this field. A basic liberalism coexists uneasily with the heritage of the Protestant conscience.

The British, then, are reasonably open in their social attitudes. But the curious thing is that reforms in social legislation—such as the laws affecting sexual conduct passed by the Wilson government—have been passed by the legislators despite the fact that public opinion polls showed the voters, on balance, to be against such reforms. Indeed, to take only Labour voters, opinion polls have shown that it is the Labour Party's economic program, rather than its social attitudes, which has attracted the mass vote. Middle-class Labour MPs tend to be poles apart, on questions such as divorce law reform or homosexuality, from their working-class constituents. Yet—up until now at least—the MPs' consciences have guided them more than the opinion poll.

No issue illustrates this better than the question of capital punishment. In the sixties there was a considerable debate over whether capital punishment—carried out in Britain by hanging—should be abolished. Yet although a majority was, and still seems to be, in favour of hanging, MPs voted in 1965 to suspend the death penalty for murder and substitute a mandatory life sentence for an experimental period of five years; in 1969 they voted to continue the suspension indefinitely. (The death sentence still remains in force for high treason.) There have been several attempts by individual MPs to get the death penalty reinstated, but none has prospered.

THE BRITISH BOBBY UNDER ATTACK

In terms of the ratio of police to population, Britain—with, for England and Wales, one police officer for every 420 people in the population—is neither as highly policed as Belgium (1:323) nor as thinly policed as the Netherlands (1:702) but more or less average, not far from the United States figure of 1:500. But the origins of the British police are totally different from those of most other forces. London's Metropolitan Police, established in 1829 as Britain's first regular police force, was carefully set up by Parliament after years of hesitation and debate over what sort of police the capital city should have. Members of Parliament were reluctant to put into the streets any body of men which might be seen as militaristic, or even smack of being an army of occupation.

The uniform of the British police officer, and his basic training and approach, date from that period. The uniform was designed not to appear military; policemen were not armed; they carried rattles rather than whistles. They were seen as the servants of society, not as its masters. The training manual of the time is still quoted in police training today:

> It should be understood at the outset that the object to be attained is the prevention of crime. To this great end every effort of the police is directed. The security of person and property, the preservation of the public tranquillity, and all other objects of a police establishment will thus be better effected than by the detection and punishment of the offender after he has succeeded in committing the crime. Every member of the Force must remember that his duty is to protect and help members of the public no less than to apprehend guilty persons.

What is more, the tradition holds that the police officer is no more than a citizen in uniform, a specialist in doing things that it is the duty of all citizens to do. In Britain a citizen may make an arrest and (in England and Wales) institute a prosecution, and must by law respond to a policeman's request for help. Indeed, the police have few legal powers ordinary citizens do not themselves possess. Police officers are told in their training sessions that they police by consent: British bobbies (so called after the founder of the Metropolitan force, Home Secretary Sir Robert Peel) can only function if they work with the support and consent of the community as a whole. The stereotype of the friendly British bobby was the hero of a popular television series, "Dixon of Dock Green," whose programmes used to begin with the greeting "Evenin', all." For politicians, nothing could be worse than a police state—something that happens in Soviet Russia, in Argentina, or in Hitler's Germany, but which on no account must come to pass in Britain. The culture, in fact, is highly anti-authoritarian, and the image, and indeed self-image, of the British police remains generally friendly and unmilitaristic.

But, in a fast-changing society, the police force is at the forefront of change. The number of police is growing—from 42,000 in

England and Wales in 1900 to 107,000 in 1977. In 1970, guns were issued to the police on 1,072 occasions (excluding those in Northern Ireland); in 1979, on 8,783 occasions. Many people in Britain are proud of the fact that there is no national police force under central government direction, yet the pressures are all working towards a central co-ordination of police work which on occasion seems to be bringing about what almost amounts to national control by the Home Secretary in London. Relations between black people and police in a number of inner-city areas reached crisis point in the anti-police riots in the early summer of 1981.

Since the first London bobbies appeared on the streets of London over 150 years ago, there have of course been great changes in the role of the police, and, in particular, a vast number of new duties have been added to their traditional role of maintaining the Queen's peace and catching criminals. Terrorism has added a new dimension to police work, and the vast rise in the number of foreign diplomats in Britain as new countries have come into being has brought new areas of diplomatic protection into the sphere of the police. Every year Parliament assigns new duties to the police, from checking up on aliens to dealing with stray dogs, from crowd control to investigating complex international frauds. The bicycle and the notebook are no longer the sole items of police equipment; a national police computer has come into being (and is a source of concern to the civil liberties lobby), and most policemen now carry a pocket radio that gives them access to the computer and enables them, for example, to check on the owners of cars by gaining immediate access to the licence records of every vehicle in the country. Few police now patrol on foot or even by bicycle. They tend to use cars, although more and more police forces are trying to get men back onto the beat as foot patrolmen, a popular move with the general public. Indeed, there has never been a time when the methods used by the police have been more controversial and their approach more discussed in the press and by the politicians.

But most British policemen are not armed. Although fires burned in the riots in 1981, and one person appears to have been run over and killed by a police vehicle in Liverpool, no rioter died and no policeman or member of the public fired a shot. *The Economist* magazine commented that the April 1981 riots in Brixton,

London, were typically British: the police and the rioters, said *The Economist,* were muddled and disorganized and there was a lack of real violence, whereas in a similar situation in Chicago or Detroit a couple of dozen people might have lost their lives. But the riots shook the complacency of the British. It was clear that, although surveys continued to show that public support of the police was still running at a high level—a poll by the London *Sunday Times* in 1980 showed policemen to have a higher standing than lawyers, businessmen, and politicians, though not such a high standing as doctors—there were important minorities in the inner-city communities with whom police relationships had reached breaking-point.

Until the 1960s police forces in Britain were locally run by a committee of councillors called the Watch Committee, under the local chief constable. In 1964 there was a major change with the passing of the Police Act; the number of separate police forces went down from 150 to 43. Training is co-ordinated nationally. Young recruits go through a thirteen-week training period in one of a number of regional police colleges, and the senior officers go to a national police college in Bramshill, Hampshire, several times during their careers. Now virtually no senior British policeman has not been through at least one course at Bramshill. The Home Secretary is responsible for overall policy and is nowadays looked on as the minister for the police. Except in London, where the Home Secretary is the person responsible, local police authorities are responsible for general police policy. But the police authorities are excluded by law from discussing "operational" matters, and the chief constables have been criticized for not being democratically accountable. Some police authorities with strong Labour Party representation have had bad relations with their chief constables; this has been the case in 1981 in both Liverpool and Manchester.

As senior British police officers see the problem, there are conflicting interests of efficiency and accountability. If the country is divided up into many different police forces, proper efficiency in combating crime will be difficult to attain, but too much police efficiency could be bought at an unacceptably high price—that of alienating the public and of destroying the basic principle of policing by consent on which the success of the whole system depends.

Chief Constable Oxford of Merseyside believes in tough policing unhampered by interference from the politicians. Chief Constable Alderson of Devon and Cornwall pioneered a new form of "community policing," encouraging his officers to get deeply involved in youth and sports activities and to visit old people's homes and the like. In the public controversy over policing methods in 1981, Alderson became the spokesman, in a strange way, both of the traditionalists who want the "bobby on the beat" back in British streets and of the liberals and civil libertarians who see the other school of thought as authoritarian and repressive. But many policemen tended to see Alderson's approach as fine for the mainly rural areas of Devon and Cornwall, but impossible or impractical in the tougher, multiracial centers of the older cities.

Race relations are undoubtedly a major crisis area for the British bobby. The British police remain almost entirely white, even though the black and brown population is approaching 4 per cent overall and can reach 40 or 50 per cent in some inner-city areas. Despite energetic attempts by the police to have a dialogue with the leaders of the black and immigrant communities, it is clear that the general pro-police attitudes of the mass of the British public are not shared by the black communities. The black people who came to Britain in the 1950s and '60s to work in public transport, the health service, and industries like the textile industries settled in the main in poor areas, parts of the older cities of Britain that the white population, newly prosperous, was leaving for the new towns and suburban housing estates. As economic decline has accelerated, these inner-city areas—parts of London such as Brixton and Notting Hill, parts of Manchester such as Moss Side, and much of the old port area of Liverpool—have become steadily more impoverished and dilapidated. There have been exceptions, in, for example, parts of London where the middle class have moved back in to buy up and gentrify the large crumbling Victorian houses found in these areas. The children of the immigrants have grown up with the same attitudes and expectations as their white compatriots, but in places where—as industry followed the whites into the prosperous suburbs—job prospects for those who remained were bad.

As one Liverpool policeman put it, "Society creates these dustbins and does nothing about it—we, the police, have to hold the lid on." There has been no Johnsonian "great society" in Britain, no major program to put government money into the inner-city areas. When riots erupted, first in Bristol in April 1980, and then, a year later, in a dozen cities around the country, many black leaders and some policemen were not surprised. Police in many areas were the only visible sign of authority, and often they seemed to act unfeelingly towards communities of the unemployed and the ethnically distinct. No one denied that there were some racist police. Extremists of the left hoped to find in the young blacks the revolutionary proletariat they had failed to find elsewhere, while extremists of the right tried to focus on crime—especially muggings—to tell a frightened white (and often elderly) community that black immigration was the culprit, and "wholesale repatriation" the answer. White liberals argued, as they have done for years, that British citizens born in Britain cannot be "repatriated" anywhere. What many commentators failed to point out was that although the riots were clearly racial in origin—the Brixton riots apparently began with a rumour that police had killed a black man, when in fact police had come to the aid of an injured black—many young whites joined the black youths who began to throw stones at police, to set buildings alight, and to loot houses and, above all, shops. Especially in Liverpool, the riots became a cry of rage, about the police but also about society in general, from white as well as black youths.

What will be done is not yet clear, but a change in the way complaints against the police are handled seems likely, and the police themselves are looking hard at their policing methods in multiracial inner-city areas. Research from Leicester University showed police recruits on occasion to be prejudiced against blacks, and moves to screen out prejudiced whites from police recruits, as well as more attempts to recruit blacks, seem inevitable. Meanwhile, though rioters have received heavy sentences, the police themselves are taking tough action against corrupt or "bent" officers. Hundreds of policemen have resigned voluntarily from Scotland Yard in the last few years, while others have been dismissed and in some cases put on trial.

So what is the image of the British bobby today? There is little doubt that the recent security lapses involving the Queen and Buckingham Palace have seriously dented the image of the police.

The resignation of the Queen's personal bodyguard because of the imminent disclosure of a homosexual affair with a male prostitute hardly helped to restore public confidence or the police force's own self-esteem. As it turned out, nothing disastrous occurred— but it could have; and the fact that someone could make his way undetected into the Queen's own bedroom despite the security precautions allegedly in operation was a serious blow to the standing of those in charge. For a time the Metropolitan Police became the butt of every comic and cartoonist, but despite this, the effects of these incidents are unlikely to be lasting. Security will doubtless be tightened and training improved—but if anything similar should happen again, then heads would have to roll, and they would have to be distinguished heads at that. So far the verdict on the police is "not proven," but the public expects matters to be now put right.

All that can be said is that, as Britain's police move to counter the influences that have made them more a subject of controversy in the past few years than ever before in their history, they have the huge advantage of a tradition and a public opinion that is solidly behind them.

THE ARMED FORCES
OF THE CROWN

In late 1981 the British defence establishment stood at 345,000 soldiers, sailors, and airmen and 265,000 civilians and had a budget of just over £12 billion. The change over the past forty years has been staggering. In 1946 there were nearly 2 million servicemen, and spending on defence made up nearly half of total public expenditures. In the late forties and early fifties military expenditure remained at around 30 per cent of all public spending, but in the sixties dropped sharply, reaching 10 per cent in 1974, now it is once again rising. For comparison, it is worth noting that British defence expenditure is, in proportional terms, 40 per

cent higher than the average for the European members of
NATO, though considerably less than in the United States. Since
Mrs. Thatcher's government came to power in 1979, only expenditure on the police has risen more than defence spending; proportionately, government spending on education and housing has actually gone down.

But the yo-yoing of public expenditure and the size of the
armed forces still tell only part of the story. At the end of World
War II, Europe was still recovering from devastation and disruption, and Britain, while still having the world-wide responsibilities
of Empire, was planning and discussing the future defence of
Europe. That was before the beginning of the cold war, the Communist takeover in Czechoslovakia, and the clear United States
commitment, in NATO, to the defence of Western Europe. In
1946 Britain's Empire included the Indian subcontinent and vast
slices of Africa; thirty years later, all this was gone. Until well
into the 1960s there were British bases "east of Suez": now, apart
from residual commitments in Belize, the Falkland Islands,
Brunei, and Hong Kong, Britain has withdrawn to the European theatre. Britain attempted, with French and Israeli support
but with the strong disapproval of President Eisenhower, to mount
a military operation against Egyptian President Gamal Abdel
Nasser in Suez in 1956; it ended in ignominious failure. Perhaps
no other event has better illustrated the decline of British world
power, and certainly, after a long post-war period of gentle but
peaceful and prosperous contraction, 1956, the year of Suez,
marked, for the British, a traumatic lesson in the limitations of
second-rank nationhood. Since then, the faltering search for a
European role has gone hand in hand with what some observers
consider to be an over-hasty retreat from a world role.

This enormously fast period of change, involving a spectacular
military victory in Europe which, paradoxically, left a nation too
exhausted to embark immediately on the creation of a new role
for itself, and a military disaster in Suez as well as the traumas
of decolonization, has been accompanied by other changing
influences on the armed forces of the Queen. The Royal Air
Force, which during the Second World War raced to build fighters
and to train airmen for dogfights with the Germans, now mans
missile bases and reconnaissance aircraft; the Royal Navy, which

was at one time thought likely to die out together with old-fashioned battleships, runs nuclear submarines which are at the heart of NATO's strategic doctrine of deterrence; while the Army, back from Empire, has a major domestic law-and-order role in Northern Ireland.

Here, as in so many spheres, the pace of change has been only less remarkable than the smoothness with which it has been carried out. There have been periods of great friction between the politicians and the armed forces, notably when a Tory defence minister in the late fifties, Duncan Sandys, implemented a policy of "big bangs and small forces" and sacked hundreds of officers, amalgamated regiments, and closed bases; and, more recently, when the Chief of the Naval Staff protested publicly against Mrs. Thatcher's cuts in naval expenditures made necessary by her decision to buy the Trident missile as the basis of Britain's ongoing independent nuclear deterrent. But there has been no military revolt and far less of the institutionalized defence leaks used in Washington to press the claims of the armed forces against their political masters' will. There has never (except briefly in 1968, when many Establishment figures were worried at the extreme unpopularity of the Wilson government and—as one observer put it—a few gin-besotted generals toyed with the idea) been any serious talk of a military coup in Britain. And no professional military man since the Duke of Wellington over a century and a half ago has been Prime Minister: there has been no British De Gaulle, Eisenhower, or Franco.

Much of the explanation for this remarkable, if not unique, relationship between military and civil power in Britain can be explained by the country's history and geography, by its island state, the relative absence of revolution and invasion. But it has been sustained through all the changes of Britain's recent history. Despite the precipitous decline of Britain, no general, no chief of staff, has seen it as his mission to intervene to save the fortunes of the nation, as happened in Spain with Franco and in France with De Gaulle—and as happens more regularly in Africa and Latin America. The military men have remained far from politics, indeed out of touch with politics, and as much of military science now involves technology and running a modern army or navy needs administrative skills more than anything else, the senior soldier, airman, or sailor is now more likely to be an unobtrusive commuter on the 8:12 from Weybridge to central London than a glamorous figure pacing the quarterdeck or dining in the officers' mess. The evidence, increasingly, is on education, with officers either being recruited as graduates or being sent to university for a period after recruitment. Much of the time is spent in planning, often in meetings with NATO colleagues. Yet glamour and tradition still coexist with change.

The colleges at Sandhurst (Army), Dartmouth (Navy), and Cranwell (Air Force) imbue their students with a sense of tradition and a strong *esprit de corps*. Fewer entrants are now public school boys than was recently the case. Though the services are now much more meritocratic than they used to be, there is still an upper-class preponderance among senior officers, and the élite Guards regiments—among the oldest regiments are the Scots Guards, the Grenadiers, and the Coldstream Guards—remain the preserve of the well-off. Their tasks include guarding the Queen and Buckingham Palace, and "trooping the colour" on the official birthday of their Colonel-in-Chief, Her Majesty herself. Guards officers play polo and shoot. They are the élite of the British Army and have probably been more sheltered from the cry for increased social mobility than any other group in the service of the state. But, as Anthony Sampson commented in 1962, in the Army "tribalism" has some justification that it cannot have elsewhere: *esprit de corps,* in a war, can be decisive. Army regiments, despite the changes and amalgamations since the last war, vary enormously in their outlook and have a symbolism and a pattern of traditional rivalries and attitudes that it is difficult or impossible for the outsider to fathom. The pageantry and drill remain important, however, and not only for tourists: for the average Briton, for whom the jargon of modern warfare is incomprehensible, the show, the uniforms, the mascots remain an important and cherished symbol of the nation and its history.

In spite of the lingering service and regimental rivalries, and the ancient traditions of the British armed forces, these forces are now perhaps more integrated, as a fighting force, than any other NATO force. The last bastion of inter-service rivalry in fighting for money in the Ministry of Defence fell in early 1981 when Mrs. Thatcher dispensed with the system of having separate ministers for the Army, Navy, and Air Force under the Secretary of State for Defence—they had often spent their time fighting each other rather than gearing up to fight the enemy. Now a single Ministry of Defence, with a team of ministers unconnected, in their formal responsibilities, with any of the three services, makes defence policy. Its boss, the Secretary of State, is a senior Cabinet minister. The service chiefs, the chiefs of staff, may seek direct access to the Prime Minister (and did in 1981 over the row about the Trident decision and the naval cuts), and they may be asked to sit in on Cabinet meetings to give specialist advice, but the Secretary of State, a civilian, is the unchallenged political head of the ministry. There is a defence select committee in the House of Commons, which reviews defence policy and financial estimates, but the British Defence Ministry does not have to contend (at least openly) with the pronouncements and lobbying of retired senior officers that are so much a part of the American political scene. Much British defence planning has traditionally been conducted in secret. A former Foreign Secretary, David Owen, has told how matters being discussed in conditions of top secrecy by the British Cabinet in the late 1970s were being discussed openly by Senate committees in the United States—while locked boxes and "for your eyes only" procedures were being used in London, readers of the Washington *Post* could find out about the same plans for nuclear warhead renewals simply by opening the newspaper!

If, in defence administration, traditional inter-service rivalries have now largely been ironed out, the basic organization of the British effort within NATO makes such divisions largely obsolete anyway. The key divisions are no longer Army, Navy, and Air Force, but nuclear strategic force, European theatre forces, and general-purpose forces. Britain is fully committed to NATO, and its forces are largely committed to the alliance. The Navy remains the largest NATO navy in Western Europe, and BAOR, the British Army of the Rhine, provides 55,000 men in Germany as part of NATO's forces. In the event of East–West hostilities up to 70 per cent of the British Army would be deployed in the central European theatre. There are British independent nuclear weapons —now the Polaris, but due to be replaced by the Trident in the 1990s—at the service of NATO, and Britain has agreed to take theatre nuclear weapons as part of the NATO modernization strategy agreed in 1979. Cruise and Pershing missiles will therefore be based in Britain, unless a Labour government returns to power and refuses to have them.

Should Britain retain an independent nuclear capacity or not? Only France and Britain retain, in Europe, an independent nuclear deterrent, and Britain's, whether the present Polaris or the future Trident, is in fact an American weapon purchased by and installed in Britain on favourable terms. In fact it is extremely difficult to envisage circumstances in which Britain, but not her NATO allies, might wish to use an independent nuclear deterrent, and the four Polaris nuclear submarines double as part of NATO strategic forces. But Mrs. Thatcher's government decided in 1980 to go for Trident, and thus prolong Britain's life as an independent nuclear-weapons state into the last years of the twentieth century. It was a controversial decision, as much on grounds of cost as for any other reason, since the government found it necessary to cut the Navy budget in order to finance Trident, but for the first time the Ministry of Defence provided information and background on why it had reached the decision. True, the "public debate" came *after* the decision, and the debate was over whether the policy was right rather than what it should consist of—but the debate over the future of Britain's independent nuclear deterrent in 1980 and 1981 was much livelier and better informed than ever before.

Mrs. Thatcher's decision to go for Trident was not, however, universally welcomed. The opposition parties opposed it, and it is clear that if the Thatcher government, or one very like it, is not returned at the next election, Britain's independent deterrent might well be cancelled. In addition, the Labour Party has resolved, at its annual conference, not to accept Cruise or Pershing missiles, and, indeed, to renounce nuclear weapons altogether. The unilateralist cause in Britain is backed by the Labour Party and considerable elements of the Liberal Party, and a number of public figures, such as Professor E. P. Thompson, a historian, have become ardent apostles of the unilateralist cause. Many British people who regard the prospect of a nuclear war as totally unacceptable have jumped to the wrong conclusion that a unilateral renunciation of nuclear weapons by Britain will of itself make a nuclear war less likely. Opponents of the unilateral cause argued that, because of its geographical position, Britain would, even if it renounced nuclear weapons, still be in the direct path of nuclear weapons used by the two superpowers, and would be affected by nuclear fall-out. The alternative course, such people argued, was for Britain to press strongly for multilateral disarmament, and for a gradually increasing measure of agreement among the superpowers to ban nuclear weapons. But Britain was no exception, within Europe, to the trend of increasing outright opposition to nuclear weapons. What former Prime Minister James Callaghan once called the "stop the world, I want to get off" approach represents a strong thread in present-day British politics. It is just conceivable that within a few years Britain could renounce nuclear weapons, evict American bases, and abandon the independent nuclear deterrent—this could happen if a hard-line Labour government came to power. But the Labour Party's difficulties in the early 1960s were principally caused because of disagreements over the nuclear defence issue. Some of us believed then, and believe now, that unilateral nuclear disarmament would be a totally retrograde and irresponsible step for Britain to take.

The Quality of Life

CITIZENS' RIGHTS
AND FREEDOMS

How free is the average Briton? How happy is the man in the street in Britain compared with his opposite numbers in France, Germany, or the United States? Foreigners, perhaps especially Americans, often find positive the very things that infuriate domestic observers: the class-consciousness, the slowness to adapt, and the preference for old ways can easily be seen as a refreshing absence of the rat race and keeping up with the Joneses. But one thing is certain. As mass poverty has been largely eliminated—and it is worth remembering that despite unemployment and recession *most* people in Britain have never known such a high standard of living—there is an increasing tendency, particularly among middle-class people, to focus less on quantitative improvements in life-styles and more on quality. This is, of course, the same trend that has been remarked upon in the United States, with Jimmy Carter and his labour union allies being seen as a partial reversion to "quantitative" politics in the Democratic Party after the "quality" people had taken over with McGovern in 1972: the third-party candidate in 1980, Anderson, was in some ways the epitome of the "Volvo and Brie" school of new "quality" politics.

Similar forces are at work in Britain and may in part lie behind the rise of the Social Democrats as a major challenge to the old class parties. But the rise of the pressure groups as major forces in politics in Britain is relatively recent. Oxfam, the third-world-development charity, began in wartime as a local famine-relief charity based in Oxford, but is now a massive national organization in receipt of regular donations from thousands and often the subject of fund-raising in schools and colleges; Amnesty International, though now an international movement campaigning on behalf of prisoners of conscience, began life in London with a campaign by a British barrister in 1961; and many other groups that play a major part in social policy lobbying in Britain, from Shelter, which campaigns for better housing, to Friends of the Earth, which campaigns for the environment, through such charities working for the old as Age Concern, are essentially products of the last twenty years in British life. Virtually every field, from pollution to third-world hunger, from gay rights to the future of nuclear power, attracts groups of activists who form into specialized organizations to campaign in the media and put pressure on governments. Formerly such people would have worked through the political parties; now the parties are often seen as "all the same"—at least when they get into office.

But for every housewife in the suburbs campaigning for old people, and for every group actively opposing government plans to extend nuclear power stations, there are new and strong forces ranged on the other side. Government has become bigger and bigger and more and more centralized. Life for many people, working in repetitive jobs and living in cheaply constructed local-council-owned "tower blocks" of apartments, or for the old, struggling on a state pension to pay ever-increasing heating bills, can be very far from the full life dreamed of by the Hampstead man of letters. The legal system may provide guarantees, but there is a backlog of cases coming to court. The National Health Service may guarantee free medical treatment according to need, but in some areas there is a waiting-list for treatment of up to five years for "routine" operations. And there are corners of British life, like the grossly overcrowded and inhumane prisons (which the Home Secretary has said are near to breaking-point) and the very low educational level of some sixteen-year-olds coming out of some comprehensive schools, that are simply scandalous. But what is the balance sheet?

It is not easy to generalize. For ordinary white Britons, to use former Prime Minister Harold Macmillan's famous phrase, there seems little doubt that they've "never had it so good." There are opportunities as never before, but the question is whether people are well placed to take advantage of these opportunities. Free education and a system of financial grants for higher education enable children from poor families to reach university. Indeed, there is clear evidence that a higher proportion of university students are from working-class families in Britain than is the case in either France or Germany. There are scholarships to enable bright students, whether in music or in the arts, to take advantage of specialist courses to develop their talents. But there is also a very high level of youth unemployment—a major problem, of course, throughout the Western world—and a general apathy, a feeling of hopelessness, seems to be feeding back into the school system. Young people seem to be beginning to wonder whether education is worth all the trouble when the dole queue is the only reward when it is all over. And for some minority groups, such as non-English-speaking immigrants from India or Pakistan, life in Britain can be very difficult and very lonely.

But for the British middle classes life continues to be extremely pleasant. They may no longer be able to afford servants, and the London middle-class housewife may not have as much to spend on clothes as her equivalent in Paris or Los Angeles, but within the society, life is good for the middle classes. They are favoured by the tax system and the mortgage system, and therefore can live in large, sometimes old but refurbished, houses. If they are working for a firm or in a professional partnership, the chances are that, even if their salary is low in comparison to that of their equivalents elsewhere in Europe or in North America, they will receive many extra benefits, such as a car and school fees for their children to go to public school. By middle age, with reasonable career success, the middle-class professional or executive may begin to think of buying a "second home"—a country cottage, possibly in Scotland or France, or a holiday chalet or villa in Spain or Portugal. And the level of cultural provision, particularly in London or one of the other major cities of the U.K., ensures that the concert-goer, theatre-goer, or frequenter of art galleries has plenty to do.

There are concerts, exhibitions, and evening classes (night school) in everything under the sun; the theatre is free from censorship, and most cultural activities are subsidized and not too expensive. The television provides cultural goodies as well as a diet of pop. But what about general freedom and political rights? Here again, the formal position is that any citizen can have recourse to law, and, despite the expenses incurred, there is a fund, provided by the state but administered by the Law Society, the solicitors' body, to help individuals involved with the law and the courts. Suing and recourse to litigation are, however, less common than in the United States, and suing for vast sums of money less of a sport in Britain than in the United States. As far as political freedoms are concerned, standing for office is possibly easier in Britain than elsewhere—provided the person concerned can get the backing of one of the major political parties. Very little political expenditure is actually allowed, and very little is incurred—certainly a minute sum compared with what someone running for Senator can expect to incur in the States.

In some fields there is no doubt that the British state is more secretive and less open than the American. The legislation affecting discrimination on grounds of sex or race has been strengthened in recent years, but there is nothing to compare with the civil rights legislation in the United States, and no way, for example, of using the courts to test the legality of school busing or to force local police forces to employ more black officers. And British civil liberties lobbyists look with envy at the Freedom of Information legislation in the States. In Britain, as we have seen, the civil service is protected from public gaze, and it is extremely difficult to find out what goes on behind Whitehall's closed doors. In the field of measures against terrorism—passed by the Labour government in 1976 mainly to deal with IRA terrorism—there is no doubt that police powers, for example, to detain a suspect without trial, have been greatly increased. On the other hand, one notorious law—the "sus" law, or law against "loitering with intent on suspicion," was repealed by Parliament in 1981 after it had been criticized by a House of Commons committee because it had been used disproportionately against black citizens.

It is only about a hundred years since women began to have rights in British society. The first Trades Union Congress, held in 1877, declared that a woman's place was in the home, and that it was the man's duty to protect and provide for her. The First World War brought a major change in attitudes, which was reflected in the victory of the suffragettes in gaining the vote for women in 1918. But the recognition that, despite their formal equality as citizens, women suffer from disadvantage and discrimination did not come until 1970 with the Equal Pay Act and 1975 with the Sex Discrimination Act. This act, which set up the Equal Opportunities Commission, makes it unlawful to treat a woman less favourably than a man would be treated in the same circumstances, and applies also to discrimination on grounds of marital status. Basically, it works through a complaints system: to the commission, in the case of allegedly discriminatory advertisements; to the industrial tribunals, in the case of alleged discrimination at work; and otherwise to the courts. There are exceptions, where sexual discrimination is lawful; they include private households, firms with fewer than five employees, and the Church. But like the 1970 Equal Pay Act, the Sex Discrimination Act can be circumvented. Equal pay still eludes women because employers tend to segregate women and pay them a low wage, in, for example, textile or clothing factories—since no men are employed there, no sex discrimination takes place. Both acts, particularly the Equal Pay Act, are extremely complicated and ways can be found to get round them.

But there is, despite the glaring inequalities that a growing women's movement constantly exposes, less sex inequality than there used to be, and probably less than there is in most countries. British men of the younger generation take their turn at housework and looking after children. There are more and more cases where the father stays at home to look after the children and the mother goes out to earn the living. Britain has a woman head of state and a woman head of government, but there remain many fields where women are very rarely to be found. Although a handful of women can now be found behind the wheel of London double-decker buses, the woman taxi-driver or printer is extremely rare, at least in London—these are both occupations where entry is tightly controlled and a measure of father-to-son recruitment goes on. More female students are being admitted to the medical schools, many of which have until very recently been observing quotas restricting the number of women students. There are only 19 women out of 635 Members of Parliament, and very few senior civil servants are female. The Anglican Church has resisted woman priests, although women ordained by the Episcopal Church in the United States have on occasion officiated at services in Church of England churches. Only 3.8 million women, compared with 9.3 million men, are members of trade unions, but more and more married women are going out to work—nearly half of married women are now economically active, a proportion that has been steadily increasing in recent years. As we noted in the chapter on unemployment, Britain's labour force has grown by over 2 million in the past twenty years; over a million women have joined the labour force in that time. We sometimes hear the absurd notion that if the number of married women in jobs had stayed the same since 1961, and the jobs they do were done by men, there would be practically no unemployment in Britain today. This illustrates the magnitude of the change in the life-style of ordinary British women in the last twenty years.

Freedoms in Britain do not depend solely on the courts, or on the House of Commons, or on the revelations of the press, but on a combination of all three. The courts may help to protect one freedom while restraining another (for example, by accepting the use of injunctions to prevent newspaper revelations about the effects of certain drugs), but the combination of legal action, the campaigning of determined Members of Parliament, and the activities of a vigilant press all combine to ensure that abuses of power do get aired in Britain.

THE PRESS
AND BROADCASTING

The politician's wife opens the front door of their house to find pressmen assembled on the doorstep. "Darling," she cries to her husband inside, "the men from the press and a gentleman from *The Times* want to talk to you." This—no doubt apocryphal—story illustrates one of the fundamental points about the British press: its division into the "quality" papers (headed by *The Times*) and the tabloids or the so-called populars. *The Times*—once called the notice-board of the Establishment—has a circulation of just over 300,000, and its rival *The Guardian* slightly more, while the other two qualities, the *Financial Times* and the *Daily Telegraph*, have

circulations of about 200,000 and 1.5 million respectively. Yet
the tabloids have huge readerships, the *Daily Mirror* averaging between 3.5 and 4 million daily sales, the *Sun* slightly ahead, and the
Daily Express about 2.25 million. More newspapers are sold per
person than in most other countries, but the difference between
papers is phenomenal.

The other important point about the British press is that although there are important regional papers (and in all there are
about 120 daily and Sunday newspapers published in the U.K.),
the London papers reach virtually the whole country. This is a
major difference from many other developed countries: in the
United States newspapers are essentially regional, although the
New York *Times* and the Washington *Post* have an importance
that goes far beyond New York or Washington, and *The Wall
Street Journal* and *The Christian Science Monitor* do have national distribution, while in some European countries, such as
Italy, different major centres have their own newspaper (*La
Stampa* in Turin, *Corriere della Sera* in Milan). In Britain *The
Times* and the other London dailies and Sundays are also called
the "national" press. The columnists of the major dailies are
themselves national figures: local newspapers tend to be owned by
chains, which maintain, for example, one staff handling parliamentary affairs or international affairs from London, but there is
no equivalent of the nationwide syndicated columns of the United
States. Advertising is also, therefore, often conceived and planned
on a national basis.

But, as the politician's wife pointed out, there really is a world
of difference between the qualities and the mass-circulation
papers. For a start, the qualities are fighting to hold their market,
while some of the populars, particularly those specializing in the
seamier side of life, are pushing their circulations upwards. *The
Times* has undergone a number of changes in recent years: the
front page, which used to carry the personal advertisements, now
carries news, and writers on *The Times* (who used to be described
simply as "our correspondent," "our own correspondent," or "our
special correspondent") now actually have names. There have
been important gestures to the advertising market, with "women's
pages" and supplements on tourism, as well as conscious attempts
to win new, young readers. *The Times,* once known as the "Thun-

derer," was founded in 1785 and is part of the Establishment: the Prime Minister, the Archbishop of Canterbury, and the editor of *The Times* have traditionally been opinion leaders in the country. *The Times* has seen its role as the responsible one of supporting whatever government is in power, but it is in no sense an official paper. Indeed, there were rumours in 1981 that *The Times* would break with tradition, oppose Mrs. Thatcher's government, and advise its readers to vote for the newly founded Social Democratic Party.

The Times's gestures to modernity have even included, in recent years, some sensational journalism—including exposures, through the use of tape-recorders, of corrupt Scotland Yard detectives—but it has also tried to maintain its reputation as a journal of record. This means that official speeches are reported in full, government changes are given in detail (always, for some reason, with the ages of newly appointed ministers and junior ministers), and cases in the law courts are reported verbatim. The correspondence columns are a unique feature of *The Times:* views are aired by all and sundry, governments are criticized or backed up, and, in addition, there is always room for the merely eccentric. For a long time letters appeared from readers with ingenious suggestions after one reader had asked how they coped with the problem, which he found insoluble, of turning the pages of his book while reading in the bath—without, of course, getting the pages wet. Another important function of *The Times* is to announce births, marriages, engagements, and deaths. Early in January each year a reader publishes an analysis of the most popular names appearing in the births columns, an interesting pointer to the fashions of the middle and upper classes. Again, the class differences are highly noteworthy. While *Times* readers' children were being called Matthew, James, and Edward, or Sophy, Amy, and Charlotte, the masses were calling their children Gary or Darren, Dawn or Cheryl. *The Times* once had an advertising campaign based on the unashamedly snobbish slogan "Top people read *The Times*" but some think it might be more accurate to say that "Top people use *The Times*."

The Times has a weekend stable-mate, *The Sunday Times,* founded in 1822 as an independent paper but now owned by the same company. The immediate past editor of *The Times,* Harold

Evans, was for many years editor of *The Sunday Times,* which he transformed from being a rather sleepy and stuffy journal for the somnolent middle-aged at weekends into a lively, radical newspaper with a line in in-depth investigations of "the facts behind the news." *The Sunday Times* is still the nearest thing we have in Britain to a campaigning newspaper; it has campaigned fearlessly on behalf of the child victims of the drug thalidomide and has exposed corruption and double-dealing. Its political reporting is of a high order. Evans had begun the task of transforming *The Times:* his changes included many more "human" stories—for example, more interviews with ordinary voters and reports from the local constituencies—but he was clever enough to make it a more lively and up-to-date newspaper without endangering the "journal of record" tradition.

The Guardian is *The Times*'s nearest rival; indeed, when *The Times* lost circulation because of an eleven-month stoppage in 1979–80, *The Guardian* picked some of it up, and *The Times* has yet to win it all back. *The Guardian* is also a paper with a fine old tradition; founded in Manchester in 1821 as the voice of Manchesterian Liberalism, it moved to London and changed its name from *Manchester Guardian* to *Guardian* in the 1960s. Now, although some of the advertisements—particularly for houses and for theatres and concerts—still have a bias towards Manchester and the North-West of England, the paper is to all intents and purposes a London-based national newspaper. Its political standpoint, too, has changed: generally speaking, it has supported Labour in recent years, and many of its journalists, as individuals, are Labour supporters, but it, like *The Times,* is showing signs of supporting the Social Democrats. Its women's page provides a forum for feminist ideas, often of an advanced type. The term *"Guardian* woman" has been coined by male chauvinist Conservatives as a term of abuse, meaning a progressive, opinionated woman.

Both *The Times* and *The Guardian* devote several pages to foreign news—*The Guardian* specializing in features on the Third World, *The Times* being rather more keen on European coverage. But *The Financial Times,* now published simultaneously in London and Frankfurt, despite its relatively low circulation, is the paper that business people and investors turn to when they want information about international affairs: it maintains more foreign correspondents abroad than any European newspaper (except perhaps the French daily *Le Monde*). The *FT*, as it is commonly known, also goes in for informed political comment. Its policies, predictably, are Conservative, and some of its best-known commentators, such as the economics writer Samuel Brittan, are close to the monetarist and free-market thinking of Mrs. Thatcher and her colleagues. *The Financial Times* is rather like the weekly journal *The Economist* in that it has built its success in recent years on a steady reputation for providing good international information and comment of the type that international business people need. And, like *The Economist, The Financial Times* has been highly successful in recent years in pushing up its circulation, especially abroad—showing that English has now become the international language of business and commerce.

Another factor that singles out Britain's press is the absence of national newsmagazines, like *Time* and *Newsweek* in the States, *L'Express* or *Le Point* in France, and *Der Spiegel* or *Stern* in West Germany. No such papers exist in Britain, and an attempt by the Anglo-French financier Sir James Goldsmith (who, incidentally, is the owner of *L'Express* in Paris) in the last few years to set up a glossy weekly, *Now!*, ended in financial failure. Why do Britons not go for the weekly newsmagazine format? There are various possible explanations—and, it must be said, there were many who believed, long before Sir James's venture got under way, that there was no place in British journalism for a magazine of the *Now!* type. Possibly the very high level of newspaper readership in Britain (where four out of five adults read a daily newspaper) and the special role of the Sunday papers in providing news and comment covering the previous week make a weekly digest unnecessary. But colour magazines attached to newspapers, which started as companions to the quality Sundays, are now being tried out by other newspapers, and the colour supplement does now seem to have a future in the more popular newspapers as well as the "qualities."

There are, of course, weekly newspapers of a more specialist and slightly old-fashioned type, devoted partly to politics, like the Socialist *New Statesman* and Conservative *Spectator*. They have relatively low circulations these days (about 30,000 and 14,000 respectively) but come from an old and venerable tradition and are required reading for those who want to keep up with what is happening in politics. *New Society,* founded only in the sixties, is proving successful in providing analysis of a more sociological type as well as facts rather than opinion. But these élite political weeklies have tiny circulations compared with mass weeklies such as *Woman, Woman's Own,* and—an eloquent commentary on where the British masses' priorities lie—the best-selling *Angler's Weekly.* Traditionally there have been other weekly papers specializing in the private lives of the stars, fortune-telling, and intimate revelations (papers with names like *Tit-Bits* and *Reveille*), but as the mass-circulation daily papers have provided more of their traditional diet they have tended to do less well. While the long-established *Punch* remains funny and enjoyable, there is not much bite in it nowadays.

No description of the British press could be complete without a mention of the satirical *Private Eye,* founded in the early sixties and still rather crudely printed and produced. *Private Eye* is not political—and certainly not of the left—but rather teases and lampoons all those whom it thinks abuse power, are too pompous, or, to use a *Private Eye* term, are simply "ludicrous." *Private Eye* has been involved in some sensational libel actions, but it has also had some fantastic successes: it was, for example, the first paper to talk about rumours of the former Liberal Party leader Jeremy Thorpe's involvement with the male model Norman Scott. It has pointed fun mercilessly at governments, whether Labour or Conservative, and its spoof letters by the wife of Harold Wilson or the husband of Mrs. Thatcher have attracted a wide readership. Denis Thatcher's letters to his erstwhile golfing companion "Bill" recounting his life as husband of the "Boss" are often hilarious; in these totally fictitious letters (which Mrs. Thatcher herself has said bear no resemblance to the real Denis Thatcher's approach or attitudes), Denis is painted as an unsophisticated suburban reactionary with a desire "to tell these Arab Johnnies where to get off" (when an Arab leader, for example, is on an official visit, it is alleged, all whisky is locked away on Mrs. Thatcher's orders to prevent Denis's tongue becoming dangerously loosened).

The other great achievement of *Private Eye* has been to add words and phrases to the British political vocabulary. Once, when Harold Wilson was in power, *The Guardian* misspelled his name as "Wislon"; *Private Eye* has made sure the name, with its delightful suggestion of twists and turns, has stuck. When George Brown was Foreign Secretary and appeared in public in a fairly merry state, the Foreign Office spokesman was quoted as saying that "the Foreign Secretary was emotional and overtired"—a euphemism that has entered *Private Eye*-ese as a non-libellous way of saying who was drunk when. If a couple are enjoying carnal relations, *Private Eye* reports them as "sharing a mutual interest in Ugandan affairs," which derives from a newspaper report some years ago of a diplomatic party in which a lady journalist was reported to be having a "lively discussion with a Ugandan diplomat." The discussion having, allegedly, been much more than merely political, *Private Eye* found a new code-word. *Private Eye* has, it should be said, also undoubtedly made some serious blunders—attacking people on the basis of false information—but its total irreverence has, on balance, added a sparkle to the British press.

While political reporting, and indeed the business news which affects the behaviour of investors and on which the stock market depends, appears in a relatively small world of up-market "quality" newspapers and weeklies, it is important to remember that the vast majority of British newspaper readers read papers of a quite different type. The mass-circulation papers aim unashamedly at the ordinary man (and woman) in the street and have a directness and a simple approach that are very different from the gentlemanly world of *The Times*. Sex, sensation, and news about pop stars and television newsreaders are the staple diet of *The Sun,* a newspaper that emerged out of the only Labour newspaper in the country, the now-defunct *Daily Herald,* transformed into a tabloid. Its "page 3 girls" appear topless, a development which would have been unthinkable only ten years ago. The *Daily Mirror* aims at much the same market, but tries to introduce more serious material and political comment. Its editorial columns tend to be addressed direct to Prime Ministers and to carry headlines like "Come off it, Maggie!" (*The Sun*'s headline today, as I write, is DENTIST DRUGGED GIRL FOR SEX.) But on occasion the *Mirror* goes in for detailed, well-researched articles analyzing current trends in, for example, the National Health Service or provision for the old. The *Mirror* has traditionally supported the Labour Party, but there is undoubtedly a bias towards the Conservative Party in the British press. But whether, as the left says, the press is totally opposed to the Labour Party is another matter.

Part of the left's attack on the press is based on the fact that the press "barons"—the major proprietors of the newspapers and newspaper chains—have often been larger-than-life, swashbuckling characters. The Beaverbrook family, whose heirs still have an interest in the *Express* group, and the Northcliffe family, who control the *Daily Mail,* have left their mark on the British press, and often used their papers for political campaigning of a frankly right-wing kind. Now the owners of the press, like the Australian Rupert Murdoch, who controls *The Times* and *The Sunday Times,* or Lord Matthews, whose firm Trafalgar House owns the *Daily Express,* tend to be tough businessmen rather than political crusaders. As recently as 1968 Cecil King, of the *Daily Mirror,* tried to use the paper to bring down the Wilson government and substitute a "businessman's coalition," and there were rumours that he was trying to encourage a military coup. Nowadays the press barons, in fact, seem more interested in balance sheets and circulation figures than in the future of the Empire (the obsession of the late Lord Beaverbrook). Indeed, the press was specifically acquitted in 1977 by the Royal Commission on the Press of anti-Labour bias. But perhaps there is something in the argument that the press in Britain has tended to become more provincial and more trivial in recent years. Since accountants rather than crusaders now hold sway, it is perhaps inevitable that the public should be getting what it wants—or what journalists and editors think it wants.

"Giving the public what they want" was, in fact, the theme of a major argument in the Conservative Party in the fifties, when the party was deeply divided over whether or not commercial television should be introduced in the country. Until then, in all sound or television broadcasting, the British Broadcasting Corporation had had a monopoly. Those who wanted to give the public what they wanted—the business lobby in the party, which correctly foresaw that huge profits were to be there for the grabbing—were opposed by the traditional, paternalist wing of the party, which thought the tone of the BBC was uplifting and that it maintained standards of culture and decorum—not to mention spoken English.

The businessmen won, and commercial television was established in 1955, to be followed by commercial radio in the 1970s. Now the "commercial" radio and television stations and the BBC national, regional, and local radio and television stations are to all intents and purposes rivals, seeking the same audiences with more or less the same techniques—different only in one major respect: while the BBC is financed by a licence (at present costing £46 for a colour TV set) the independent companies are financed by advertising revenues.

Thus the popular radio stations of the BBC and private companies offer the same diet of pop music and disc jockeys; independent television companies fight the BBC's viewing figures with identikit serials, quiz shows, and situation comedies and try to put on livelier news presenters than the rival channels. Even in current affairs there is acute competition. The BBC's Monday night programme "Panorama" is probably the leader in the field, but the independent companies have developed highly successful and lively political and current affairs programmes such as Granada Television's "T.V. Eye" or the London Weekend Television Sunday lunchtime programme "Weekend World." But accusations of political bias, so frequently made against the British press, are rarely made against the television companies, which have maintained high standards of objectivity. The tradition of balance so important to the BBC as public service broadcasting in its monopoly days seems to have been inherited by the commercial television stations as well. Indeed, there is some evidence that the public takes little notice of newspaper editorials anyway and gets much of its politics from television.

It used to be said that in the thirties, when BBC radio had an unchallenged place in the nation, announcers were required to don tuxedos before entering the studio, and books of acceptable pronunciation and phraseology were kept to ensure that high standards of taste and decorum were maintained. Indeed, the Queen's English is, as we shall see, often regarded as the hallmark of what is linguistically acceptable in polite society, but the BBC became the standard-setter in the thirties and subsequently. If the BBC decided to say "*con*troversy" rather than "con*tro*versy," then only "*con*troversy" was acceptable. Now, however, notions of the BBC's role in the maintenance of good English have changed. The

BBC has its English language expert, Dr. Robert Burchfield, but he sees it as the BBC's role to reflect current English in all its bewildering variety, as an evolving organism—not as something whose features can be artificially preserved by maintaining a single standard. This is a major and significant change, mirroring the change in the BBC from being some sort of guardian of the nation's cultural standards to just another provider of entertainment to the public.

But if the good old days of BBC paternalism seem to have gone for ever, there are at least some corners of the corporation where standards are still maintained in the old way. One is Radio 3—a national station catering for the "highbrow" audience, broadcasting music and concerts all day and either music or serious plays and talks at night—which opens at seven in the morning and closes at eleven at night. Radio 3's audience is not large—a few hundred thousand, compared with the millions who listen to Radios 1 (pop), 2 (light music), or 4 (news and talk)—but it is a devoted audience which regards its programmes with all the seriousness of the teenagers who tune obsessively to Radio 1. Not only is there a steady stream of classical music, but regular programmes feature, for example, early or very modern music.

The other area of traditional BBC standards is the BBC World Service. Financed by the Foreign Office (and not, like all the domestic services, by licence revenue), the World Service programmes, like the BBC's short-wave broadcasts in nearly forty foreign languages, are beamed from Bush House in central London to listeners abroad. But, because the medium-wave transmitter to Europe can be picked up in most of the U.K. (though not for long—the new transmitter that the BBC is planning will be beamed away from Britain so listeners at home cannot pick it up), there are an increasing number of British people who find the Overseas or World Service broadcasts much better in terms of international news and comment than the material actually put out for the home audience. For a start, the World Service news is actually world news, whereas the home news tends to be more provincial and inward-looking. There are longish commentaries on world affairs on the World Service that the programme organizers at home would presumably find too boring for their listeners. And the announcers on the World Service speak old-fashioned BBC English, with no concession to regional or pseudo-proletarian forms of speech at all.

Most international observers find the standard of drama and music on the BBC to be very high indeed. The BBC has an important role as a patron of the arts and has a number of orchestras—including four symphony orchestras—of its own, while its patronage of young writers and playwrights, particularly in the regions, is crucially important. "Play for Today" each week on BBC 1 is important; frequently drama productions on the BBC are of a very high artistic standard and present ideas or challenge accepted notions in a way that the overtly political programmes find difficult to do. And this is despite the pressure of the anti-pornography and "clean up television" campaigners mentioned earlier.

The extraordinary thing about the BBC is its relationship with the government. It is not state-owned, but depends on Parliament to raise its revenue through the annual licence fee. The government advises the Queen on whom to appoint as chairman and governors of the BBC. The traditional doctrine is that the BBC is not a state-controlled organization, but is accountable to the people through Parliament; its charter requires it to maintain balance in its presentation of programmes. Yet it is generally accepted that, during the period when the BBC is negotiating with the government to fix the level of the licence fee, it is very careful to avoid upsetting ministers by needling criticism or hostile reporting. Again, a confused and unclear situation that seems to work out very well in practice.

THE ARTS AND SPORT— THE BRITISH AT LEISURE

There have been few great British composers: no Bach, Beethoven, or Mozart such as the German-speaking world has produced, and even Handel, the composer of the *Messiah,* was only a naturalized Briton. Of course, there have been distinguished British composers, from the early Tudor composers of English church music, such as Byrd and Tallis, through Orlando Gibbons and Purcell, to Elgar, Walton, and Benjamin Britten. It is a distinguished, if not outstanding, record. But today the extraordinary thing is that Britain is a nation of music-makers and concert-goers. Though statistical comparisons are impossible, there seems to be no doubt that—taking, for instance, the number of different concerts being put on in London on any one day—there is much more public music in London each day than in almost any other European capital. Major musical festivals are held each year in places such as Edinburgh and Bath.

And if London is one of the musical capitals of the world, exactly the same can be said of the theatre. There are 50 theatres in London and over 250 in professional use in the country as a whole. Touring companies take plays to distant parts of the country or try out productions before they are launched in London's West End. There is a National Theatre with three different theatres in its complex on the South Bank of the River Thames, and the Royal Shakespeare performs not only in Stratford-on-Avon but also in its Aldwych Theatre in London. Many of the most distinguished actors in the modern world—from Laurence Olivier to Richard Burton, not forgetting film stars from Charlie Chaplin to Peter Sellers—were British-born, even if much of their careers were actually carried out in the United States. And recently British pop singers have enjoyed a phenomenal success, though none greater than the Beatles' world-wide success in the sixties.

Statistics about how the British spend their leisure time tell much the same story. Libraries in the U.K. have a total stock of over 132 million books; as for book publishing, 24,893 book titles were issued in 1961, but 41,940 in 1979, a rise of 68 per cent. Attendance at art galleries is also rising, with all the major art galleries and museums registering large increases in visitors throughout the seventies. Visits to "stately homes" also increased. Some of these figures may reflect an increase in the number of tourists visiting Britain—and their numbers have certainly risen—but even so, the picture that emerges is of a people increasingly taking their leisure time seriously. Outdoor activities have all become much more popular in recent years. Water sports such as sailing and yachting are ever more popular, and membership of the Royal Society for the Protection of Birds has mushroomed from 66,000 in 1970 to 320,000 in 1979.

Compared with some other countries, the picture is of a serious people, much given to reading, enjoying good music (whether classical or popular), and the theatre, and increasingly looking to nature for relaxation and recreation. But why should Britain, with considerable economic, social, and political difficulties at the present time, produce such a high level of public and private music, and such high-quality drama? It is, of course, also noteworthy that the great interest in wild life and the environment comes when the British Isles have never been so crowded and it has never been so difficult to get away from it all into the wilds. Perhaps escapism has something to do with it—perhaps personal fulfilment is sought by individuals when collectively the national identity seems to offer little that is satisfying to ordinary people.

Although there are some professionals—the artists, the writers, the composers, and their exponents and interpreters—there is also a great deal of amateur music-making and amateur dramatics. Schools will regularly perform a full-length play, and there are amateur dramatic groups all over the country. Besides school and church choirs, a host of local choral societies exists to put on several performances a year of the great oratorios. Handel's *Messiah* is a great and traditional favourite throughout the land. The local amateur choir will provide the chorus, but frequently the soloists will be professionals doing the job for a fee and moving around all over the country during the *"Messiah* season." As for favourites in the drama field, offerings such as *Major Barbara* or *The Importance of Being Earnest* or a sprightly Agatha Christie or Noël Coward are the very stuff of which British amateur dramatics are made.

At national level the arts are subsidized: in addition to indirect support from the patronage of the BBC and the other television companies, orchestras, theatre companies, ballet, and even local arts centres receive government subsidies. These government grants are administered through the Arts Council, which was set up in 1946 and is the main channel of official support to the arts. Its total budget in 1980–81 amounted to £70 million, with about a quarter going as direct support to national companies such as the English National Opera, the National Theatre, the Royal Shakespeare Company, and the Royal Ballet. In addition, there are scholarship and bursary schemes to support young writers, artists, and film-makers, among others, and the council promotes art exhibitions and provincial tours by opera, dance, and drama companies. Through regional arts associations the Arts Council tries to ensure a fair division of funds across the nation.

Whether the Arts Council's grants and bursaries actually aid the creation of art is hotly contested. There are frequent reports in the press about alleged misuse of Arts Council funds—the man whose artistic creation is a pile of bricks and stones will be certain to get the full treatment in the pages of *The Sun* or the *Daily Express* and it is quite common to hear disgruntled authors or would-be authors accusing the Arts Council of subsidizing the wrong people. But one thing is certain: there are plenty of people writing in Britain.

The sheer professionalism of the British theatre—and this would include the drama departments of the television companies—never ceases to amaze. The standard of acting is high, and the sets and costumes are unparalleled for their splendour and excellence. Here again, the skill and the technical quality seem to disguise the fact that, as far as one can tell, little original creation is actually happening at the present time. It is almost as though this were an age that specializes in interpreting what past figures have said rather than in saying anything itself. Is it perhaps an age which fears to speak out, which is afraid of commitment to any clear set of values? Obviously the flowering of the musical and dramatic arts is connected with Britain's general political and social predicament, but only one tentative conclusion is possible: in the theatre and in drama generally, the British (to use the French terms) are dazzlingly successful at *la forme,* but much less accomplished where *le fond* is concerned.

Compared with the flourishing world of artistic and leisure pursuits in general, attendance at spectator sports has fallen off in recent years. Soccer is far and away the most popular spectator sport, yet the number attending league matches has fallen from 28 million in 1961–62 to 24.5 million in 1978–79. Various reasons have been given, including the good coverage of football on television, the widespread publicity given to soccer hooliganism, and the allegedly uncomfortable accommodation available at stadiums for the spectators. Nevertheless, important football matches, such as the Cup Final between the two finalists from all the competing teams, held at Wembley Stadium in London each year at the end of the football season, are always well attended, not only by the public but also by members of the Royal Family and political leaders. Soccer—or association football as it is called officially, to differentiate it from Rugby football—remains the most popular sport, followed by cricket and Rugby.

Britain gave football to the world: the very name and most of the vocabulary of the sport are British and have been taken up enthusiastically wherever football itself has been taken up (even if they do spell football *fútbol* in South America). Sociologists of the game have divided its history into three distinct phases. The first, from the fourteenth century until well into the nineteenth, saw football as what one writer, Eric Dunning, has called "a relatively simple, wild and unruly folk game played according to unwritten, customary rules." From 1750 until 1840, according to Dunning, the game evolved, mainly because it was taken up by the public schools, into a rather more organized sport; while from 1840 to about 1860 it developed formal rules. Subsequently it became organized and professionals came into existence as men engaged full-time in the sport. During this period there was intense competition between those who saw football as a leisure pursuit for gentlemen and those who wanted to develop it as a mass spectator sport. For Dunning, the rise of professional football teams with enormous numbers of supporters was a direct result of the urbanization and industrialization of the nineteenth century. As he puts it in his book *The Sociology of Sport:* "Gradually, . . . the ceremonial battles of the local football team came to form a major outlet for the need for leisure-time excitement and to provide a partial focus for the regular and ritualised expression of identity with the community, thus helping to counter alienation and anomie."

The development of "Rugby" football as a distinct sport—a sport which, except in South Wales, has never become a mass spectator sport like soccer—is also deeply bound up with English social history. Rugby was, of course, developed at Rugby, the public school, as simply one form of traditional English football, codified and played in that way at that school. But today Rugby is very much the middle- and upper-class sport in England, a game played at public schools but not, normally, at state comprehensive schools. Soccer, meanwhile, is the working-class sport, steeped in traditional working-class culture and values, and with genuine mass appeal throughout the country. But the fall-off in attendance at soccer matches may show that the old working-class

football culture is on the wane, as urbanization and industrialization are followed in their turn by de-industrialization and
suburbanization. Football fever seems now to be a disease more
appropriate to countries like Brazil. In Britain, meanwhile, the
ugly face of soccer hooliganism has appeared.

Soccer hooliganism is, unfortunately, like strikes and inner-city
riots, very much part of the unacceptable face of modern Britain.
Invasions of football pitches are only part of the story—fans have
smashed trains and buses, attacked innocent passers-by in the city
(or countryside) of the opposing team, and indulged in mini-riots
with the fans of the other side. It has, literally, been impossible to
move about in central London after important football matches in
recent years, as bus and underground staff have gone home rather
than risk contact with rampaging fans. English fans have recently
disgraced themselves in continental cities, Turin and Paris, for example, and the government has given high priority to trying to
understand the phenomenon and bring it under control. No one
can agree on any simple explanation. It seems to be the case, however, that the traditional working-class, respectable, middle-aged
football fan is being replaced by a more contemporary creature:
the rootless youth seeking, not loss of himself in the greater whole
as he yells support for "his" team, but thrills, spills, excitement,
and a fight with the police. Football has certainly changed and
become more of a popular entertainment than the sociological phenomenon Dunning described.

Cricket, on the other hand, never had the proletarian associations of traditional football. Cricket was always played by gentlemen or amateurs: professionals are a relatively recent innovation. Cricket teams were, and are, organized into county teams,
there being one major league and one minor league; and international, or "test," matches are held each season with one of the
other major cricketing nations: Australia, New Zealand, India,
Pakistan, the West Indies, and—until its departure from the Commonwealth in 1961—South Africa. Huge crowds were never attracted to cricket matches, which have always been spread over
several days, including working days, unlike football matches,
which have traditionally taken place on Saturday afternoons.

But cricket is changing fast, too. The arrival of immigrants from
Jamaica and Trinidad and other West Indian countries where

cricket is a popular sport has introduced a new and lively dimension to the hitherto restrained and gentlemanly behaviour of the English cricket crowds as bells and rattles are used and excited cries and howls of delight echo round the pitch when good moves are made. Cricket entrepreneurs, like Australia's Kerry Packer, have introduced one-day matches and tried to speed up and enliven the proceedings in order to attract larger crowds. In 1981 England beat Australia for the first time for years, at least two English players became popular heroes, and it seemed as though cricket was set to enjoy a new lease on life as a popular sport with the British public.

Are the British a sporting nation? Apart from inventing most sports and exporting them to the colonies—tennis is a very old Norman game, while golf has its origins in the stony and rough ground of upland Scotland—the British remain very active in most international sports, including equestrian events (where the Royal Family, especially Princess Anne and her husband, Captain Mark Phillips, give a national lead) and athletics (where Sebastian Coe is the current hero). Government sponsorship is patchy and works by providing assistance through the Sports Council. In 1980–81, grants for sports development, coaching, and administration to the various sports totalled £24.7 million; but private sponsorship for sport is much more plentiful than it is for the arts, with £30 million being made available for sports events by private sources in 1979, compared with between £4 and £5 million for the arts. The provision of sports fields and swimming pools is patchy, too, and is left to local authorities; there seems to be no doubt that facilities are less plentiful than, for example, in the United States. What is certainly true is that there is no national network of facilities to encourage and bring on the young sportsman or sportswoman. Those who rise through the system by their own determination are certainly helped, but without initial personal determination, whatever the talent, it is hard for sports stars to rise in modern Britain. There is certainly nothing approaching the highly organized preparation and selection of Olympics participants that seem to be such a feature of the Eastern European countries.

What of our typical modern Briton? He enjoys pop music but is not a fan of classical music; nevertheless, he does occasionally go to brass band concerts. At school he was taken in a party on several occasions to see live performances of Shakespeare plays, and very occasionally has joined a group from a local youth club to go by coach to London to see a live play. He follows football fairly actively, but rarely sees a live football match. Though he lives in the East of England, he has followed some of his old school friends (who were originally from the East End of London) in developing a strong loyalty for the First Division London football club Arsenal. He would certainly try to get tickets for the Cup Final next May if Arsenal got through to the final. He enjoys watching television and has taken up model-making lately, but his grandfather used to breed rabbits and pigeons and—if ever he gets a place of his own—he would like to give that a try. He will also probably enjoy a weekly flutter on the football pools—a weekly bet on goals scored in the big-league matches—and maybe on the odd horse- or dog-race.

As George Orwell wrote, the English in their leisure pursuits are essentially *private* rather than social. It is this *privateness* that we once again find to be all-pervasive in British life.

ENGLISH AS SHE IS SPOKEN

Standard English, or BBC English, or the Queen's English, is not spoken by most of the British population. Though there are few dialects as such—one major exception being Lowland Scots, the language of the poet Robert Burns, which still maintains major differences in vocabulary and construction from standard English —the English language throughout Britain is pronounced in a wide variety of different ways. Regional accents instantly identify a speaker, and vary still, despite radio, television, and mass communications, within a few miles. The accent of rural Kent, never more than seventy miles from London, is different from the "cockney" accent of the London East Ender, and different again

from the Hertfordshire or Bedfordshire accent spoken only twenty
or thirty miles to the north.

As fans of Professor Higgins know, accent in Britain, and particularly in England, is an important indicator of social class.
George Bernard Shaw said that in England you can tell a man's
social origins from his speech the moment he opens his mouth
rather than from his clothes or his bearing, and the same remains
broadly true today. But social attitudes to speech, as in so much
else, have changed. As we have seen, the BBC, generally speaking,
no longer seeks to impose a pure BBC or "Oxford" accent on the
population. It has to some extent legitimized the use of regional
accents in news and other broadcasts, while recent political leaders, from the former Conservative leader Edward Heath with his
clear Kentish vowels to Harold Wilson with his homely Yorkshire
ones, have had obvious regional accents. There is even a tendency
among some young people from the public schools to try to cast
off the accents their parents have paid so much for them to acquire, and to try to speak instead a form of fashionable proletarian
English. Disc jockeys and pop stars, on the other hand, go in for a
form of "mid-Atlantic" English—American in some if not all of its
pronunciation and some of its specialist vocabulary. Accent remains important in Britain, though the possession of a monolithic
pronunciation is no longer the aid to success in public life that it
once was.

Nowadays English, the language, originally, of a few thousand
square miles in the British Isles, is a world language—the language
of one of the major superpowers; the second language of the
educated and the international business classes in most of the
Western world; and, increasingly, supplanting French as the language of diplomacy. In a remarkable way, the language that the
early colonists took to the New World, having acquired a new
vigour and adaptability, is now returning to its place of origin
to enrich the original tongue. As Professor Albert Baugh, the
great American historian of the English language, has remarked:
"Those who are familiar with the pronounced dialectal differences
that mark the popular speech of different parts of England will
know that there is nothing comparable to these differences in the
United States." Baugh quotes an early English traveller in the
United States, Isaac Candler: "As far as pronunciation is con-

cerned, the mass of the people speak better English than the mass of the people in England. . . . We hear nothing so bad in America as the Suffolk whine, the Yorkshire clipping, or the Newcastle guttural."

In other words, the English taken to the United States developed a standard form that, for historical reasons, is still absent from Britain. In addition, English in America absorbed concepts and vocabulary from successive waves of immigrants from other linguistic traditions, who themselves absorbed and, simultaneously, influenced the English language. English in the United States also had to evolve to take account of new needs imposed on the language as the New World was opened up and colonized. Mario Pei, the American linguist, lists as typical new words from that period: *clearing, underbrush, garter snake, groundhog, sidewalk, hitchhike, low-down, have an axe to grind, fly off the handle, bury the hatchet;* while imports or borrowings included (from the Indians) *wigwam, warpath, paleface;* (from the Dutch) *cole-slaw, cookie, boss,* and *scow;* (from the blacks) *banjo, hoodoo, jazz,* and so on. A large number of these words entered English in America and have travelled back across the Atlantic to become part and parcel of "standard" English. Some of the more colourful examples listed by Pei are: *bulldozer, caboodle, gobbledegook,* and *snollygoster* (not, in fact, a common word in England!), as well as idioms which many of the British probably think are their own, like *to make a bee-line, to hold one's horses, stag party, to talk turkey, assembly line, trouble-shooter, lockout, lame duck,* and *to sit on the fence.*

Of course, there are variations in speech within the United States, and at least three identifiable regional groupings, but if we consider English as a world language the trend that seems to be emerging is that—despite the BBC—the standard form of the language is becoming that spoken in the United States. This evolves and innovates in its own way and travels back across the Atlantic to modify the original source. But if Shaw said that England and America were two countries separated by the same language, are there not many more differences between British and American English than meet the eye?

In fact, those differences which do exist are often in fields that have evolved their own vocabulary since the English colonists arrived in North America. Transport is a typical example, since means and methods of transport have been revolutionized since the seventeenth century. The American air traveller will deplane on arrival at the airport, go to the baggage claim to hand over the check in order to claim his baggage, and leave the airport in his automobile (having loaded his cases into the trunk); alternatively he might use the downtown limousine service in a major American city. His British opposite number will alight from the aircraft, proceed to hand over the ticket in order to claim his luggage, and either go by car (having loaded his luggage into the boot) or use the airport coach service. As for his evening meal, our American traveller may simply buy some cookies or a little candy, or find a take-out and eat on his own; our Briton may have some biscuits or sweets, or perhaps patronize a take-away. Housing vocabulary also differs. If our American friend is in his home city, he may go to the apartment he has just purchased through a local realtor. His British friend, if he is in his home town (only cathedral or university cities are cities in Britain) may well go straight to his new flat, just purchased from a local estate agent. Unless our American drives carefully, he may be involved in an accident that will need a wrecking crew to come and take away his automobile, and he may need to be hospitalized: our British friend's car, in similar circumstances, may need the services of a breakdown van even if he is not to be admitted to hospital. If, on the other hand, the damage is slight, in America there may be a passing trucker or patrolman to lend a hand—a lorry-driver or policeman may be available in Britain.

British English is normally more formal and less relaxed than American English. Officialese is a particular English bugbear, forming another language. One wag translated "There's no place like home" into officialese as "It has not come to our notice in the course of exhaustive enquiries, made through appropriate channels, that there is any unit to come within the same residential category as an accommodation unit." One of the great hazards of British politics is that politicians who gain office sometimes lapse into "officialese" and lose contact with the everyday, ordinary language. It is often said that the best English is spoken in the Inverness area in the North of Scotland, where there is very little accent at all and language is clear but simple, making use of verbs and prepositions (go along, up, round, etc.) rather than Latin or Germanic circumlocutions.

In sum, the British are the heirs of a great international language, one which, because it is a living language for millions beyond the shores of the British Isles, is constantly being refreshed and invigorated by new forms and new idioms. This has a peculiar effect on the modern-day British: it tends to reinforce their self-esteem, but, since English is now spoken virtually throughout the world, it has encouraged them to be lazy about learning other languages. Any other people in a country with Britain's real power, but lacking the heritage of the international language, would have to pay much more attention to learning foreign languages. In a paradoxical sense, the language reinforces what is best about the British, giving them a lively and international medium of communication and expression, but, like many of the inheritances of the imperial past, it does tend in other ways to make adaptation to the modern world just that little bit more difficult.

* * * * *

As readers who have persevered thus far will appreciate, this book was not designed to be a comprehensive socio-economic study of contemporary Britain, a detailed political analysis of our system of government, or a profound historical treatise. It was intended to give the flavour of a country that on any view remains, in its richness and diversity, one of the most fascinating nation-states in the world. While it is no more possible to condense this into one volume than it is to sum up a meal, one can, I think, discern certain characteristics, many of which are inevitably contradictory.

I suspect that if one scratched the "average" Briton (if indeed one such exists), and then categorized his or her responses to the question "What are the qualities you perceive in our contemporary society?" among those enumerated would tend to be national unity, though with strong regional diversities; centrism and moderation in politics; a tradition of free speech and responsible journalism; a broadly tolerant society; a country that is basically law-abiding and one policed firmly but gently; a nation conscious of its cultural heritage and one in which the arts now flourish; a system of government which is adaptable and which has allowed the United Kingdom to come to terms with its changing role in the world; a local bureaucracy which, despite its imperfections, is honest and on the whole uncorrupt; an urban planning system that has allowed our cities to develop while still preserving the countryside; and possibly the high quality of British radio and television.

Yet for each of these there is the other side. National unity is threatened in Northern Ireland, and there are active nationalist movements in Scotland and in Wales. Political moderation is no longer the most obvious quality within the Labour Party, which in recent years has been in danger of a take-over by extreme Trotskyist and Marxist elements, though even there they describe themselves in delightfully archaic terms as "the militant tendency." On the extreme right, we have seen a revival of an incipient fascism in the activities of the National Front.

Our traditions of free speech and responsible journalism have produced tabloids of a ferocity yet trivialization unique in Europe. The way in which we treat our black and brown citizens is hardly indicative of a tolerant society, nor was the extreme Protestant agitation against the visit of His Holiness the Pope. The continuance of the British class structure is difficult to equate with a society that is genuinely accepting or equal. The crime statistics, particularly for muggings, in our cities do not entirely bear out the somewhat cosy belief we have that Britain is a more law-abiding society than our European neighbours. The police, and their methods of law enforcement, have come in for much complaint recently, particularly in urban areas, where there is a high concentration of blacks, and the recent report by Lord Scarman on the causes of the riots in Brixton was particularly critical on this point. The arts and music do flourish in Britain—punk rock is but one of our latest offerings. The political system is so unadaptable that some claim it to be in danger of ossification, and it has cer-

tainly not allowed the United Kingdom to come to terms with our
changing role in the world if, for example, national disenchantment
with the EEC is anything to go by. (Of all the ten nations in the
European Community we are, according to recent opinion polls,
the least enthusiastic.) Our uncorrupt local bureaucracies have
produced municipal scandals which, while perhaps lacking the pa-
nache of similar events in the United States, have nevertheless
shown that all is not always well in our town halls. Our town
planning structures have produced monstrosities, such as some of
the municipal housing of the 1960s, to be seen in many of our
cities. Radio and TV in the United Kingdom are by no means a
continuous diet of "Civilisation," "Upstairs, Downstairs," "Pride
and Prejudice," or "Brideshead Revisited," and the BBC at times
has such a tendency towards impartiality that it appears stagnant.

And yet there is sufficient truth in the initial responses to make
contemporary Britain a fascinating and rewarding place to ob-
serve. The flavour is gentler than in America, more New England
than Manhattan. But the regional diversities and accents are still
there.

From Cornwall to Newcastle-upon-Tyne, the distance is only
500 miles, yet the difference in accent is far greater than that between San Diego and Detroit. From Glasgow to Cardiff, the mile-
age is even less, but the difference in speech is immense, and we
are, after all, talking about a country whose total area is only one-
fortieth that of the United States, though with one-quarter of its
population. That it has maintained its diversity is remarkable, at-
tributable either to the stubbornness or the immobility of the population.

While personal diversity exists, however, the basic unity of the
state remains unimpaired, and, in my view, unimpairable. Save for
Ulster, which is, to put it mildly, a highly individualistic phenomenon, the cement has so far held, and looks like holding. The recent election to Parliament for a Glasgow seat of Roy Jenkins, a
Welshman by origin, who for many years sat for a Birmingham
constituency before a tenure as President of the European Commission in Brussels, and who had no known prior connection with
Scotland, is perhaps one more example of the extraordinarily "national" character of British politics. That election was fought on
national issues, not local ones: unemployment, the government's

economic strategy, the appeal of his new party (the Social Democrats), Britain's attachment to Europe and membership of the
EEC. Scottish affairs were incidental to the campaign, and a candidate of the Scottish National Party did badly in the final count.

And, just as the cement seems to be holding fast, the edifice itself is still standing firm. The British seem to feel psychologically
secure in their Britishness. While the other side of security may be
insularity (and the British are confirmed navel-watchers), there is
still a feeling that, despite all our problems, the U.K. is a good
place to live and bring up one's children.

Security, tradition, history, civilization, and tolerance are national qualities that cannot be acquired quickly. They need slow
husbandry, and just as much do they need a recognition that our
economic, social, and political systems are on the whole moderate
and generally acceptable. There is in contemporary Britain a tendency, perhaps, towards over-blandness. Free-booting capitalism
is now almost as rare (or, as in the case of Freddie Laker, as unsuccessful) as revolutionary Marxism is unpopular—the Communist Party in the United Kingdom is openly tolerated and elec-
torally disastrous. It is true that our educational system is too rigid
and class attitudes persist, and we are still a very long way from a
society in which there is genuine equality of opportunity. There is,
I fear, a streak of the patrician as well as the Puritan in many living in Britain, which makes us a country slow to change and mad-
dening to those who are trying to change it.

Our national characteristics are perhaps a reflection of the
country in which we live. Writing in 1940, Vera Brittain in her au-
tobiography *England's Hour* tried to sum up this strange attachment. She wrote:

> When, as so often, I am abroad, and especially in the United
> States where I contemplate, overwhelmed, the harsh spectacular
> outline of its Western lands, England does not mean for me the
> government at Westminster, nor even London's historic land-
> marks—Westminster Abbey, Big Ben, the Houses of Parliament,
> St Paul's Cathedral—now threatened with annihilation by a for-
> eign power. It certainly does not signify Winston Churchill, Stan-
> ley Baldwin, Ramsay MacDonald, David Lloyd George, or who-
> ever may be the political Colossus of the moment; still less does it

mean the Royal Family, now so conscientiously doing its best in circumstances always overwhelming for national figure-heads who serve the State by their continuous performance of expected duties. Least of all does it stand for government officials, those worthy, over-worked men and women whose nervous fear of out-stepping public opinion has so often resulted in bureaucratic cru-elty, and is displayed in the self-protective devotion to "Red Tape", "passing the buck", and every other conceivable form of the procrastination so peculiarly British.

To a limited degree, England does mean for me the process of British justice, which on two occasions—once at a provincial As-size Court, and once in the Police Court of a London magistrate —I have seen function in a fashion as close to the ideal of human decency as the present stage of our spiritual development can be expected to achieve. It means still more the tolerant endurance of British men and women; their patient amusement in Hyde Park or on Tower Hill when open-air orators proclaim opinions to which they are diametrically opposed; their brave, grumbling sto-icism in danger and adversity; their staunch refusal even in max-imum peril to become panic-stricken refugees.

But more than all, England for me means the fields and lanes of its lovely countryside; the misty, soft-edged horizon which is the superb gift to the eyes of this fog-laden island; the clear can-dour of spring flowers; the flame of autumn leaves; the sharp cracking of fallen twigs on frosty paths in winter. These are the things which, no matter where I may travel, I can never forget; this is the England which will dwell with me until my life's end.

Others, from Shakespeare to the Lake poets, have told the same tale; despite the industrialization of the last two centuries, it remains true. The British have by long association come to terms with their environment in ways perhaps unappreciable in many much newer countries. This is not unique to Britain; one finds it also in France or in Italy, this sense of mutual accommo-dation of humans and land and history. But it is important. It helps to give us continuity and tolerance, qualities essential if a nation is to be more than an accumulation of people living in one defined geographical area. A country that has, let us say, survived for nine centuries (English history tends to be taught as if it started with William the Conqueror in 1066) is bound to have developed certain persisting characteristics. And, for all its problems, Britain remains a pleasant country in which to live.

Despite our economic decline (which is in any event relative rather than absolute), despite the loss of power that accompanied our loss of Empire, and despite the social problems that we are now experiencing, the quality of life remains high. The British are by and large a kindly, unextreme, law-abiding, and moderate people, and these characteristics surface in our institutions, education, art, and culture. We do seem to value privacy and personal independence more than most. Personal freedom is no mere catchword in Britain today. It is safeguarded, and jealously so, by Parliament, the courts, and the press. Human rights are not enshrined in any legislative instrument in the United Kingdom. That we do not have a bill of rights in the American sense is not a defect in our apparatus of legal protections, it is rather that we have never felt the need to codify those basic rights which Parliament and the courts now accept as axiomatic. Perhaps also there is a feeling, present though usually unexpressed, that a written constitution or bill of rights gives too much power to an unelected group, the judiciary, and who then shall keep the judges in check? No one born in Britain may have his passport withdrawn or be deprived of his citizenship. An Englishman can, with impunity, vote in a foreign election if he happens to possess dual citizenship. No one can be prevented from leaving the country unless there is a valid warrant out for his arrest. No one can be prevented from saying what he will, writing what he will, or publishing what he likes—rights which have been hard won in the past but which are now accepted as being unarguable. If he wishes, an Englishman can even burn the Union Jack in public without committing an offence.

Voting is free and secret, and rarely indeed are our elections as such questioned as being unfairly held or improperly counted. Imprisonment without trial is of course illegal, and no one may be deprived of liberty without a trial openly conducted and impartially judged. Despite what many consider to be the historical anomaly of an established Church, religious freedom in Britain is total.

Many of these rights are not, of course, confined to Britain. They exist in North America, Western Europe, and a few other parts of the world. It is just that we have perhaps had them longer and more continuously than most, so that they have become part of the fabric of our society. The fact that they are rarely talked about is not indifference but rather acceptance as part of the natural order of things. This may be one reason why the obsession with individual rights that one detects in the United States seems not to be shared in the United Kingdom.

But if the price of liberty is eternal vigilance, the cost of vigilance is a ferocious press and an unpredictable and rowdy House of Commons. It is very good for ministers to have to submit themselves regularly to the judgement of that elected body. It can be stormy, tempestuous, angry, undignified, frivolous, even childish. The one thing no government can ever do is to take it for granted.

Britain is, then, a country that has given the world much, from parliamentary democracy and the rule of law to Shakespeare and Dickens. We are perhaps too conservative in our ways, and over-cautious in our readiness to support fundamental political or social changes. We have perhaps not yet fully come to terms with the latter part of the twentieth century, and our view of international politics remains too insular. But, despite this, we play our part fully in world affairs. As a nation, we are the product of centuries of patient development, from which we have emerged in 1983 as a nation which is free, diverse, active, interesting, and, on the whole, civilized.

FOR FURTHER READING

STANDARD FACTS

Her Majesty's Stationery Office. *Britain 1981: An Official Handbook*. London.

Her Majesty's Stationery Office. *Social Trends 11*. London: A Publication of the Government Statistical Service.

Hey, John D. *Britain in Context*. Oxford: Basil Blackwell.

GENERAL WORKS

Birch, A. H. *The British System of Government*. 4th ed. London: Allen & Unwin, 1980.

Blondel, Jean. *Voters, Parties and Leaders: The Social Fabric of British Politics*. Harmondsworth, England: Penguin, 1966.

Booker, Christopher. *The Seventies*. Harmondsworth, England: Allen Lane/Penguin, 1980.

Brogan, D. W. *The English People: Impressions and Observations*. New York: Alfred A. Knopf, 1943.

Butterworth, E., and Weir, D., eds. *Social Problems of Modern Britain*. London: Fontana, 1971.

Caves, Richard E., and Krause, Lawrence B., eds. *Britain's Economic Performance*. Washington, D.C.: The Brookings Institution, 1980.

Hanson, A. H., and Walles, M. *Governing Britain*. 3rd ed. London: Fontana, 1980.

Punnett, R. M. *British Government and Politics.* 4th ed. London: William Heinemann, 1980.

Rose, R. *Politics in England.* 3rd ed. London: Faber & Faber, 1980.

Rundle, R. N. *Britain's Economic and Social Development: From 1700 to 1975.* Sevenoaks, England: Hodder & Stoughton, 1976.

Ryder, Judith, and Silver, Harold. *Modern English Society.* Rev. ed. Andover, England: Methuen, 1977.

Sampson, Anthony. *The Anatomy of Britain.* London: Hodder & Stoughton, 1962.

Shonfield, Andrew. *British Economic Policy Since the War.* Harmondsworth, England: Penguin, 1958.

"Whatever Happened to the British Constitution?" *The Economist,* Dec. 13, 1979, pp. 21–23.

INDEX

294

INDEX

BBC. *See* BBC
officialese, 277
in U.S., 275–77
Environmentalists, 94
Episcopal Church in Scotland, 219
Equal Pay Act (1970), 253
Equestrian sports, 272
Eton (school), 115, 116, 118
Euro-currency market, 76, 77
European Airbus, 71
European Common Market, 94, 95, 192, 193
European Court of Human Rights, 65
European Economic Community (EEC), 39, 54, 69, 71, 150, 281, 282
European Monetary System, 77
European theatre, British Army NATO forces and, 243
Evans, Sir Geraint, 112
Evans, Harold, 257–58
Exchange rate, 75, 77
Exports, 71–72, 124
coal, 92
food, 94–95
and foreign policy, 90
natural gas, 91
oil, 90
Eye care, under National Health Service, 131

Factory conditions, 142
Fairness concept, 133
Falkland Islands, 5, 195
Falklands factor, in British politics, 195
Fascism, 280
Feather, Lord, 63
Festival of Light, 228
Films, 121
*Financial Time*s (newspaper), 255, 258–59
Fog, 102
Food, exporting, 94–95
Foot, Michael, 21, 117
Football, 269–71
Rugby, 270–71
soccer, 6, 23, 25, 269–71
Foreign Office, 106, 112, 180

Foreign policy
and exporting, 90
and importing, 93
Forestry Commission, 78
Founding Fathers (U.S.), 105, 201
"Four-wheeler" Christians, 216, 222
France, 240, 241
electricity exchange cable with, 93
Freedom, personal, 284
Freedom of Information legislation (U.S.), 253
Free speech, 280
Friendly Society of Agricultural Labourers, 140–41
Friends of the Earth (activist group), 250
Fuller's earth, 93
Fulton, Lord, 181

Gaelic language, 6, 14, 23
Gaitskell, Hugh, 43
Garter, Order of the, 111
General Medical Council, 119
George III, 136
George V, 150, 151
Germany, West, 52–54
Gibbons, Orlando, 220, 266
Gibraltar, population of, 5
Gilbert, W. S., quoted, 142, 199
Girls' education, 116
Gladstone, William, 142, 175
Glasgow, 30
Gloucester, Duke of, 108
Goldsmith, James, 259
Gold standard, 76
Golf, 272
Goronwy-Roberts, Lord, 21
Government of Ireland Act (1920), 34
Grand Consolidated Trades Union, 140
Gray's Inn, 209
Great Depression, 53
Greater London Council, 75
Greene, Graham, 221
Grenadier Guards, 242
Guardian, The (newspaper), 255, 258
"*Guardian* woman," 258
Guards regiments, 242